A NOTE ON THE AUTHOR

AMY CHUA is the John Duff Jr. Professor of Law at Yale Law School. She is the author of *World on Fire*, *Day of Empire*, *Battle Hymn of the Tiger Mother* and *The Triple Package* (with Jed Rubenfeld) and is a noted expert in the fields of international business, ethnic conflict and globalisation. She lives in New Haven, Connecticut, with her husband and two daughters.

POLITICAL
TRIBES

Group Instinct and the Fate of Nations

AMY CHUA

BLOOMSBURY PUBLISHING

LONDON · OXFORD · NEW YORK · NEW DELHI · SYDNEY

BLOOMSBURY PUBLISHING
Bloomsbury Publishing Plc
50 Bedford Square, London, WC1B 3DP, UK

BLOOMSBURY, BLOOMSBURY PUBLISHING and the Diana logo are
trademarks of Bloomsbury Publishing Plc

First published in 2018 in the United States by Penguin Press
An imprint of Penguin Random House LLC
First published in Great Britain 2018
This edition published 2019

A catalogue record for this book is available from the British Library

ISBN: HB: 978-1-4088-8157-6; TPB: 978-1-4088-8154-5;
eBook: 978-1-4088-8156-9; PB: 978-1-4088-8153-8

2 4 6 8 10 9 7 5 3 1

Printed and bound in Great Britain by CPI Group (UK) Ltd, Croydon CR0 4YY

MIX
Paper from
responsible sources
FSC® C020471

To find out more about our authors and books visit
www.bloomsbury.com and sign up for our newsletters

For

Mom and Dad

Sophia and Lulu

Coco and Push

and Jed

Contents

Introduction

Humans are tribal. We need to belong to groups. We crave bonds and attachments, which is why we love clubs, teams, fraternities, family. Almost no one is a hermit. Even monks and friars belong to orders. But the tribal instinct is not just an instinct to belong. It is also an instinct to exclude.

Some groups are voluntary; some are not. Some tribes are sources of joy and salvation; some are the hideous product of hate mongering by opportunistic power seekers. But once people belong to a group, their identities can become oddly bound with it. They will seek to benefit their group mates even when they personally gain nothing. They will penalize outsiders, seemingly gratuitously. They will sacrifice, and even kill and die, for their groups.

In many parts of the world, including the regions of greatest national security interest to the United States, the group identities that matter most are ones that Americans are often barely aware of. They are not national, but ethnic, regional, religious, sectarian, or clan based.

In our foreign policy, for at least half a century, we have been spectacularly blind to the power of tribal politics. We tend to view the world in terms of territorial nation-states engaged in great ideological battles—Capitalism versus Communism, Democracy versus Authoritarianism, the "Free World" versus the "Axis of Evil." Blinded by our own ideological prisms, we have repeatedly ignored more primal group identities, which for billions are the most powerful and meaningful, and which drive political upheaval all over the world. This blindness has been the Achilles' heel of U.S. foreign policy.

Take the Vietnam War, arguably the greatest and most humiliating military defeat in the history of the United States. It's by now well known that we underestimated the extent to which the Vietnamese people were fighting for national independence, as opposed to Cold War Marxism. But here's something most Americans, experts and novices alike, don't know, not even today. Inside Vietnam, a deeply resented 1 percent Chinese minority historically controlled as much as 70 to 80 percent of the country's commercial wealth. Thus, a hugely disproportionate number of Vietnam's "capitalists" were ethnic Chinese, despised by the Vietnamese, both northern and southern.

Because we completely missed the ethnic side of the conflict, we failed to see that virtually every procapitalist step we took in Vietnam was guaranteed to inflame popular resentment. If we had actively wanted to turn the Vietnamese people against us, we could hardly have come up with a better formula.

This is part of a consistent pattern. To give just one more fateful example: on the eve of the Iraq War, the Washington establishment was aware of a divide between Sunnis and Shias, but repeatedly minimized its significance. At the same time, we failed to understand the centrality of Iraq's tribal structures and how they were key to where Iraqi loyalties would fall. As former Secretary of State Condoleezza Rice acknowledged in 2017, "We didn't probably understand fully the role of the tribes." American policy in Iraq was based on the conviction that ethnic, tribal, and sectarian divisions would dissipate in the face of democracy and market-generated wealth. In President George W. Bush's words, "freedom and democracy will always and everywhere have greater appeal than the slogans of hatred." Instead, Iraq descended into a maelstrom of escalating conflict and violence from which it has still not recovered.

A handful of critics had warned of this danger. I was among them. In 2003, in my book *World on Fire*, I urged caution, warning that in Iraq "everything—even freedom and wealth—has ethnic and sectarian ramifications." Because Iraq's Shias formed a 60 percent majority long oppressed by Saddam Hussein's reviled Sunni Baathist regime, I cautioned that democracy could actually catalyze historic enmities, with elections producing not a unified Iraq but rather a sectarian Shia government that excluded and retaliated against the Sunnis. These circumstances would be ripe for the rise of "powerful fundamentalist movements" that "are intensely anti-American." Unfortunately, this precise scenario unfolded.

Domestically as well, elites in the United States have either not cared about or been remarkably oblivious to the group identities that matter most to large segments of ordinary Americans, including people they are supposedly trying to help.

Occupy Wall Street, for example, was a movement intended to

3

help the poor—but which did not actually include the poor. On the contrary, it was overwhelmingly driven and populated by the relatively privileged. It's not just that working-class Americans did not participate in Occupy; many, if not most, of them intensely dislike and spurn activist movements. As a student from rural South Carolina put it, "I think protesting is almost a status symbol for elites. That's why they always post pictures on Facebook, so all their friends know they're protesting. When elites protest on behalf of us poor people, it's not just that we see them as unhelpful; it seems they are turning us, many of whom have a great deal of pride, into the next 'meme.' We don't like being used as a prop for someone else's self-validation."

For a blast of irony, contrast Occupy Wall Street with a movement that actually is enormously popular among America's have-nots and have-lesses. The prosperity gospel is one of the fastest-growing movements in the United States. It teaches that being rich is godly and that God will make people rich if they pray (and tithe) correctly. The number of poor and working-class African and Hispanic Americans who belong to prosperity churches is growing exponentially. Three out of four Hispanic Christians in the United States believe that "God will grant financial success and good health to all believers who have enough faith." A Mexican American student of mine—whose family members are now in danger of being deported by the Trump administration—recently wrote to me: "In my opinion, the Prosperity Gospel explains how much of my Hispanic family can be anti-Obama and pro-Trump, despite that being so obviously against their self-interest. It's a coping mechanism for poor people who feel hopeless in this world. Just a few weeks ago, my mom sent me a video of one of her favorite pastors snapchatting from Trump's inaugural ball. My mom was so excited to see Trump welcoming in men she considers to be 'holy.' For me, this is frustrating to no end."

But the most important tribal identity missed by America's elites was the powerful antiestablishment identity forming within the working class that helped elect Donald Trump. Right up until election night, U.S. elites—pundits, pollsters, major media outlets, economic analysts—on both sides of the political aisle had no idea what was coming.

Race has split America's poor, and class has split America's whites. Even today, the tribal politics behind President Trump's election still baffles many. How could so many in America's working class have been "conned" by Trump? How can lower-income Americans possibly fail to see that Trump is not one of them?

What these elites don't see is that Trump, in terms of taste, sensibilities, and values, actually *is* similar to the white working class. The tribal instinct is all about identification, and Trump's base identifies with him at a gut level: with the way he talks (locker room), dresses, shoots from the hip, gets caught making mistakes, and gets attacked over and over by the liberal media for not being politically correct, for not being feminist enough, for not reading enough books. His enemies, they feel, are their enemies. They even identify with his wealth, because that's what many of them want, along with a beautiful wife and big buildings with their names on them. For many working-class Americans, being antiestablishment is *not* the same as being antirich.

Tribal politics demand group markers, and the difference

between elites and nonelites is always partly aesthetic. America's elites today, especially progressive ones, often don't realize how judgmental they are. They disdain tacky things, and, not coincidentally, those tacky things—fake tans, big hair, pro wrestling, chrome bull testicles hanging from the back of a big truck—are usually associated with lower-income Americans.

For many elites, so is patriotism—at least of the "USA!"-chanting, Budweiser-drinking, Make-America-Great-Again variety. American elites often like to think of themselves as the exact opposite of tribal, as "citizens of the world" who celebrate universal humanity and embrace global, cosmopolitan values. But what these elites don't see is how tribal their cosmopolitanism is. For well-educated, well-traveled Americans, cosmopolitanism is its own highly exclusionary clan, with clear out-group members and bogeymen—in this case, the flag-waving bumpkins. When former Republican Speaker Newt Gingrich declared in 2009, "I am not a citizen of the world," he was instantly attacked. One writer in the *Huffington Post* called him "supremacist," "regressive," "elitist," and "racist," concluding, "Mr. Gingrich, if you are **not** a citizen of this world, then stay the *eff* out of it"—hardly the most inclusive of sentiments.

There is nothing more tribal than elite disdain for the provincial, the plebian, the patriotic. Without taking anything away from their important contributions across the globe, U.S. elites often seem to have more compassion for the world's poor than America's poor, perhaps because the former are easier to romanticize. Meanwhile, for their part, many ordinary Americans have come to view the elite as a distant minority controlling the levers of power from afar, ignorant about and uninterested in "real" Americans. America's elites miscalled the 2016 election in part because they don't understand—even look down on—what matters most to America's nonelites.

Americans tend to think of democracy as a unifying force. But under certain conditions, including inequality that tracks racial, ethnic, or sectarian divides, democracy can actually ignite group conflict. In 2009, in a speech in the Grand Hall of Cairo University, President Barack Obama said, "[I] have an unyielding belief that all people yearn for certain things: the ability to speak your mind and have a say in how you are governed; confidence in the rule of law and the equal administration of justice; government that is transparent and doesn't steal from the people; the freedom to live as you choose. Those are not just American ideas, they are human rights, and that is why we will support them everywhere."

These stirring words—echoing similar declarations by presidents George W. Bush and Bill Clinton, as well as by many leading figures of the U.S. foreign policy establishment—express the fundamental hope that freedom will speak to people's deepest yearnings. Unfortunately, people have other yearnings as well.

The great Enlightenment principles of modernity—liberalism, secularism, rationality, equality, free markets—do not provide the kind of tribal group identity that human beings crave and have always craved. They have strengthened individual rights and individual liberty, created unprecedented opportunity and prosperity, transformed human consciousness, but they speak to people as individuals and as members of the human race, whereas the tribal instinct occupies the realm in between. (In Hollywood movies, the only time Earth is united is when it is under attack by another species from another planet.) Especially in societies where people fear for their safety or some struggle just to survive, idealistic principles will often ring hollow—and in any case have a hard time competing with appeals to more primordial group passions. Universal brotherhood is incompatible with gross inequality.

We are at an unprecedented moment in America. For the first time in U.S. history, white Americans are faced with the prospect of becoming a minority in their "own country." While many in our multicultural cities may well celebrate the "browning of America" as a welcome step away from "white supremacy," it's safe to say that large numbers of American whites are more anxious about this phenomenon, whether they admit it or not. Tellingly, a 2011 study showed that more than half of white Americans believe that "whites have replaced blacks as the 'primary victims of discrimination.'" Meanwhile, the coming demographic shift has done little to allay minority concerns about discrimination. A recent survey found that 43 percent of black Americans are skeptical that America will ever make the changes necessary to give blacks equal rights. Most disconcertingly, hate crimes have increased 20 percent in the wake of the 2016 election.

When groups feel threatened, they retreat into tribalism. They close ranks and become more insular, more defensive, more punitive, more us-versus-them. In America today, every group feels this way to some extent. Whites and blacks, Latinos and Asians, men and women, Christians, Jews, and Muslims, straight people and gay people, liberals and conservatives—all feel their groups are being attacked, bullied, persecuted, discriminated against. Of course, one group's claims to feeling threatened and voiceless are often met by another group's derision because it discounts their own feelings of persecution—but such is political tribalism.

This—combined with record levels of inequality—is why we now see identity politics on both sides of the political spectrum. On the left, "inclusivity" has long been a progressive watchword, but today's antioppression movements are often proudly exclusionary. The stubborn persistence of racial inequality in the wake of Barack Obama's supposedly "postracial" presidency has left many young progressives disillusioned with the narratives of racial progress that were popular among liberals just a few years ago. When a grand jury failed to indict a white cop who was videotaped choking a black man to death, black writer Brit Bennett captured this growing mistrust in an essay entitled, "I Don't Know What to Do with Good White People":

> We all want to believe in progress, in history that marches forward in a neat line, in transcended differences and growing acceptance, in how good the good white people have become. . . . I don't think Darren Wilson or Daniel Pantaleo set out to kill black men. I'm sure the cops who arrested my father meant well. But what good are your good intentions if they kill us?

As a result, many on the left have turned against "inclusive," universalist rhetoric (for example, All Lives Matter), viewing it as an attempt to erase the specificity of the experience and oppression of historically marginalized minorities.

The new exclusivity is partly epistemological, claiming that out-group members cannot share in the knowledge possessed by in-group members ("You can't understand X because you are white"; "You can't understand Y because you're not a woman"; "You can't speak about Z because you're not queer"). The idea of "cultural appropriation" insists, among other things, "These are *our* group's symbols, traditions, patrimony, and out-group members have no right to them." Not long ago, it was considered left wing and a sign of multicultural openness—a rejection of ethnocentrism—for a Caucasian person to wear a sari or a kimono, or to sport cornrows or dreadlocks. Today, any of these acts might be considered a "microaggression," a transgression of group boundaries by members of a dominant group.

Meanwhile, with a disturbing rise in white nationalist, anti-Muslim, anti-Mexican, anti-immigrant rhetoric, identity politics has also seized the American Right; mainstream politicians speak of "taking back" the country and warn of a "war on whites." All this is making a hash of core conservative values. For decades, the Right has claimed to be a bastion of individualism and color blindness. This is why the emergence of white identity politics is typically painted by conservatives as having been forced on them by the tactics of the Left. Just after the 2016 election, a former Never Trumper explained his change of heart in the *Atlantic:* "My college-age daughter constantly hears talk of white privilege and racial identity, of separate dorms for separate races (somewhere in heaven Martin Luther King Jr. is hanging his head and crying). . . . I hate identity politics, [but] . . . [w]hen everything is about identity politics, is the left really surprised that on Tuesday millions of white Americans . . . voted as 'white'? If you want identity politics, identity politics is what you will get."

This leaves the United States in a perilous new situation: with nearly no one standing up for an America without identity politics, for an American identity that transcends and unites the identities of all the country's many subgroups.

Most European and all East Asian countries originated as, and continue to be, *ethnic* nations. In these countries, the population is overwhelmingly composed of a particular ethnic group, which typically supplies the country's name as well as its national language and dominant culture. Thus China is politically and culturally dominated by ethnic Chinese, speaking Chinese; Germany by ethnic Germans, speaking German; Hungary by ethnic Hungarians, speaking Hungarian; and so on.

By contrast, America's national identity is not defined by the identity of any one of the innumerable ethnic subgroups that make up the U.S. population. Instead we are a tribe of tribes, with citizenship equally open to anyone born on our soil, no matter what their ancestry. It would be odd to refer to "Irish French" or "Japanese Korean." But in the United States, you can be Irish American, Japanese American, Egyptian American, or whatever American, and intensely patriotic at the same time.

Alone among the major powers, America is what I will call a super-group. A super-group is first of all a group. It is not universal; it does not include all humanity. It has a "We" and an "Everyone Else." But a super-group is a distinctive kind of group: one in which membership is open to individuals from all different backgrounds—ethnic, religious, racial, cultural. Even more fundamentally, a super-group does not require its members to shed or suppress their subgroup identities. On the contrary, it allows those subgroup identities to thrive, even as individuals are bound together by a strong, overarching collective identity.

America was not a super-group for most of its history. On the contrary, the United States became one only through a long and painful struggle, involving a civil war and a civil rights revolution. But America's continued existence as a super-group is under tremendous strain today.

America is beginning to display destructive political dynamics much more typical of developing and non-Western countries: ethnonationalist movements; backlash by elites against the masses; popular backlash against both "the establishment" and "outsider minorities" viewed as disproportionately powerful; and, above all, the transformation of democracy into an engine of zero-sum political tribalism.

Donald Trump may seem utterly unprecedented in the United States, but there's a startling parallel from the developing world. Trump was neither the world's first "tweeter-in-chief" nor the first head of state to have had a reality TV show. Venezuela's Hugo Chávez was. Like Trump, Chávez was elected to the shock and horror of elites, sweeping to victory in 1998 on an antiestablishment platform, attacking the mainstream media and a slew of "enemies of the people." Like Trump, who catapulted himself to the White House 140 characters at a time, Chávez was a master at communicating directly to the populace, winning over millions of the country's have-nots with unscripted rhetoric that struck elites as vulgar, outrageous, absurd, and often plainly false. Finally, like Trump, Chávez's appeal had a racial dimension. But whereas Chávez's base consisted primarily of the country's long excluded darker-skinned masses, Trump's base was white.

Interestingly, Washington completely miscalled Venezuela too. Seeing Chávez through the usual anti-Communist lens, U.S. foreign policy makers in 1998 were oblivious to the deep racial tensions in Venezuelan society and the intense, tribal, antielite resentment building up just below the surface. As a result, we repeatedly made bad foreign policy calls—like hailing a 2002 coup against Chávez as a "victory for democracy"—undermining our legitimacy in the region and our ability to combat today's real attack on Venezuelan democracy.

If we want to get our foreign policy right—if we don't want to be perpetually caught off guard, fighting unwinnable wars, and stuck having to choose between third- and fourth-best options— the United States has to come to grips with political tribalism abroad. And if we want to save our nation, we need to come to grips with its growing power at home.

CHAPTER ONE

American Exceptionalism and the Sources of U.S. Group Blindness Abroad

America is God's Crucible, the great Melting-Pot where all the races
of Europe are melting and re-forming!
—ISRAEL ZANGWILL, *The Melting Pot*

Daddy once told me there's a rage passed down to every black man
from his ancestors, born the moment they couldn't stop the slave
masters from hurting their families.
—ANGIE THOMAS, *The Hate U Give*

Great Britain's acute group consciousness during its imperial heyday contrasts jarringly with America's group blindness today. The British were minutely knowledgeable about, almost obsessed with, the ethnic, religious, tribal, and caste differences among their subject populations. They studied and cataloged, harnessed and manipulated, often deliberately pitting groups against each other. They also left behind time bombs that are still exploding today.

From a cold-blooded, strategic point of view, Britain's divide-and-rule policies were astonishingly successful. In India, some forty thousand British officers and soldiers governed approximately 200 million Indians for nearly two hundred years. By contrast, America couldn't hold Vietnam for ten years, couldn't stabilize Afghanistan for five, couldn't unify Iraq for even one.

Why didn't America follow the British model? Part of the answer may simply be timing. Great Britain's shrewd divide-and-conquer strategies arose out of the practical necessity of colonial governance—of having to administer large numbers of colonial subjects with a relatively small occupying force. By the time the United States emerged as a Cold War superpower, supplanting Great Britain on the world stage, the rules of the imperial game had changed. Conquest and territorial occupation were out of favor. The challenges of governing tens of millions of foreign subjects never faced postwar America, which constructed its "empire" very differently—by engineering coups, installing friendly regimes, building military bases, opening up markets, and establishing spheres of influence, rather than actually occupying and ruling foreign territory.

But the timing explanation is incomplete at best. There are deeper reasons for the group blindness of U.S. foreign policy, rooted in America's distinctive history—at both its best and its worst.

n 1915, addressing several thousand recently naturalized citizens, President Woodrow Wilson said:

> You cannot dedicate yourself to America unless you become in every respect and with every purpose of your will thorough Americans. *You cannot become thorough Americans if you think of yourselves in groups. America does not consist of groups.* A man who thinks himself as belonging to a particular national group in America has not yet become an American. . . .

This is a classic expression of American group blindness, and it is astounding that Wilson could make this comment at a time when many Native Americans were still denied citizenship, Jews were subject to quotas, Asian immigrants were barred from owning land in California, Mexican Americans were being lynched in the Southwest, and blacks faced violence, terror, and degradation throughout the country in almost every aspect of life. Wilson was claiming that "America does not consist of groups" when he was himself a beneficiary and practitioner of tribal politics: like every president before him, as well as nearly every holder of an important public office, Wilson was a white, Protestant male. It was Wilson, moreover, who oversaw the racial resegregation of the civil service.

Racism is group consciousness at its most repugnant, built on the premise that human beings can be divided by skin color into innately superior and inferior groups. Yet, paradoxically, racism is also a form of group blindness. Racial categories like "black," "white," and "Asian" erase ethnic differences and identities. The original African slaves brought to America knew—and might have tried to tell their children—that they hailed from the Mandinka tribe or the Ashanti people, or that they were descended from a long line of Yoruba kings. But even as they were stripped of their rights to life, liberty, and the pursuit of happiness, America's slaves were also stripped of these ethnic identities. Slave families were deliberately broken up, and heritages were lost, reduced by the powerful to a pigment and nothing more. Even now, immigrants from, say, Ghana, Jamaica, or Nigeria are often stunned to discover that in America they are just "black."

Something similar can be said about Native Americans and Asian Americans. To see all Native Americans as "savages that delight in war and take pride in murder," as Benjamin Franklin put it, is to *not* see or care about the differences among the Cherokee, Lakota, Ojibwa, Choctaw, and Navajo. (In the United States today, there are 566 federally recognized tribes.) One of the biggest objections Asian Americans have to the "model minority" stereotype is that it reduces them to a giant undifferentiated group of "abused, conformist quasi-robots," running roughshod over the stark ethnic and socioeconomic differences among, say, Taiwanese Americans, Hmong Americans, and Cambodian Americans. This was part of our problem in Vietnam: one of the reasons we couldn't tell the difference between the Chinese and Vietnamese was because they were all "Gooks" to us.

But Wilson's assertion that "America does not consist of groups" is remarkable not only because of how false it was, but also because of how much truth it holds, at least for certain major segments of the population. Of all the nations in the world, none has succeeded more than the United States in bringing together immigrants from diverse backgrounds and joining them in a new identity—American.

This was true even in the founding era. "What then is the American, this new man?" asked Crèvecoeur in 1782. The American, he answered, was a "strange mixture of blood, which you will find in no other country. I could point out to you a family whose grandfather was an Englishman, whose wife was Dutch, whose son married a French woman, and whose present four sons have now four wives of different nations. *He* is an American . . . leaving behind him all his ancient prejudices and manners."

This is what's so peculiar about America. We have been both exceptionally racist and exceptionally inclusive.

Alone among modern Western democracies, America had extensive race slavery inside its borders, which it did not abolish until 1865, nearly a century after a British court ruled slavery illegal inside England and thirty years after Great Britain abolished slavery in its colonies. We then replaced bondage with a legalized system of "separate but equal," which was not equal at all, and which effectively implemented apartheid in many parts of the country. Even today, the aftereffects of slavery still haunt America in the form of systemic inequality and injustice.

But America is exceptional in another, seemingly contradictory, way as well. Over the centuries, through the alchemy of markets, democracy, intermarriage, and individualism, America has been uniquely successful in attracting and assimilating diverse populations. The proverbial "nation of immigrants," the United States has always been one of the most ethnically and religiously open countries in the world. Today, in terms of absolute numbers, the U.S. population includes 47 million people born abroad, hailing from more than 140 countries—a full 19 percent of the world's migrants, putting us in first place by far. Germany, the next closest country, has just 12 million immigrants.*

America's distinctive history—its ethnicity-transcending national identity and its unusual success in assimilating people from diverse origins—has shaped how we see the rest of the world and has deeply influenced our foreign policy. It's not just ignorance, racism, or arrogance that predisposes us to ignore ethnic, sectarian, and tribal divisions in the countries where we intervene. In the United States, immigrant communities from all sorts of backgrounds have become "Americans"; why wouldn't Sunnis and Shias, Arabs and Kurds, all similarly become "Iraqis"?

It's in this sense that our blindness to political tribalism abroad reflects America at both its best and worst. In some cases, like Vietnam, ethnically blind racism has been part of our obliviousness. But American group blindness abroad is also rooted in some of our noblest ideals: tolerance, equality, individualism, the power

---

* Relative to total population, however, other countries take in a greater percent of immigrants. In 2014, Australia and Canada admitted 1.0 percent and 0.7 percent, respectively, of their total population in immigrants, compared to just 0.3 percent in the United States. As of 2015, 28 percent of Australia's population and 22 percent of Canada's were born outside the country. In America, the figure is 14 percent.

of reason to triumph over irrational hatred, and the conviction that all men are united by their common humanity and love of liberty.

THE RARITY OF SUPER-GROUPS

America is exceptional in yet another way that has also dramatically shaped our foreign policy. Perhaps the best way to see this is to return not to the 2016 presidential election but to the two before that.

In 2008, Barack Obama was elected president of the United States. In 2012, he was reelected. It's worth pausing a moment to register just how exceptional this is. Obviously, Obama's presidency was so striking in part because of America's history of racism. Racial bloc voting, the systemic denigration of blacks, their relative exclusion from the country's higher strata of power and wealth—all this was so deeply entrenched that only a couple of years before Obama's rise, the election of an African American to the White House seemed to many Americans, as the *New York Times* put it in 2008, "unthinkable."

But especially in light of the 2016 presidential election, we should also remember what a testament to American exceptionalism the elections of 2008 and 2012 were from a world-comparative point of view. No other major power in the world has ever democratically elected a racial minority head of state.

Just try to imagine the United Kingdom electing a black prime minister or Germany electing an ethnic Turkish chancellor. Or Russia, if it ever held real elections, electing an ethnic Korean as president.

America was able to elect Barack Obama as president because this country is a super-group, a group in which membership is open to individuals of any background but that at the same time binds its members together with a strong, overarching, group-transcending collective identity.

Historically, there have been super-group empires—Rome, for example, and, arguably, Great Britain. In theory, there have been super-group ideological movements (communism, for example) and super-group religions (Christianity, for example), although of course ideological movements and religions are not open to individuals with the wrong beliefs. But for a *country* to be a super-group is extremely rare.

China, for example, is not a super-group. One ethnicity, the Han Chinese, represents 92 percent of the population and effectively defines the national identity. Minority cultures are routinely suppressed. Thus, the Muslim Uighurs are banned from wearing veils and long beards; children under eighteen are prohibited from entering mosques and must sometimes be renamed in order to attend school.

None of the East Asian countries is a super-group. On the contrary, Japan and Korea are among the most ethnically homogenous countries on the planet, with powerful, ethnically defined national identities. For the same reason, most European nations aren't super-groups either. Strongly ethnic nations, like Poland or Hungary, obviously aren't super-groups. But interestingly, neither is France or the United Kingdom. Both countries have quite diverse, multiethnic populations; both are at least nominally constitutionally committed to minority rights and equal liberty. Yet neither is a super-group, although for opposite reasons.

France has a powerful national identity, but insists that its ethnic and religious minorities must thoroughly assimilate, at least publicly. Even putting aside the openly anti-immigrant National Front party—which explicitly calls for a return to a "pure French" national identity—France strongly discourages the expression of subgroup or tribal identities. Modern French law disallows any "ostentatious" displays of religion, including religiously symbolic clothes and demonstrations, in public places such as schools and government offices. While Christians are permitted to wear crosses (apparently not "ostentatious"), Jews may not be allowed to wear yarmulkes (though that rule is rarely enforced), and Muslims have been banned from wearing head scarves and face veils. Even the Socialist prime minister Manuel Valls said that Muslims must give up head scarves in universities in order to demonstrate that their religion "is fundamentally compatible with the Republic."

In other words, it's *laïcité*—the French form of political secularism—or nothing. As former French president Nicolas Sarkozy declared in 2016, "If you want to become French, you speak French, you live like the French and you don't try and change a way of life that has been ours for so many years." The "burkini ban" made headlines in the summer of 2016. In the latest controversy, a number of French towns stopped providing pork-free meals in public schools; Jewish and Muslim children must "eat like the French" or not eat at all. Many believe that such attempts at forced assimilation have backfired with France's Muslims, contributing to poor Muslim migrants feeling excluded from and hostile to the nation in which they now reside. In short, France has a strong national identity, but it doesn't let ethnic or religious minority cultures freely flourish.

Conversely, while the United Kingdom embraces several different "tribes" with their own intense subgroup identities—Irish, Scottish, Welsh, and so on—the grip of its national identity is surprisingly weak. In part, this is because "Britishness" is linked to "Englishness" (the English make up about 84 percent of the total population), and for obvious reasons an English-centered identity does not appeal to most Irish, Scots, and Welsh. At the same time, invoking a "British" identity based on Britannia's glorious history would necessarily celebrate empire, which is anathema in polite circles. The result is on the one hand repeated secessionist movements—most of Ireland is already gone; Scottish independence was narrowly defeated in 2014—and on the other hand the recent emergence of a nativist Little England movement led by the UK Independence Party, which led the charge for Brexit.

With respect to immigrant groups, Great Britain today takes a hands-off, or "multicultural," approach similar to that of the United States—but without the strong overarching national identity. Unlike France, Britain has no restrictions on religious clothing or other public expression of cultural identity. Indeed, Britain often bends over backward to accommodate religious minorities. To the dismay of some community members, for example, a growing number of schools have actually removed pork from lunch menus altogether—banning traditional sausages, ham, and bacon—out of deference to Muslim and Jewish students, even when they represent only a minority of the student body.

Unfortunately, instead of promoting cohesion, the result has been what David Cameron in 2007 (three years before he became prime minister) called "cultural separatism." Comparing Great Britain to the United States, and specifically addressing the problems of Muslim assimilation, Cameron said:

> [America] does succeed in creating, to an extent far more evident [than] we have achieved here, a real sense of common identity—about what it means to be an American. . . . It is this strong sense of inclusive identity that has helped make so many people feel part of American society. In Britain, we have to be honest: we have failed to do the same.

Growing numbers of Muslims in Great Britain live in largely Muslim neighborhoods and, as Clive Crook puts it, "feel little sense of community and solidarity with their fellow Britons, and vice versa." Second- and third-generation Muslims in Great Britain seem to be more religious and more alienated from British society than first-generation immigrants. Many worry that this state of affairs is fueling the growth of homegrown jihadis. The 2017 Manchester suicide bomber was born and raised in the city he later terrorized. Similarly, as Crook puts it, "The July [2005 London] bombers were not foreigners who had sneaked in from abroad. They sprang from local Muslim communities." As of 2015, more British Muslims had joined militant Islamic groups than were serving in the British armed forces.

For similar reasons, the European Union also fails to qualify as a super-group. Some people, mostly elites and well-educated students, do feel a strong sense of collective "European" identity and pride. But as Brexit and the explosion of anti-EU, Far Right nationalist movements all over Europe show, a great number of Europeans, particularly in the working class, feel little allegiance to or identification with Brussels. As Italy's populist leader Matteo Salvini declared: "It is not for a European bureaucrat to decide our future, and that of our children."

Even America, for much of its history, was not a super-group, excluding large numbers of people from citizenship (and freedom) on the basis of race, ethnicity, and gender.

THE EMERGENCE OF AMERICA AS A SUPER-GROUP

America was founded by mainly white, Anglo-Saxon Protestants, who dominated the country politically, economically, and culturally for most of its history. Until the late nineteenth century, the vast majority of immigrants to the United States were people we would today consider "white"—with "white" always a moving target. The Irish, Italians, Hungarians, Jews, Greeks, and Poles were all groups not considered fully white when they first arrived.

From the nation's founding until 1920, immigration from Europe continued almost unrestricted. Whether fleeing persecution or drawn by America's freewheeling capitalism, waves of immigrants of increasingly diverse backgrounds—Danes, Swedes, Czechs, Slovaks, Finns, Ukrainians, Serbs, Syrians, Basques, Russians, Armenians, Lithuanians—continued to pour in, often intermarrying within a few generations. The total numbers were breathtaking. Between 1820 and 1914, more than 30 million people arrived in the United States—the largest human migration in the history of the world. For purposes of comparison, between 1871 and 1911, some 20 million immigrants arrived in the United States, while over the same time frame, Argentina and Brazil together received 6 million immigrants, Australia and New Zealand 2.5 million, and Canada fewer than 2 million.

Yet during this period, for all its openness to immigrants, the United States continued to build ethnic and racial exclusions into every aspect of society, from the education system, where quotas were pervasive, to our immigration and citizenship laws, which explicitly discriminated against nonwhites. But as the twentieth century unfolded, and especially after the Civil Rights Act of 1964, America underwent another profound transformation: from a multiethnic nation into something even more unusual: a super-group.

This transition had its roots in the Civil War, when America not only abolished slavery but passed the Fourteenth Amendment, establishing that anyone born in the United States was an American citizen. The significance of birthright citizenship cannot be overstated. It means that as a *constitutional* matter, citizenship—being American—does *not* pass by blood, as it does in most of Europe. (Most Americans may not realize it, but the rule that children of U.S. citizens are also U.S. citizens, even if they are born abroad, is not constitutionally mandated; it is the result of statutory provisions.) As far as the U.S. Constitution is concerned, if you're born on American soil, then you are equally a U.S. citizen, whether your parents were born in Mexico, Libya, or Iowa. In other words, being American is not a matter of ancestry, but rather a matter of connection to the land, and of being bound by a shared constitution.

The Fourteenth Amendment was not only revolutionary in its own time. Birthright citizenship remains extremely rare even today. No Asian country grants it. No European country grants it. In fact, the United States is one of only a very few developed nations to recognize birthright citizenship (Canada is another). If anything, the trend is in the opposite direction. France eliminated birthright citizenship in 1993; Ireland, in 2005; New Zealand, in 2006.

But it would take another century for the United States to begin dismantling the legalized racism that continued unabated after the Civil War. In the 1954 landmark case *Brown v. Board of Education*, the Supreme Court struck down race-based school segregation, rejecting the doctrine of "separate but equal" in public education. A decade later, Congress passed the 1964 Civil Rights Act, which enacted sweeping voting reforms and prohibited discrimination on the basis of race in employment and in public places such as hotels, restaurants, and theaters.

Around the same time, the Ivy League universities—historically the grooming grounds for America's leaders—embarked on un-precedented institutional reforms aimed explicitly at building more diverse student bodies. Yale, for example, eliminated geo-graphical factors for admission—which had been a way to limit Jewish students—and reduced preferences for alumni legacies and prep school students. This resulted in a spike in the percentage of Jewish students (from 16 percent in the freshman class in 1965 to about 30 percent in 1966) and students from public schools. The number of minority students accepted to Ivy League schools also rose dramatically. In 1960, the "Big Three" had collectively just 15 African American freshmen; in 1970, there were 284 (83 at Yale, 98 at Harvard, and 103 at Princeton). Overall, between 1970 and 1980, the number of African American college gradu-ates increased by 91 percent.

The changing face of U.S. higher education was part of a much more radical transformation of American society. The 1960s and their aftermath did not end the primacy of white Anglo-Protestant men in the corporate world or in Washington, but women, blacks, and other minorities made impressive inroads in American business, politics, and culture. At the same time, new immigration policies dramatically changed the demographics of American society.

The 1965 Immigration and Nationality Act abolished the ra-cially and ethnically discriminatory national-origin quotas insti-tuted in the 1920s. Immigration rates exploded, from roughly 70,000 annually during the quota years to about 400,000 annu-ally by the early 1970s, 600,000 annually by the early 1980s, and more than 1 million in 1989. From 1990 to 2000, the United

States admitted approximately 9 million immigrants—more than any other country in the world, and more than in any other decade of U.S. history except the heyday of Ellis Island at the turn of the previous century. The vast majority of these newcomers, moreover, were non-European, mostly from Latin America and Asia. The rise in legal migration was accompanied by an increase in illegal entries. In 1960, foreign-born residents of the United States were distributed principally as follows:

Italy	1,257,000
Germany	990,000
Canada	953,000
United Kingdom	833,000
Poland	748,000

In 2000, the distribution was very different:

Mexico	7,841,000
China	1,391,000
Philippines	1,222,000
India	1,007,000
Cuba	952,000

With these demographic shifts have come enormous cultural transformations as well. Although white Protestants, especially male, continue to wield considerable influence all over America—with disproportionate representation in the U.S. Congress, for example—their dominance has waned in recent years. For example, white Protestants are today disproportionately *under*represented at our institutions of higher learning. A 2014 Pew Research Center study found that around 46 percent of Americans were Protestant, but at Harvard University—named after Puritan pastor John Harvard—only 20 percent of the class of 2017 described themselves as Protestant. Although most U.S. Supreme Court justices since 1789 have been white Protestants, after Justice John Paul Stevens retired in 2010, the court became entirely comprised of Catholics and Jews, and remained so until the 2017 appointment of Neil Gorsuch (who was raised Catholic but who now worships with an Episcopal congregation).

Perhaps most strikingly, on the day of this writing, *Billboard*'s top 10 musical artists included only one singer and one duo of white Protestant descent (Taylor Swift and Twenty One Pilots). This brings us back to the heart of today's tribal politics—the fact that every group in America today feels threatened, whatever the reality. Although it may seem preposterous given the persistence of racism in the United States—and the fact that nonwhites continue to be underrepresented at the highest levels of many fields—many white Americans now feel the country is culturally and socially dominated by blacks and other minorities. They experience their world as being swallowed up by a popular culture that equates coolness with multiculturalism and lionizes hip-hop music and movies like *Moonlight* (about a gay black man). Needless to say, many on the left deride this view, pointing out that Hollywood is still very male and very white (the hashtag #OscarsSoWhite went viral during the 2016 Academy Award season) and decrying the fact that Adele instead of Beyoncé won Album of the Year at the 2017 Grammys.

Nevertheless, from the point of view of many white Americans—ones who think the world of *Mad Men* wasn't necessarily all that bad—they've lost their cultural primacy. Now, it seems, everything they see—TV programming, commercials, pop music, ads on the subway—is influenced and increasingly flavored by minority culture.

A merica's national identity is no longer exclusively defined by WASPs, nor by whites more generally, nor by any of America's countless other ethnic subgroups. The 97 percent white population of Kennebunkport, Maine, is of course part of American identity and culture, but so are Cuban Americans in Miami's Little Havana and Iranian Americans in L.A.'s Little Persia. Americanness embraces everyone born in this country, from the children of Jamaican immigrants to the grandchildren of Vietnamese immigrants to the great-great-grandchildren of Jewish immigrants, from *Mayflower* descendants to the descendants of slaves.

American society remains shot through with racism, and things may be getting worse, not better. A super-group is not a perfect group; it is not "postracial"; it can be full of violence and inequality. But no one can doubt that Barack Obama, Oprah Winfrey, and Derek Jeter are American. Indeed, they are all symbols, faces of America. What it means to be American is not the preserve of any particular racial, ethnic, or religious subgroup.

In a 1990 speech, Ronald Reagan gave eloquent expression to the extraordinary expansiveness of being American—and how that makes the United States different from other countries:

> [Y]ou can go to live in France, but you can't become a Frenchman. You can go to live in Germany or Italy, but you can't become a German, an Italian. . . . [But] anyone, from any corner of the world, can come to live in the United States and become an American. . . . [I]f we take this crowd and if we could go through and ask the heritage, the background of every family represented here, we would probably come up with the names of every country on [E]arth, every corner of the world, and every race. Here, is the one spot on [E]arth where we have the brotherhood of man.

By the twenty-first century, however imperfectly and haltingly, the United States of America had become a super-group—the only one among all the world's great powers.

FOREIGN POLICY IMPLICATIONS

Precisely because it's so unusual, America's status as a super-group has led us astray when it comes to assessing the tribal politics of other nations. We forget how unusual it is to have both an extremely diverse, multiethnic population *and* a strong overarching national identity capable of binding the people together. Libya,

Syria, and Iraq are all, like the United States, postcolonial, multi-ethnic nations, but none of them has a national identity anywhere close to as strong as ours.

In countries like these, it can be a catastrophic mistake to imagine that through democratic elections, people will suddenly rally around a national identity and overcome their preexisting ethnic, religious, sectarian, and tribal divides. On the contrary, in sharply divided societies, democracy often galvanizes group conflict, with political movements and parties coalescing around these more primal identities. America has made this mistake over and over again.

Thus American exceptionalism, in its different facets, both at its ugliest and most inspiring, lies at the root of our obliviousness to the tribal identities that matter most intensely to people abroad. Sometimes racism blinds us. But most fundamentally, we tend to assume that other nations can handle diversity as we have, and that a strong national identity will overcome more primal group divisions.

This mentality suffers from two fatal flaws. First, it's a naïve view of the world. After a U.S.-led coalition toppled Colonel Gaddafi in 2011, President Obama declared, "[O]ne thing is clear—the future of Libya is now in the hands of the Libyan people. . . . [I]t will be Libyans who build their new nation." But "the Libyan people" hail from some 140 different tribes, and they did not come together to "build their new nation." On the contrary, the country began a slow descent into fragmentation and eventually a bloody civil war. As Obama would later say, "The degree of tribal division in Libya was greater than our analysts had expected." In 2016, the top U.S. general in Africa declared Libya "a failed state," and it is now a hotbed of radicalism. Obama himself has said that "failing to plan for the day after" in Libya was probably the worst mistake of his presidency. If we are to get things right in our foreign policy, we need to be much more alert to the destructive potential of the group instinct abroad.

Second, it's a naïve view of ourselves. The belief that other countries can handle diversity as well as America assumes that *we* can handle our own diversity. But the United States is not immune to the destructive forces of political tribalism—the forces that have repeatedly torn other nations apart and turned our foreign interventions into catastrophes.

CHAPTER TWO

Vietnam

Vietnam is too close to China, too far from heaven.
—VIETNAMESE PROVERB

We will drive the Americans into the sea.
—PHAM VAN DONG,
North Vietnamese premier

In Henry Kissinger's words, "No war since the Civil War has seared the national consciousness like Vietnam." Even as the war was unfolding, Hans Morgenthau, one of the leading international-relations experts of the twentieth century, wrote: "We are humiliated in the eyes of the world. What is worse and graver is that we humiliate ourselves in our own eyes because we betray the moral principles, the ideals on which this country was founded." Arguably the first war lost in American history, the Vietnam War was, to quote George McGovern, "an utter, unmitigated disaster."

Fifty years later, the question remains: how did superpower America, with its formidable military, lose to what Lyndon

B. Johnson called "a piddling, piss-ant little country"—or, actually, half that country?

It's by now widely recognized that the decision makers in Washington, DC—David Halberstam's "the best and the brightest"—overlooked the potency of Vietnamese nationalism, instead interpreting events through the Cold War lens of a worldwide struggle between freedom and communism. As Thomas Friedman puts it, the United States failed "to understand that the core political drama of Vietnam was an indigenous nationalist struggle against colonial rule—not the embrace of global communism, the interpretation we imposed on it."

But that's still not the complete picture. To this day, we don't fully understand what we got so badly wrong in Vietnam. Driving and shaping Vietnamese nationalism was a millennia-old *ethnic* conflict going back far longer than resentment against the West.

The core reason we lost in Vietnam is that we failed to see the ethnic dimension of Vietnamese nationalism. But to understand this phenomenon, we need to understand ethnicity itself—its basis, its internal logic, and the source of its primal appeal, which goes to the heart of political tribalism.

THE TRIBAL INSTINCT AND ETHNICITY

In a recent study, children between the ages of four and six were randomly assigned to a red or blue group and asked to put on a T-shirt of the corresponding color. They were then shown edited computer images of other children—half of whom appeared to be wearing red T-shirts, the other half blue—and asked about their reactions to these children.

Even though they knew absolutely nothing about the children in the photos, the subjects consistently reported that they "liked" children of their own group better, allocated more resources to them, and displayed strong unconscious preferences for in-group members. In addition, when told stories about the children in the photos, these boys and girls exhibited systematic memory distortion, tending to remember positive actions of in-group members and negative actions of out-group members. Without "any supporting social information whatsoever," the researchers concluded, the children's perception of other kids was "pervasively distorted by mere membership in a social group, a finding with disturbing implications."

The impulse to form group identities and favor in-group members has a neurological basis. Using functional magnetic resonance imaging (fMRI), scientists have scanned people's brains while conducting experiments similar to the one just described. Their findings, as one writer puts it, suggest that: "group identification is both innate and almost immediate."

In social psychologist Jay Van Bavel's recent experiments, participants randomly assigned to different groups were placed under an fMRI and shown photos of supposed rivals and teammates. When participants saw members of their own team, certain sections of the brain—the amygdala, fusiform gyri, orbitofrontal cortex, and dorsal striatum—tended to "light up." These areas of the brain are thought to be associated with distinguishing between relevant and irrelevant stimuli and with perceptions of value. What this suggests is that our brains are hardwired to identify, value, and individualize in-group members, while "outgroup members are processed as interchangeable members of a general social category," making it easier to negatively stereotype them. Even more striking, seeing other members of our in-group prosper seems to activate our reward centers—generating emotional satisfaction—even if we receive no benefit ourselves.

The neurological processes of in-group recognition and favoritism start extremely early. Newborns shown images of people's faces do not respond differently based on race. But as early as three months later, in Yale psychologist Paul Bloom's words, "Caucasian babies prefer to look at Caucasian faces, as opposed to African or Chinese faces; Ethiopian babies prefer to look at Ethiopian faces rather than Caucasian faces; Chinese babies prefer to look at Chinese faces rather than Caucasian or African faces." While we can take comfort in the fact that humans aren't born racists, it's unnerving to realize that racial preferences develop so early.

Racial in-group empathy can operate neurologically even when we don't realize or acknowledge it. When scientists showed Caucasian and Chinese college students images of a person being pricked by a large needle, the students' *reported* pain evaluations showed no racial disparities; but fMRIs taken at the same time showed significantly increased activity in the subjects' ACC/supplementary motor cortex—the area of the brain most associated with empathy for pain—when they were viewing people of their own race being injured.

Perhaps most troubling, recent studies by Mina Cikara, the

director of the Harvard Intergroup Neuroscience Lab, show that under certain circumstances our brains' "reward centers" will activate when we see members of an out-group failing or suffering a misfortune. Normally, Cikara stresses, "very few people actually go out of their way to harm the outgroup." But when one group fears or envies another—when, for example, "there's a long history of rivalry and not liking each other"—it seems that schadenfreude has a neurological basis. Group members will take "sadistic pleasure" in the pain of their perceived rivals.

Humans aren't just a little tribal. We're *very* tribal, and it distorts the way we think and feel.

But not all group identities are equally potent. Some have a much stronger grip than others and are more politically galvanizing. Very few people have ever given their lives for the American Podiatry Association. One of the most powerful forms of group identity—and the focal point of political tribalism and violence all over the world today—is ethnicity.

The key to ethnic identity is that it's built around the idea of shared blood; in political scientist Donald Horowitz's words, ethnicity is a sense of belonging to a people that is experienced "as a form of greatly extended kinship." For most human beings, the family is primal—the ur-group—and ethnicity taps into those primal feelings. "The ethnic tie," as Horowitz puts it, "is simultaneously suffused with overtones of familial duty and laden with depths of familial emotion." Mixed together with the idea of shared blood is a sense of a shared heritage and history, a common culture, and a common language, all typically viewed as passed down from parent to child.

It's easy to scoff at myths of common ancestry. Little or no historical evidence supports the claim that today's 1 billion Han Chinese all descend from the Yellow Emperor, a legendary figure who supposedly reigned five thousand years ago. The same is true of the claim that Jews all share the common forefather Jacob or that the Yoruba all descend from the emperor Oduduwa. But beliefs in "shared blood" are no less powerful for being mythic.

Whether biologically based (as "primordialists" believe) or constructed by elites, culture, and power seekers (as "instrumentalists" believe), the experience of ethnic identification exists everywhere human beings do. It is one of the most combustible sources of political mobilization, and it is at its strongest when one group feels threatened—in danger of being extinguished—by another.

VIETNAMESE IDENTITY

Like China, Vietnam is a quintessentially ethnic nation, rooted in a form of "identity-by-blood." The vast majority of the population are ethnic Vietnamese, who also give the country its name and language. At the same time, Vietnam's national identity is practically defined in opposition to a Chinese enemy.

China, of course, dwarfs Vietnam. In terms of size, China is roughly to Vietnam what the United States is to Ecuador. The two countries are also contiguous; if you look at a map, China looks vaguely like a five-hundred-pound genie sitting on top of a tiny tilted lamp, which is Vietnam. Because of its looming proximity and size, China is not just an enemy to Vietnam, but a constant threat to its very survival.

In 111 B.C., China conquered the Viet people, incorporated Nam Viet (which in Chinese translates to "land of the southern barbarians") into the Chinese empire, and for the next thousand years ruled it as a province of China. Under Chinese rule, the Vietnamese adopted much of Chinese culture, including Buddhism, Taoism, and Confucianism, with its imperial examination system and mandarin bureaucracy. But the Vietnamese refused to become Chinese. On the contrary, they became all the more "[i]ntensely ethnocentric." Although Chinese was the official language during Chinese rule, widely used among the elite, the Vietnamese preserved their own language along with memories of pre-Chinese civilization. They never lost their veneration for local heroes who resisted the Chinese.

Even after Vietnam won independence from China in 938, it remained under Chinese domination, paying tribute to the Chinese emperor for another millennium. During this period, China repeatedly invaded Vietnam, but against all odds China's forces were repelled over and over again. Tales of Vietnamese bravery and David-versus-Goliath ingenuity in beating back Chinese invaders lie at the heart of Vietnamese lore.

Contemporary Vietnamese national identity is also in part a twentieth-century construction. In the 1920s, during French colonial rule, a group of young Vietnamese intellectuals emerged, calling for "a new Vietnam, free of colonial domination and the weight of the past." These intellectuals not only opposed the

French; they zeroed in on China as well. Influential nationalists reminded the Vietnamese of their ancient struggle against China, resurrecting legendary figures like the Trung sisters, who in A.D. 40 freed Vietnamese lands from Chinese occupation, ultimately losing their lives (and supposedly their heads). The nationalists also attacked Confucianism as a "suffocating" tradition that stifled individual liberty and thought. According to historian Christopher Goscha, the nationalists' message was simple: "Individual men and women had stood up in the past to resist a thousand years of Chinese occupation; they could do it again."

Mythic or not, every Vietnamese child learns of the heroic exploits of their forerunners, who are always fighting the same enemy: China. Indeed, the protracted fight against Chinese domination has been central in generating a sense of kinship and ethnic nationalism among the Vietnamese. As Vietnamese historian Tran Khanh writes, "The struggle for the survival of the Viet people against the [Chinese] enhanced the community spirit of the Viet people. They felt that they were brothers and sisters with common ancestors and did their utmost to safeguard their culture and race."

Yet astonishingly, U.S. foreign policy makers during the Cold War were so oblivious to Vietnamese history that they thought Vietnam was China's pawn—merely "a stalking horse for Beijing in Southeast Asia." This was a group-blind mistake of colossal proportions.

In 1995, Robert McNamara, who was secretary of defense during the Vietnam War, met his former counterpart, the foreign minister of North Vietnam. "Mr. McNamara," he recalls his former enemy saying, "you must never have read a history book. If you'd had, you'd know we weren't pawns of the Chinese . . . Don't you understand that we have been fighting the Chinese for 1000 years? We were fighting for our independence. And we would fight to the last man. . . . And no amount of bombing, no amount of U.S. pressure would ever have stopped us."

Cold War America saw North Vietnam's revolutionary leader Ho Chi Minh as a "puppet of China." Again, this was a staggering mistake. As a child, Ho too had been raised on tales of Vietnamese heroes expelling hated Chinese oppressors. He had spent at least thirteen months in Chinese prisons, sometimes in solitary confinement and often forced to walk twenty-five to thirty miles in leg irons. Ho is often described as "soft-spoken" and has been compared to Gandhi, but lest it be thought that Ho was above anti-Chinese animus, after World War II, when one of his underlings suggested turning to China to fend off the French, Ho barked: "You fools! . . . Don't you remember your history? The last time the Chinese came, they stayed a thousand years. . . . I prefer to sniff French shit for five years than eat Chinese shit for the rest of my life."

Ho was also undoubtedly a Marxist. But if we had understood the Vietnamese people's deep distrust of the Chinese, is it possible that when Ho wrote to President Truman pleading for support in Vietnam's struggle against the French, a different strategy might have been open? Ho repeatedly likened Vietnam's fight for independence to America's; he even quoted the U.S. Declaration of Independence in Vietnam's own Declaration of Independence. An OSS report from the Truman era, which would remain classified for many years, described Ho as saying that "although he formerly favored Communist ideals, he now realized that such ideals were impracticable for his country." Could we have supported Ho against the French, capitalizing on Vietnam's historical hostility toward China to keep the Vietnamese within our sphere of influence?

We'll never know. Somehow we never saw or took seriously the enmity between Vietnam and China. Thirty years after the Vietnam War, former South Vietnam premier Nguyen Cao Ky wrote:

> To many Americans in Vietnam we were just vaguely "Chinese." We are not. We are Vietnamese. The Americans did not realize that . . . we almost alone in Asia, defeated [China], when the Viets, as we were then called, beat the soldiers of the T'ang dynasty and a century later defeated the troops of the Sung dynasty.

Not only did we miss the animosity between Vietnam and China. We also missed an additional ethnic dimension, internal to Vietnam, which doomed us from the beginning in the battle for the hearts and minds of the people. Vietnam had within its borders a market-dominant Chinese minority.

MARKET-DOMINANT MINORITIES IN THE DEVELOPING WORLD

In 2003, I coined the term "market-dominant minority" to describe an ethnic minority that tends, under market conditions, to dominate economically, often to a startling extent, the poor "indigenous" majority around them, generating enormous resentment among the majority, who see themselves as the rightful owners of the land under threat from "greedy" exploitative outsiders.

Market-dominant minorities are pervasive in the developing world. Examples include ethnic Chinese throughout Southeast Asia, Indians in East Africa and parts of the Caribbean, Lebanese in West Africa and parts of the Caribbean, Igbo in Nigeria, Bamileke in Cameroon, Kikuyu in Kenya, whites in South Africa, whites in Zimbabwe, whites in Namibia, Croats in the former Yugoslavia, Jews in post-Communist Russia, Parsis and Gujaratis in Mumbai—the list goes on and on.

Groups can be market dominant for very different reasons, some completely unrelated to economics, including colonial divide-and-conquer policies or a history of apartheid. If, as was true of whites in South Africa, a minority uses brutal force and the powers of the state to relegate the majority to inferior education and inhuman conditions for more than a century—that minority is likely to be market dominant for reasons having nothing to do with superior entrepreneurialism.

On the other hand, to be clear, market dominance does not refer to vague ethnic stereotypes, but rather to *actual, starkly disproportionate control of major sectors of the economy.* In Indonesia, Vietnam's neighbor, the Chinese comprise just 3 percent of the population, but control as much as 70 percent of the private economy, including virtually all of the country's largest conglomerates. For most of Bolivia's history, a tiny minority of light-skinned, "Europeanized" elites controlled almost all of the nation's wealth, while the indigenous majority lived in abject poverty. In the Philippines, the

2 percent Chinese minority controls the country's corporate, banking, airline, shipping, and retail sectors; according to *Forbes*, in 2015 the top four wealthiest people in the Philippines (and ten out of the top fifteen) were ethnic Chinese.

Market-dominant minorities are one of the most potent catalysts of political tribalism. When a developing country with an impoverished majority has a market-dominant minority, predictable results follow. Intense ethnic resentment is almost invariable, leading frequently to confiscation of the minority's assets, looting, rioting, violence, and, all too often, ethnic cleansing. In these conditions, the pursuit of unfettered free-market policies makes things worse. It increases the minority's wealth, provoking still more resentment, more violence, and, typically, populist anger at the regime pursuing such policies. All this held true in Vietnam.

VIETNAM'S CHINESE MINORITY

The Chinese in Vietnam—called the Hoa—have been market dominant for centuries, historically controlling the country's most lucrative commercial, trade, and industrial sectors. Resentment against their success, coupled with repeated Chinese invasions, sparked recurrent anti-Hoa reprisals, including the 1782 massacre in Cholon, Saigon's sister city (often called Saigon's Chinatown), in which an estimated ten thousand Chinese were slaughtered. According to official Vietnamese records, Chinese shops were burned and looted, and the victims, including "men, women, and children," were indiscriminately "killed and their corpses thrown into the river. For more than one month no one dared to eat shrimp or to drink water taken from that river."

When the French arrived in the nineteenth century, they shrewdly cultivated Chinese entrepreneurship—in typical colonial divide-and-rule fashion—and welcomed Chinese immigrants. Under French colonial rule, the Hoa population rose from 25,000 in the 1860s to more than 200,000 in 1911. By the 1950s, the Hoa had amassed such "vast economic power" and political influence, they were viewed as "a state within a state." Chinese magnates, almost all located in southern Vietnam, were known as "kings"—the "Petrol King, the Oil King, the Rice King, the Scrap Metals King, and so on."

The extent of Hoa economic dominance is hard to overstate. While the Vietnamese elite filled the ranks of the civil service, colleges, the military, and the professions, the Chinese had a "stranglehold" on Vietnam's business and commerce. Although still only a tiny percentage of the population, the Chinese controlled a staggering 80 percent of South Vietnam's industry. The Hoa also dominated Vietnam's retail trade, its financial and transportation sectors, and all aspects of the rice economy. On top of that, they were disproportionately represented in the services sector; as of the mid-twentieth century, they owned more than 50 percent of all large hotels, and 90 percent of small hotels in the Saigon area, in addition to 92 large restaurants, 243 tea and beer shops, and 826 eating houses. According to one estimate, the Chinese in Vietnam controlled 90 percent of non-European private capital.

Not only did Hoa wealth inflame local resentment; their

attitude added fuel to the fire. The Hoa tended to live apart from the Vietnamese, often in wealthy enclaves, attending their own schools and temples, typically marrying only among other Chinese, and projecting a sense of "ethnic and cultural exclusivism." Rightly or wrongly, the Hoa were seen as exploiting the native Vietnamese, the vast majority of whom were impoverished peasants. When the Vietnamese went to war against the French, the Chinese minority stayed "apolitical," infuriating the Vietnamese.

It does not appear that America knew anything about these ethnic realities when we went to war—or if we did, it certainly wasn't reflected in our policies.

THE AMERICAN INTERVENTION

In 1954, the Vietnamese defeated the French after eight years of war. Under the U.S.-backed Geneva Accords, Vietnam was divided in two, with Ho's Communist Democratic Republic of Vietnam (DRV) government ruling the north from Hanoi, and the America-backed Republic of Vietnam (ROV) ruling the south from Saigon.

The Geneva Accords gave all Vietnamese people three hundred days to move freely to their zone of choice; while only about 120,000 moved from south to north, some 800,000 moved in the other direction. Cold warrior Americans no doubt saw the Vietnamese as voting with their feet for capitalism, but a more group-conscious lens reveals a very different picture. Many of those migrating south were Chinese (the vast majority of Chinese in the north relocated), and most of the ethnic Vietnamese who went south were Catholics, including the "Frenchified" Vietnamese elite, who feared Communist persecution. By the end of the relocation period, the overwhelming majority of the Hoa—about 1 million out of 1.2 million—lived in South Vietnam.

Ho was a passionate believer in the idea of a unified Vietnamese tribe. "We have the same ancestors, we are of the same family, we are all brothers and sisters," he once declared. "No one can divide the children of the same family. Likewise, no one can divide Viet-Nam." In 1959, Ho committed North Vietnamese forces to "liberating" the South.

The United States responded with escalating military involvement. In 1965, we began sending thousands of troops. We fought in Vietnam for a decade, and we lost. We weren't prepared for, and didn't adjust to, guerrilla warfare. We backed the wrong leaders. Some argue that we could have won had we only sent more troops. But one of the most important reasons for our devastating defeat remains largely unrecognized.

Most of Vietnam's "capitalists" were not Vietnamese. On the contrary, capitalism in Vietnam was associated with—and seen as chiefly benefiting—the Chinese, a fact that Hanoi repeatedly played up. Although there were also wealthy Vietnamese in the commercial class, Hanoi exaggerated the extent of Chinese dominance, claiming, for example, that "the ethnic Chinese controlled 100 per cent of South Vietnam's domestic wholesale trade," and at one point even calling the largely Chinese city of Cholon "the capitalist heart beating within socialist Vietnam's body."

Our wartime policies intensified the wealth and power of the already resented Hoa. America poured more than $100 billion into the war effort, and insofar as this money reached the local population, it ended up wildly disproportionately in the pockets of the ethnic Chinese. Americans required enormous amounts of supplies and services, and the Chinese were in the best position to deliver. The Chinese "handled more than 60 per cent of the total volume of goods imported into South Vietnam through U.S. aid." Many Chinese made fortunes as middlemen. Of the direct and indirect importers in Vietnam, 84 percent were ethnic Chinese in 1971. In addition, a flourishing black market controlled almost exclusively by the Chinese provided GIs with "[g]old watches, diamonds, cars, minks, marijuana, opium, heroin," and prostitutes. (In 1966, Cholon's red-light districts employed roughly thirty thousand "war-orphaned prostitutes," and one out of every four GIs had venereal disease.)

It wasn't just American dollars enriching Vietnam's Chinese minority. It was capitalism itself. In the financial sector, by 1972 the local Chinese effectively owned twenty-eight of the thirty-two banks in South Vietnam (although many of these banks were nominally owned by Vietnamese). Moreover, with economic power comes the ability to buy political influence, and the Chinese in Saigon notoriously cultivated and bribed South Vietnamese politicians and military leaders. "[T]he slime of corruption oozed into every crevice" of wartime South Vietnam.

The Chinese not only profited from America's intervention; they seemed ruthlessly impervious to the suffering of the Vietnamese around them. At one point, Chinese rice moguls intentionally created a rice shortage to jack up prices, compounding the hunger and malnourishment already caused by the war. They hoarded rice and even tried to throw it in the river to avoid government searches. Worse still, the Chinese systematically avoided the draft through bribery. Being police chief of the Cholon precinct became one of the most lucrative positions in the country; ultimately, more than one hundred thousand Chinese in Cholon dodged the draft. In effect, the U.S.-backed regime was asking the South Vietnamese to fight and die—and kill their northern brethren—in order to keep the Chinese rich.

We completely missed this ethnic dimension. Most American military personnel on the ground in Vietnam couldn't tell the difference between Chinese and Vietnamese; they may not even have been aware there was a difference. All Asians were "Dinks and Gooks, Slants and Slopes." As one American in Vietnam put it, "We didn't even think they were human—it was 'Gooks don't bleed, gooks don't feel pain, gooks don't have any sense of loyalty or love.'"

From Washington's point of view, we were battling the evil of communism, sacrificing American soldiers for Vietnam's freedom. But from the Vietnamese point of view, the idea that America was offering them "freedom" was absurd. Their experience of the American intervention was the destruction of their way of life. U.S. firepower destroyed the homes of more than 2 million South Vietnamese, most of whom were forced to relocate to urban areas, leaving behind their ancestors' graves. In addition, they endured indiscriminate bombing, napalm, and horrific civilian deaths. In

South Vietnam, a staggering 1 million civilians died and another million were wounded, mostly from U.S. "friendly fire."

And for what? The group identity America offered the Vietnamese was membership in a puppet state—the ultimate affront in a country where many Vietnamese soldiers wore trinkets dedicated to the Trung sisters, symbolizing resistance to foreign invaders at all costs. Henry Kissinger saw this as early as 1969, when he warned that "[u]nfortunately our military strength has no political corollary; we have been unable so far to create a political structure that could survive military opposition from Hanoi after we withdraw." As Guenter Lewy wrote in 1978, "The South Vietnamese soldier, in the end, did not feel he was part of a political community worth the supreme sacrifice; he saw no reason to die" for the U.S.-backed regime.

Materially, apart from a tiny upper crust, the Vietnamese people received no benefits from America; on the contrary, they lost their sons and their homes, and the only people they saw profiting were the hated Chinese and corrupt politicians. And yet as the war progressed, and more and more South Vietnamese went over to the other side, U.S. foreign policy makers were baffled; they couldn't fathom why the Vietnamese hated us so much and didn't want their "freedom." If we'd understood Vietnam's history and its ethnic realities, we wouldn't have been so mystified.

From a tribal politics perspective, virtually every step we took in Vietnam was guaranteed to turn the Vietnamese against us. The regimes we supported, the policies we promoted, the money we spent, and the attitudes we brought made the Vietnamese hate us, hate capitalism, and only enhanced the appeal and status of the charismatic Ho Chi Minh.

THE AFTERMATH: ETHNIC CLEANSING

The last U.S. troops left Saigon in 1973, and after that Americans tried to forget Vietnam. But it was then that the ethnonationalist dimension of the war became most glaringly clear.

In September 1975, the new Socialist government launched an anticapitalist campaign under the code name "X1." Chinese businesses were raided or shut down, and 250 wealthy Chinese were arrested. Many Chinese tycoons fled overseas; a number committed suicide. Chinese-language newspapers and Chinese-run schools were closed, and Chinese hospitals were taken over by the state. Although wealthy Vietnamese were also targeted, the Hoa suffered the most by far; 70 percent of those officially condemned in the campaign against "compradore bourgeoisie" were ethnic Chinese. All told, the Chinese in South Vietnam lost an estimated $2 billion because of the nationalization of their assets in the late 1970s—an astounding sum, considering Vietnam's overall poverty at the time.

Anti-Chinese sentiment worsened as relations between China and Vietnam deteriorated. In 1977, "the campaign against all ethnic Chinese in Vietnam was stepped up and became nationwide in scope." In the south, the Chinese were physically harassed, their homes and property seized. In the north, all working

Chinese were placed under surveillance and prohibited from speaking Chinese—even though most of the relatively few Chinese who remained in the north were not wealthy capitalists, but fishermen, foresters, craftsmen, and laborers. In the provinces abutting China, Hanoi began "purifying the border areas," expelling the Chinese for alleged security reasons.

But the real ethnic-cleansing policies began under "X2," a second anticapitalist campaign, launched in early 1978. On March 23, a paramilitary force of thirty thousand cordoned off Cholon—the Chinese area of Saigon—and ransacked every house and shop there. Goods and valuables were confiscated from fifty thousand Chinese businesses, and clashes between the Chinese and the police left the streets of Cholon "full of corpses." Similar raids took place all over the country, and ethnic Chinese were purged from the party, government administration, and the army. The government began arresting and relocating Chinese at alarming rates; "thousands of Chinese either died laboring in Vietnam's 'new economic zones' or fled the country." Even Chinese in the north who had been loyal revolutionaries were arrested as spies. "My uncle was arrested at that time," one Vietnamese Chinese later recalled. "He had been working for the revolution . . . at least forty years. He had been awarded the First Rank Revolution Medal [by the Vietnamese Communists themselves]." Employing "techniques Hitler used to inflame hatred against the Jews," reported *U.S. News & World Report* in 1979, "Hanoi is blaming day-to-day problems in Vietnam on resented Chinese control of commerce and the Mekong Delta."

Beijing accused Hanoi of mass killings and atrocities committed against the ethnic Chinese. Although long denied by Vietnam, experts agree that "China's allegations have now been largely substantiated." By late 1978, more than 250,000 ethnic Chinese had been driven out of Vietnam, and an estimated 30,000 to 40,000 had died at sea. Americans heard in the late 1970s a great deal about "Vietnamese boat people";* rarely, if ever, was it reported that most of those refugees were in fact ethnic Chinese. In 1978, for example, 85 percent were Chinese. In 1979, Vietnamese foreign ministry officials effectively admitted to foreign journalists that Vietnam "intended to get rid of all Chinese in Vietnam."

Thus Vietnam's Communist revolution was not only nationalist but intensely *ethno*nationalist. We completely missed the heart of Vietnamese political tribalism. Far from being a pawn of Communist China, as the United States imagined, Vietnam would by 1979 be at war with China. It would be difficult to come up with a more effective strategy for shooting ourselves in the foot, undermining our own objectives, and maximizing popular resistance against us.

---

* Since the Vietnam War, there have been three main waves of Vietnamese refugees. A first wave left Vietnam in 1975, immediately after Saigon fell. The second wave occurred in 1978–79, around the time that Vietnam and China went to war. Approximately 70 percent of the refugees in these two waves were ethnic Chinese, most of whom eventually resettled in the West. In 1988–89, a third wave of refugees left Vietnam; this group was primarily ethnic Vietnamese.

CHAPTER THREE

Afghanistan

*In Afghanistan, you don't understand yourself solely as an individual
. . . . You understand yourself as a son, a brother, a cousin
to somebody, an uncle to somebody. You are part of something
bigger than yourself.*

—KHALED HOSSEINI

*May God keep you away from the venom of the cobra, the teeth of the
tiger, and the revenge of the Afghans.*

—PROVERB

For most Americans, Afghanistan is a black box. We know that our soldiers have died there, that there are mullahs and caves, and that both may have harbored Osama bin Laden. We're vaguely aware that the war we're fighting in Afghanistan is the longest in our history. We've all heard of the Taliban, an organization that destroys art and bans girls from school, and that wears black or possibly white. Our dim memory is that we beat them once, but now for some reason they are back, and we have no idea what's going on, and we just want to forget about the whole country.

Yet we keep hearing ominous warnings from people in the know that things are going badly there and are likely to get worse—that Afghanistan is "a foreign policy disaster," a "never-ending war." Or as one congressman recently wrote in the *National Interest*, "Fifteen years, thousands of lives and tens of billions of dollars later, the United States has failed to meet most of its key objectives in Afghanistan. Mission failed."

As in Vietnam, the core reason for America's failures in Afghanistan is that we were oblivious to the most important group identities in the region, which do not fall along national lines, but instead are ethnic, tribal, and clan based. Afghanistan's national anthem mentions fourteen ethnic groups, the largest four being the Pashtuns, Tajiks, Uzbeks, and Hazaras. There is a long history of animosity among these groups. For more than two hundred years, the Pashtuns dominated Afghanistan, but during the Cold War their dominance began to decline, and in 1992, a Tajik- and Uzbek-led coalition seized control. The Taliban, supported by Pakistan, emerged against this background.

The Taliban is not only an Islamist movement but also an *ethnic* movement. The vast majority of its members are Pashtuns. It was founded by Pashtuns, it is led by Pashtuns, and it arose out of—and derives its staying power because of—threats to Pashtun dominance.

American leaders and policy makers entirely missed these ethnic realities, and the results have been calamitous. Our blindness to tribal politics allowed Pakistan to play us badly, turned large numbers of Afghans against us, and led us inadvertently to help create the Taliban, arming, funding, and training many of its key figures.

The problem in Afghanistan is not just radical Islam. It's also an ethnic problem. And it's rooted in a cardinal rule of tribal politics: once in power, groups do not give up their dominance easily.

AFGHANISTAN AND PAKISTAN

Afghanistan is landlocked. It shares its western border with Iran (indeed, Afghanistan's Tajiks speak Dari Persian and are often described as "Eastern Iranians"). To its north lie the former Soviet Central Asian republics of Turkmenistan, Uzbekistan, and Tajikistan. To its east and southeast sits Pakistan, with which it shares a fifteen-hundred-mile-long border, known as the Durand Line.

The state of Afghanistan was established in 1747 by a Pashtun, the celebrated king Ahmad Shah Durrani. From 1747 to 1973, Pashtun leaders ruled Afghanistan almost continuously. Pashtuns pride themselves on being great warriors; Europeans never conquered Afghanistan—although the British and Russians certainly tried. Pashto is the mother tongue of the Pashtuns, who also have their own code of conduct, known as Pashtunwali, which is difficult to translate into Western terms but roughly includes honor, hospitality, reciprocity, and revenge among its key components. Many Pashtuns think of Afghanistan as "their country," and even today, the terms "Afghan" and "Pashtun" are often used interchangeably.

But Pashtuns don't live only in Afghanistan; they also live in Pakistan. Indeed, the name "Pakistan" is an acronym, invented in Cambridge, England, in 1933, denoting the country's major ethnic regions. *P* stands for Punjab, *A* for Afghan (referring to Pashtuns), *K* for Kashmir, *S* for Sindh, and *tan* for Balochistan.

While Pashtuns have politically dominated Afghanistan, Punjabis have politically dominated Pakistan. Representing somewhere around half the population, Punjabis control Pakistan's famous military as well as most state institutions. Punjabis are also intensely ethnocentric. They speak Punjabi, and they are highly endogamous, typically marrying other Punjabis, often their own cousins. This practice is common even among Punjabis in Great Britain, where first-cousin marriages among Pakistanis are leading to an "appalling" and "absolutely unacceptable" incidence of "disability among children," as a (Lahore-born) member of the House of Lords recently warned.

Ever since independence, the Pakistani government has viewed the Pashtuns as a major threat. This is because there are *a lot* of Pashtuns in Pakistan. In fact, although Pashtuns comprise only 15 percent of Pakistan's total population, there are actually *more* Pashtuns in Pakistan (about 28 million) than in Afghanistan (about 15 million). Worse, most of Pakistan's Pashtuns live clustered near the Afghanistan border, along the Durand Line, which British colonialists drew in 1893 and which Pashtuns scorn as illegitimate. Indeed, Pashtuns on both sides of the border cross the Durand Line at will, which is not difficult given that the "line" runs through rugged terrain practically impossible to police. A common saying among Pashtuns holds that "[y]ou cannot separate water with a stick," and many Pashtuns in Pakistan still identify themselves as Afghan.

Pakistani fear of Pashtun nationalism and irredentism grew

even more acute after 1971, when Pakistan's Bengalis broke away in a violent, successful attempt to establish Bangladesh as an independent country. Pakistan's Punjabi elites were determined not to let that happen again with the Pashtuns.

"THE SOVIET UNION'S VIETNAM"

In 1978, Afghanistan's president was overthrown and brutally murdered in his palace along with most of his family members, their bodies thrown in a ditch. Although pro-Communist rebels led the coup, it took not only the United States but also the Soviet Union by surprise. According to one historian of the Soviet Union, "even the KGB learned about the leftist coup ex post facto." Fortunately for the United States, the Soviet Union was as ethnically blind as we were during the Cold War, similarly viewing world events in terms of a grand battle between communism and capitalism. After the 1978 coup, the Soviet ambassador to Afghanistan tried valiantly to interpret what had happened in orthodox Marxist terms. In a letter to Moscow, he explained that the previous government had accelerated the contradictions of capitalism, leading to a proletariat revolution sooner than anyone had expected. This assessment bore no resemblance to reality. There was no proletariat in Afghanistan. The coup was the culmination of a festering feud between one faction dominated by rural Pashtuns (who were behind the coup) and another dominated by urban Tajiks.

The new government in Afghanistan was a disaster. While its

leaders might have been nominally Communist, they were also, first and foremost, Pashtun nationalists who "viewed 'Afghan' as synonymous with 'Pashtun.'" To consolidate power, they embarked on a campaign of terror, hunting down rival religious and tribal leaders, and torturing and executing more than fifty thousand people. The Soviet Union's new "Afghan clients" became totally unmanageable. Moscow feared that the growing turmoil would bring anti-Communist, pro-American forces to power.

In December 1979, the Soviet Union invaded Afghanistan. "It'll be over in three to four weeks," Leonid Brezhnev told the Soviet ambassador to the United States. Nine years later, the Soviets left Afghanistan with their tail between their legs, having been defeated by the U.S.-backed mujahedin. At the time, Washington policy makers were thrilled; we had beaten our rival superpower practically on their own turf. But the Soviet defeat was a Pyrrhic victory for America.

THE UNITED STATES AS PAKISTAN'S
GEOPOLITICAL PAWN

The Soviet invasion of 1979 alarmed the Carter administration. Zbigniew Brzezinski, Carter's national security adviser, was simultaneously hopeful that Moscow had overreached but fearful of a reprise of 1956, when the Soviets invaded Hungary and crushed the resistance there, or of 1968, when they did the same in Czechoslovakia. At the same time, we were still stinging from Vietnam, and direct military involvement was out of the question. So we opted to covertly arm the anti-Soviet Afghan mujahedin, through Pakistan. All decisions about "who got the most guns, the most money, the most power" were left to Pakistan's anti-Communist dictator, General Muhammad Zia-ul-Haq.

In other words, we outsourced our Cold War policy in Afghanistan to Pakistan. In turn, Pakistan took us for a ride, making the United States its geopolitical pawn. Pakistan knew exactly how to manipulate ethnic politics in Afghanistan.

Zia's strategy was classic divide-and-conquer. The Pashtun people are not homogeneous. On the contrary, they are notoriously internally fragmented, with a maze of hundreds of smaller tribes and clans, many with longstanding rivalries and conflicts. Indeed, the Pashtuns are the world's largest tribally organized society. Although virtually all Pashtuns are Sunni Muslims, some tribes (often rural) are more religious, while others (typically urban) are more secular. Zia shrewdly favored and empowered Islamist Pashtuns, splitting them off from moderates and allying them with his own Islamist regime. He built madrassas throughout the Pashtun regions. These Islamic schools cultivated an extremist and virulent fundamentalism among young Pashtun men. As former Afghan president Hamid Karzai would later put it, "Pakistan set out to destroy Pashtun nationalism by Islamizing Pakistani Pashtuns and killing Afghan Pashtun nationalists. Pakistan's goal was to have Afghanistan dominated by radical Islam."

U.S. policy makers, focused on the battle against communism, barely knew anything about the Pashtuns. On the contrary, the United States romanticized the Pakistan-supported Afghan mujahedin as soldiers fighting for the free world. (Congressman Charlie

Wilson had floor-to-ceiling framed photographs of mujahedin warriors in heroic pose hung on his office wall.) Even in the face of the stunning upheaval of the Islamic Revolution in Iran in 1979 and the taking of American hostages there, U.S. foreign policy in Afghanistan never saw the potent anti-American, anti-Western group identity fueling the Islamic fundamentalist fighters. Fixated on the Cold War, we were heedless of the monster we were helping to create.

Between 1980 and 1992 we funneled through Pakistan almost $5 billion worth of weapons and ammunition—including heavy machine guns, explosives, antiaircraft cannons, wireless interception equipment, and twenty-three hundred shoulder-fired Stinger missiles—to anti-Soviet mujahedin fighters, paying no attention to whom we were arming. The recipients included the likes of Mullah Mohammed Omar, who would eventually land on America's most-wanted list and become the Taliban's intensely anti-Western supreme commander. It's not an exaggeration to say that the United States was in significant part responsible for the rise of the Taliban and for turning Afghanistan into a hospitality suite for Osama bin Laden's al-Qaeda militants.

After the Soviet withdrawal in 1989, Afghanistan descended into years of brutal civil war. The U.S. government lost interest in the country, even as Pakistan and Saudi Arabia each continued to aggressively finance and arm their favored Afghan jihadist leaders. In 1996, America was caught completely off guard when a group of barefooted mullahs calling themselves the Taliban captured Kabul and took over two thirds of Afghanistan.

THE TALIBAN: PLAYING THE ETHNIC CARD

Afghanistan in the early nineties was lawless. Warlords ruled practically every city and town. Racketeers and drug mafias reaped enormous profits. Kidnappings, extortion, and rape—including of young girls—were rampant. One reason so many war-weary Afghans initially supported the Taliban was that it provided security where previously chaos reigned, even if security under the Taliban came with a strict Islamic dress code and bans on television, music, cards, kite flying, and most sports.

But the Taliban was able to provide security—to amass power and popular support broad and deep enough to establish law and order—because of its appeal to Pashtun ethnic identity.

For hundreds of years, the ruler of Afghanistan was always Pashtun. After the fall of the Afghan monarchy in 1973, the Soviet invasion, and years of civil war, Pashtun dominance was suddenly upended. In the early 1990s, much of the country was controlled by members of the Tajik minority. The Pashtuns had lost control of Kabul, the nation's capital, where Burhanuddin Rabbani—a Tajik—was now president. They had lost control of the state bureaucracy, to the extent that it was still functioning. The Pashto language, once dominant in the nation's government-run television, radio, and newspapers, had lost status and declined dramatically. The Pashtuns had even lost control of their core power base, the Afghan military, which had fragmented, leaving non-Pashtun generals in command over the remaining units. As a result, deep resentment and fear of marginalization, of being eclipsed, had become widespread among Pashtuns of all different clans and tribes. Into this breach stepped the Taliban.

Virtually all of the Taliban leadership, and most of its rank and file, are Pashtuns—typically Ghilzai Pashtuns, from the "lowest socio-economic rung of society." The Taliban uses Pashto as its exclusive language of communication, and "[t]heir Pashtun identity is also obvious from their dress and individual behavior." The promise to restore Pashtun dominance in Afghanistan was a key part of the Taliban's rise to power.

Going from village to village, clan to clan, Taliban leaders combined their call for a simpler, purer Islam with appeals to Pashtun pride and resentment, offering Pashtuns a chance to reclaim their proper place. As Seth Jones writes:

> The Taliban's strategy was innovative and ruthlessly effective. Unlike the Soviets, they focused their initial efforts on bottom-up efforts in *rural* Afghanistan, especially the Pashtun south. They approached tribal leaders and militia commanders, as well as their rank-and-file supporters, and . . . they offered to restore Pashtun control of Kabul, which was run by the Tajik Rabbani. . . . It was a strategy accomplished on a very personal level: Taliban leaders who spoke the local dialect traveled to the Pashtun villages and district centers.

This is also why the Taliban was able to take over Afghanistan so quickly, catching the U.S. government unaware. "[T]he Taliban's Pashtun identity allowed them to sweep through the Pashtun areas relatively easily—in many cases without a shot being fired." It was primarily in non-Pashtun areas that the Taliban met with strong resistance. In the words of the influential Pashtun thinker Anwar-ul Haq Ahady (who later became head of Afghanistan's central bank under President Hamid Karzai), for many Pashtuns, fears of Pashtun marginalization were "more significant than the fall of communism. . . . The rise of the Taliban generated optimism among the Pashtuns about a reversal of their decline."

The Taliban's leader, Mullah Mohammed Omar, understood better than anyone the art of Afghan tribal politics. As Steve Coll writes in *Ghost Wars*, the poorly educated, one-eyed cleric from an undistinguished Pashtun clan "was an unlikely heir to Pashtun glory." But Omar was a master at interweaving fundamentalist Islam with Pashtun pride and symbolism. On the day he assumed leadership in the spring of 1996, he convened in Kandahar an audience of more than a thousand Pashtun leaders and religious scholars. There he called them to the tomb of the great Pashtun king Ahmad Shah Durrani, who after unifying the Pashtun tribes in 1747 had gone on to occupy Delhi and extend Afghan rule as far as Tibet. As Omar figuratively wrapped himself in Durrani's mantle, he climbed on the roof of the adjacent mosque and literally wrapped himself in the supposed "Cloak of the Holy Prophet." The crowd exulted and named him "Commander of the Faithful."

Ultimately, the Taliban never succeeded in unifying Afghanistan's Pashtuns. In part, this is because Pakistan's divide-and-conquer policies worked exactly as planned. More moderate, pro-Western Pashtuns found the Taliban's fanaticism increasingly repulsive. The Taliban's close ties with Pakistan also undermined its appeal to ordinary Afghans, who feared the "Pakistanization" of their country. Nevertheless, the Taliban's Pashtun identity and its readiness to exploit Pashtun ethnonationalism have been essential to its appeal, drawing large numbers of Pashtuns into its orbit from a surprising range of tribal, economic, and, to some extent, ideological backgrounds.

The ethnic side of the Taliban was even starker for the country's non-Pashtuns, who were systematically targeted. In 1998, for example, the Taliban massacred 2,000 Uzbeks and Hazaras (who for their part had massacred Taliban Pashtuns in 1997) and tried to starve another 160,000. The Taliban also persecuted and killed Tajiks, particularly in the country's rural areas.

The United States never saw the ethnic side of the Taliban. In the eighties and early nineties, we saw the mujahedin only as anti-Communist and therefore as friends. Needless to say, we quickly soured on our "freedom fighter" allies—especially after we learned that they weren't allowing girls to attend school, had slaughtered entire communities, and had barbarically destroyed the ancient Buddha statues in the Bamiyan Valley. Osama bin Laden officially launched al-Qaeda from Taliban-controlled Afghanistan, announcing to the world that it was the duty of "every Muslim" to kill Americans "in any country in which it is possible to do it." But when it became clear that the Taliban were not our friends—specifically, when they refused to turn over bin Laden after he took down the World Trade Center—we simply traded in our Cold War lens for an antiterrorist or anti-Islamist one. We recast the Taliban as a bunch of cave-dwelling mullahs and once again failed to see the central importance of ethnicity.

THE U.S. INVASION OF AFGHANISTAN

In October 2001, just a few weeks after the 9/11 attacks, on a wave of collective grief and anger, we sent troops to Afghanistan. We continued to make terrible miscalculations, repeatedly underestimating the importance of ethnic and tribal identity.

Impressively, we toppled the Taliban in just seventy-five days. But in doing so, we joined forces with the Northern Alliance, led by Tajik and Uzbek warlords and widely viewed as anti-Pashtun. According to counterterrorism expert Hassan Abbas, the Uzbek warlord Abdul Rashid Dostum, one of the Northern Alliance's commanders, "mercilessly killed thousands of Taliban foot soldiers," even though many had already surrendered. Dostum "was known for such tendencies, but on this occasion he did it on the payroll of the CIA." In another horrific episode, Dostum's soldiers packed thousands of Taliban prisoners in shipping containers for transport, with no food or water. Although Dostum later insisted that the deaths were unintentional, "hundreds suffocated in the containers. More were killed when Dostum's guards shot into the containers. The bodies were buried in a mass grave. . . . [A]bout 1,500 Taliban prisoners died."

Most Pashtuns—including many who were not sympathetic to the Taliban—saw Dostum's brutality as an act of ethnic revenge.

For them, he was an anti-Pashtun mass killer. When Dostum became one of "America's warlords," it didn't exactly endear us to the Pashtuns.

We compounded the problem with the post-Taliban government we helped set up, alienating Pashtuns all over the country by appearing to exclude them while favoring their rival ethnic groups. At a heavily U.S.-influenced postwar conference convened in Bonn to determine the "future of Afghanistan," Afghanistan was represented by a team consisting primarily of Uzbeks, Tajiks, and Hazaras from the Northern Alliance, along with a smaller number of exiled Pashtuns. American policy in Afghanistan was effectively to exclude almost anyone "remotely associated with the Taliban"—including thousands of more moderate Pashtuns who were connected to the Taliban through clan ties or who had worked with the Taliban without necessarily accepting its jihadist ideology.

Moreover, the United States was seen (to some extent correctly) as turning over the country's key positions of power to the Pashtuns' archrival ethnic group, the Tajiks, many of them known for corruption and patronage. Although President Hamid Karzai was a Pashtun, Tajiks filled most of the top ministry positions, such as army chief of staff, director of military intelligence, army inspector general, and director of counternarcotics forces. Only 24 percent of the population, Tajiks made up 70 percent of the army's corps commanders in the new U.S.-supported Afghan National Army. As Tajiks appeared to grow wealthy while U.S. airstrikes pounded primarily Pashtun regions, a bitter saying spread among Afghan Pashtuns: "[t]hey get the dollars, and we get the bullets." Many who had initially welcomed the U.S. military intervention in 2001 grew increasingly alienated from the new U.S.-backed regime, which has left Pashtuns at the very bottom of global human development.

After U.S. and coalition troops "defeated" the Taliban—actually just sending many of its foot soldiers into hiding in the mountains—we effectively turned our back on the country. With our eyes set on Iraq, we failed to implement any measures ensuring security or basic services for the Afghan people. This was a grave error. One of the Taliban's main strengths was that it had put a stop to the previously rampant extortions, rapes, gang robberies, and abductions, and after the United States routed the Taliban, corruption and lawlessness surged anew.

In December 2001, Vice President Cheney declared, "The Taliban is out of business, permanently." By 2010, the Taliban had regained control of major swaths of eastern and southern Afghanistan—despite the United States having spent a staggering $650 billion on the war and sacrificed more than 2,200 American lives. In 2016, U.S. Forces Afghanistan reported that about 43 percent of the country's districts were either "contested" or back under insurgent control or influence. In March 2017, the Taliban recaptured a key area in Helmand Province—an area known for opium poppy production that U.S. and British troops had defended at great human cost. According to a CNN security analyst, the Taliban was able to do so in part because "the Taliban have popular support, the government in Kabul [doesn't]. The further away from Kabul you get the worse it becomes." Meanwhile, Afghanistan has once again become an epicenter for terrorism, attracting members of al-Qaeda, ISIS, and the Pakistani Taliban (which killed 132 schoolchildren in Peshawar in 2014).

From the Cold War through the present day, our foreign policy in Afghanistan has been a colossal failure. In daunting part, this is because we either failed to understand or chose to ignore the country's complex tribal politics. What General Stanley Mc-Chrystal said of the NATO-led security forces in 2009 was surely true of the United States as well: We had "not sufficiently studied Afghanistan's peoples, whose needs, identities and grievances vary from province to province and from valley to valley." Consequently, as with Vietnam, nearly every move we made in Afghanistan was practically designed to turn large segments of the population against us.

Specifically, we never saw and never solved—in fact, never really even tried to solve—the Pashtun problem. The Pashtuns see Afghanistan as *their* country. They founded it and ruled it continuously for more than two hundred years; they defeated two world superpowers—the British and the Russians. However much they loathe the Taliban, Pashtuns are not going to support any regime they view as subordinating the Pashtun people to their deeply resented ethnic rivals.

Today, there are a host of excellent and insightful books and articles with titles like "The Pashtun Dilemma," "The Pashtun Problem," and "The Pashtun Question," which, hopefully, U.S. foreign policy makers are now paying attention to. But, as always, it's a little late.

CHAPTER FOUR

Iraq

A group of imams turned up to see me, introducing themselves as Kurds, Arabs and Turkmen, and both Sunni and Shia. . . . I asked them how I could help. "You know our needs," one retorted. "America would not have invaded without knowing everything about us and what we need."

—EMMA SKY, *The Unraveling*

You don't kill or capture your way out of an industrial-strength insurgency.

—GENERAL DAVID PETRAEUS

In 2003, U.S. leaders and policy makers thought they had the right foreign policy models for the invasion of Iraq: post–Second World War Germany and Japan. In both countries, we overthrew an authoritarian regime, liberated the populace, democratized, and introduced a liberal constitution—all with extraordinary success, leading to peace and prosperity. As President Bush put it, "There was a time when many said that the cultures of Japan and Germany were incapable of sustaining democratic values. Well, they were wrong. Some say the same of Iraq today. They are mistaken."

As a result, the United States invaded Iraq with enormous optimism. "We will help the Iraqi people establish a peaceful and democratic country in the heart of the Middle East," President Bush said, later adding, "The rise of freedom in this vital region will eliminate the conditions that feed radicalism and ideologies of murder and make our nation safer." Similarly, Vice President Cheney predicted that after the United States liberated Iraq, "the streets in Basra and Baghdad are sure to erupt in joy," and "the freedom-loving peoples of the region will have a chance to promote the values that can bring lasting peace." In the months before the war, CIA analysts were so confident that Iraqis would warmly welcome U.S. soldiers that one operative suggested "sneaking hundreds of small American flags into the country for grateful Iraqis to wave at their liberators."

Of course, none of this happened. On the contrary, as in Vietnam and Afghanistan, we soon found ourselves in an unwinnable war, hated by the people we were supposedly trying to help. Instead of establishing a shining model of free market democracy in the Middle East, we produced ISIS.

The problem was that postwar Japan and Germany were the wrong "comparables." From a tribal politics point of view, they could not have been more different from Iraq. Both countries were strikingly ethnically homogeneous—Japan because it had always been that way, and Germany because by 1945 it had exterminated most of its non-Aryans. In other words, postwar democratization in both those countries took place in the relative absence of ethnic or religious division.

Unfortunately, a much better comparison was staring us right in the face: 1990s Yugoslavia. Like Iraq, Yugoslavia was a multi-ethnic nation (Serbs, Croats, Slovenes, Bosnians, and so on) with a long history of ethnic enmity. To give just one example, Croats, with Nazi support, slaughtered thousands of Serbs in concentration camps in World War II. Yugoslavia had deep religious divides (Catholics, Eastern Orthodox, and Muslims). It had a market-dominant minority (the Croats, who, along with the Slovenes, were far wealthier than the more populous, less economically developed Serbs). It had a relatively weak national identity (like Iraq, the state of Yugoslavia was created after the First World War). And all this had been held together by the iron hand of a charismatic military dictator (Josip Broz Tito) with considerable success. Under Tito's decades-long rule, although ethnic tensions simmered just below the surface, Yugoslavia's different groups had lived together relatively peaceably, with Serbs and Croats often intermarrying.

But when democratization came to Yugoslavia in the early 1990s, the result was not peace and prosperity. It was ethnic demagoguery, ethnic warfare, and ethnic cleansing—a kind of violence not seen in Europe since the Holocaust. Concentration camps appeared. Serbs killed Croats, Croats killed Serbs, Serbs slaughtered Bosnian Muslims. Serbs who had lived as neighbors with Croats for years were suddenly roaring with approval as their leaders shouted, "We will kill Croats with rusty spoons because it will hurt more!"

Yugoslavia, not Japan or Germany, would have been a far more instructive comparison for Iraq. In 2003, Iraq too was a multiethnic nation, with cross-cutting ethnoreligious divisions among Sunni Arabs, Shia Arabs, Kurds, and Christians. (Although most Kurds in Iraq are also Sunni, I will use the term "Sunnis" to refer to Sunni Arabs.) Iraq too was a country with a relatively weak national identity, ruled for decades with an iron fist by a military dictator. And, like Yugoslavia, Iraq had its own equivalent of a market-dominant minority.

SUNNI MINORITY DOMINANCE IN IRAQ

On the eve of the U.S. invasion, Iraq's roughly 15 percent Sunni minority dominated the country economically, politically, and militarily. By contrast, Shias comprised the vast majority of the country's rural poor as well as most of the urban poor living in slums on the outskirts of Baghdad and other major cities.

Sunnis had dominated Iraq for centuries, first under (Sunni) Ottoman rule, then under the British, who, in signature divide-and-rule fashion, favored and governed indirectly through Sunni elites, while marginalizing Shias and Kurds. In 1968, the Baath Party took control of Iraq and, despite its nominal emphasis on secularism and Arab unity, quickly became an organ for Sunni hegemony.

But Saddam Hussein, the almost cultlike leader of the Baathists, took Sunni favoritism—and subjugation of the Shia majority—to a whole new level. After becoming president in 1979, Saddam filled the ranks of Iraq's military, civil service, and intelligence with Sunnis. Under his regime, Sunnis—especially from his own hometown and clan—occupied the most powerful government posts and controlled the country's vast oil wealth, with Baathists holding the key positions in the nationalized oil company.

At the same time, Saddam ruthlessly crushed and persecuted the country's Shias and Kurds. Threatened by the rising influence of Shia clerics and the large Shia population, Saddam banned Shia religious holidays and arrested and executed prominent Shia clergy. Entire Shia villages were burned to the ground, and hundreds of thousands of Shias and Kurds were expelled or killed. After the Kurds and Shias rose up in 1991, Saddam retaliated mercilessly, using chemical weapons and executing untold numbers— including women and children—whose corpses were thrown into mass graves.

These were the conditions when U.S. troops invaded in 2003, overthrowing Saddam in a matter of weeks. The Sunnis were a privileged ruling minority, and the Shias a long-oppressed 60 percent majority with deep feelings of resentment and a desire for revenge. The dangers of rapid democratization—especially given the recent events in Yugoslavia—should have been obvious. The Shias had a collective ax to grind, and the Sunni minority had every reason to resist and fear majority rule. Yet most of America's foreign policy makers, politicians, and thought leaders seemed to think that the Sunni-Shia divide was no big deal, repeatedly minimizing its significance.

"There is not a history of clashes that are violent between Sunnis and Shias," Senator John McCain stated in 2003, "so I think they can probably get along." "Most Arab countries have Shiites and Sunnis, and a lot of them live perfectly well together," said conservative commentator William Kristol. Testifying before the House Budget Committee, then deputy secretary of defense Paul Wolfowitz noted that, compared to the Balkans, "[t]here has been none of the record in Iraq of ethnic militias fighting one another. . . . These are Arabs, 23 million of the most educated people in the Arab world, who are going to welcome us as liberators."

Worse, American policy makers believed that democratization was the *solution* to Sunni-Shia tensions. Harvard professor Noah Feldman, one of the principal authors of the new Iraqi Constitution, expressed confidence that the democratic process would unite Sunnis and Shias: "[O]ne can predict with some confidence that ordinary politics will eventually take effect, and the Shi'a will divide into multiple political parties that will, in the end, have to look for Sunni partners to create parliamentary majorities." Sadly, democratization had the opposite effect.

BRINGING DEMOCRACY TO IRAQ

Practically from the moment U.S. troops arrived, Sunni insurgents began waging war against the American invaders who they believed (correctly) would bring the majority Shias to power. The on-the-ground American ignorance of local group conditions is hard to overstate. Only one senior official in the U.S.-led Coalition Provisional Authority (CPA) spoke any Arabic. The main selection criteria for staffing the CPA were conservative credentials and loyalty to the Bush administration; applicants were asked whether they had voted for Bush and "if they supported *Roe v. Wade.*" The CPA's ignorance about Iraq, especially the Sunni-Shia dynamic, resulted in a series of catastrophic decisions.

For example, Sunni fears and opposition were exacerbated by the disastrous "de-Baathification" order issued by the CPA in May 2003, which stipulated that anyone "in the top four ranks of the Baath party should be dismissed from their jobs and never allowed to hold public office again." As General Stanley Mc-Chrystal put it a decade later, de-Baathification "reinforced Sunnis' fears that the fall of Saddam would leave them disenfranchised in the face of Shia dominance." De-Baathification also stripped the country—already in economic ruin from the war—of desperately needed skills. Hospitals found themselves without doctors, and government ministries lost expertise overnight.

But perhaps the worst U.S. decision was disbanding the entire Iraqi army. Overnight, we produced a pool of some 250,000 to 350,000 unemployed, frustrated Sunni men who owned weapons and had no marketable skills other than their military training, leaving them with no means of earning a livelihood. Many of these men joined Sunni insurgency groups, including al-Qaeda and ISIS, and took up arms against the United States. In 2015, one expert estimated that over 60 percent of ISIS's most prominent leaders were former Baathists. A former Iraqi army intelligence officer, who lost his job when the army was disbanded, commented that "[t]he people in charge of military operations in [ISIS] were the best officers in the former Iraqi army."

Back in 2003, the U.S. solution for this massively unstable

state of affairs was—immediate democratization. With practically no guidance or knowledge of local conditions, coalition military commanders were ordered to schedule provincial elections and to print ballots. Danger signs appeared immediately. In Najaf, for example, in June 2003, the coalition set up elections, but then, embarrassingly, had to cancel them when it became clear that "[t]he most organized political groups in many areas are rejectionists, extremists and remnants of the Baathists. . . . They have an advantage over the other groups."

Nevertheless, the United States pressed on with democratization, and in December 2005, three days before the country's first national elections, President Bush hailed the upcoming vote as "a remarkable transformation for a country that has virtually no experience with democracy and which is struggling to overcome the legacy of one of the worst tyrannies the world has known." He spoke with pride of the "hundreds of parties and coalitions" that registered for the election and the candidates "holding rallies and laying out their agendas" across the country.

Unfortunately, the political parties that emerged tracked and galvanized Iraq's ethnic and sectarian divisions. Shias voted for Shias, Kurds for Kurds, and Sunnis for Sunnis. As General David Petraeus later put it, "The elections hardened sectarian positions as Iraqis voted largely based on ethnic and sectarian group identity."

In other words, the 2005 elections did nothing to unite the people or ameliorate sectarian violence. On the contrary, violence quickly escalated. In Baghdad, roaming Shia death squads began terrorizing and murdering Sunnis. At the same time, militant

Sunnis commenced their own campaign of terror. One of their leaders, Abu Masab al-Zarqawi, declared "all-out war" on Shias, on democracy, on the coalition, and on America. The 2006 bombing of the al-Askari shrine, one of Shia Islam's holiest sites, set off vicious sectarian warfare, as furious Shias retaliated by bombing more than twenty Sunni mosques over the next few days. More than a thousand people died, pushing Iraq to the brink of a Sunni-Shia civil war.

What was the United States doing, militarily, in response to this violence? By 2006, the American populace was sick of the war, and the U.S. military was largely in "exit-strategy" mode. The orders from Washington were to minimize U.S. casualties, so most American troops had retreated into sealed-off forward operating bases (FOBs). In other words, as Iraq descended into chaos, U.S. troops were holed up, essentially trying to avoid contact with Iraqis. When a confused soldier in an FOB near Tikrit asked his captain what they were supposed to be doing, his superior replied, "We're here to guard the ice-cream trucks going north so that someone else can guard them there."

Could we have done better if we hadn't been so blind to tribal politics in Iraq—if we had paid more attention to, and worked with, the most important group ties and loyalties on the ground? There's very good evidence that the answer is yes.

THE 2007 SURGE

In a sea of foreign policy failures, the United States enjoyed a brief moment of success in Iraq when President Bush ordered an influx of twenty thousand additional troops in 2007, dramatically reducing sectarian violence and both civilian and U.S. casualties. Most Americans, however, have a very poor understanding of the surge, in part because it's been dragged through the mud of partisan spin and finger-pointing. But the surge is worth examining in detail, because it offers a concrete example of what a more effective, tribal-politics-conscious U.S. foreign policy might look like.

While the additional U.S. soldiers—sent primarily to Baghdad and Al Anbar Province—were of course a critical factor, the surge succeeded only because it was accompanied by a 180-degree shift in our approach to the local population. For the first time in Iraq, the U.S. military pursued explicitly group-focused, ethnically conscious policies on the ground. The surge was won tribe by tribe, leader by leader, neighborhood by neighborhood.

The story begins almost two years earlier and involves a then-little-known colonel by the name of H. R. McMaster, who would later become national security adviser in the Trump administration.

In the spring of 2005, McMaster and thousands of troops arrived in the northern Iraqi city of Tal Afar, at the time largely controlled by Sunni insurgents and awash in beheadings and bloodshed. After two demoralizing years in Iraq, McMaster had become acutely aware of the failings of U.S. policy: "When we came to Iraq, we didn't understand the complexity—what it meant for a society to live under a brutal dictatorship, with ethnic and sectarian divisions . . . [W]e made a lot of mistakes. We were like a blind man, trying to do the right thing but breaking a lot of things." Known for being a contrarian, McMaster decided to take a totally different approach—one that tried to understand and work with Iraq's complex group divisions and identities.

To begin with, McMaster required his troops to take detailed crash courses in local group customs, practices, and attitudes. As George Packer writes:

> [T]he regiment bought dozens of Arab dishdashas, which the Americans call "man dresses," and acted out a variety of realistic scenarios, with soldiers and Arab-Americans playing the role of Iraqis. . . . Pictures of Shiite saints and politicians were hung on the walls of a house, and soldiers were asked to draw conclusions about the occupants. Soldiers searching the house were given the information they wanted only after they had sat down with the occupants three or four times, accepted tea, and asked the right questions.

McMaster prohibited his soldiers from using derogatory terms, like "hajjis," for Arabs and told them, "Every time you treat an Iraqi disrespectfully, you are working for the enemy." He also had some troops take Arabic language classes, and ordered hundreds of copies of *The Modern History of Iraq* by Phebe Marr. Moreover, instead of cordoning them off, McMaster sent his troops to interact with the local population, to cultivate trust and to figure out Tal Afar's complex group dynamics and power structures. One of McMaster's squadron commanders spent forty to fifty hours a week meeting one-on-one with the leaders of the city's dozens of tribes: "first the Shiite sheikhs, to convince them that the Americans could be counted on to secure their neighborhoods; and then the Sunni sheikhs, many of whom were passive or active supporters of the insurgency."

McMaster began building alliances with crucial tribal leaders. He recognized that the only way to defeat the insurgency was to get Sunnis and Shias to work together against the extremists, whose brutality and indiscriminate killing had left a terrorized Tal Afar strewn with headless corpses. His task was enormously difficult: the insurgents were Sunni, and the local Sunni tribes hated and feared the Shias, who controlled the local police. But against all odds, through painstaking on-the-ground persuasion, often one tribal leader at a time, McMaster succeeded. By driving a wedge between moderate and extremist Sunnis, and by persuading Sunni and Shia tribal sheikhs to cooperate, McMaster and his men cleared Tal Afar of insurgents block by block. Within just six months of McMaster's arrival, Tar Afar had stabilized, and sectarian violence had fallen precipitously.

Tal Afar was the U.S. military's first successful large-scale counterinsurgency initiative in Iraq—a lonely bright spot in a year of sustained losses. Drawing on McMaster's success, U.S. forces pursued similar tactics in Ramadi, capital of the Al Anbar Province in central Iraq.

By 2006, many Anbari Sunnis who originally supported the

insurgents had become disgusted with al-Qaeda's savagery and utter disregard for human life. "[A]nyone who was caught smoking had his or her fingers chopped off," writes retired colonel (and now professor) Peter Mansoor. "The corpses of assassinated Iraqis were booby-trapped so that family members coming to collect them for burial would be killed and injured in the process." Moreover, many of al-Qaeda's senior leaders were foreigners, who executed even widely respected Sunni tribal leaders if they refused to cooperate. In what is now known as the "Sunni Awakening," many Anbari Sunnis turned against al-Qaeda.

Colonel Sean MacFarland, a brigade commander in charge of Ramadi, seized this opening. By cultivating and working closely with Sunni tribal sheikhs, MacFarland brought one Sunni tribe after another into the U.S. fold. He drew on the talents of men like Captain Travis Patriquin, who spoke Arabic and was highly knowledgeable about Iraqi tribal culture and who, "[o]ver countless cups of tea and hundreds of cigarettes . . . worked magic with the tribal leaders." (Patriquin was killed by a roadside bomb in December 2006.)

Crucially, MacFarland and his troops persuaded Sunni chieftains to recruit their fellow tribespeople to serve on new local police forces trained and armed by the U.S. military. It made all the difference to have local police who actually knew the neighborhoods and who could identify the insurgents and criminals. The new police protected local citizens from retaliation by al-Qaeda and provided the U.S. military with "cultural savvy and local knowledge that opened the door to enormous amounts of intelligence on al-Qaeda and other insurgent groups." Suddenly, the U.S. military and its partners were able to capture hundreds of al-Qaeda suspects along with large caches of al-Qaeda weaponry.

Instead of viewing Iraq's tribes as anachronisms, as the CPA initially did, or dismissing their importance, as Wolfowitz had in 2003, the new leaders of the U.S. effort, such as Brigadier General John Allen, understood that "[t]ribal society makes up the tectonic plates in Iraq on which everything rests." With its new Sunni partners, U.S. forces cleared neighborhoods one by one, then "gated" them, allowing only those with registration cards to enter. By November 2006, the area around Ramadi was largely free of al-Qaeda insurgents. And by summer of 2007, coalition forces had reclaimed much of Al Anbar Province.

Tal Afar and Ramadi became blueprints for General David Petraeus when he took over command of coalition forces in Iraq as well as responsibility for the surge in February 2007. The challenges facing Petraeus at the time could not have been more daunting. The country was still reeling from the sectarian warfare unleashed by the 2006 bombing of the Shia al-Askari mosque, and nearly four hundred thousand Iraqis had been forced out of their homes. Violence was at surreal levels, with "well over fifty attacks and three car bombs per day on average in Baghdad alone."

It was clear to Petraeus that the strategy the United States had been pursuing for years in Iraq—basically using overwhelming force to try to kill as many insurgents as possible—was failing.

"An operation that kills five insurgents," he observed, would still be counterproductive if it led "to the recruitment of fifty more." Instead, Petraeus adopted the radically different approach pioneered by McMaster and MacFarland. As Petraeus saw it, the "big idea" emerging from Tal Afar and Ramadi "was that stability would be achieved by the bottom-up engagement of tribes and other Sunni groups as well as through the pursuit of top-down reconciliation via the Iraqi government."

The focus of the surge was Baghdad, which was on the verge of disintegration and seen by all sides as the "key to victory or defeat." The plan embraced by Petraeus was extremely attentive to Iraq's tribal politics. One of the principal documents underlying the surge, a strategy paper by military historian Frederick Kagan of the American Enterprise Institute, included a color-coded map dividing Baghdad district by district, sometimes block by block, into "Sunni Dominated," "Shia Dominated," and "Sunni/Shia Mixed" areas.

As in Ramadi, U.S. commanders now made a point of using men and women highly knowledgeable about Iraq's ethnic and sectarian dynamics. This included Petraeus's so-called "brain trust": academics, journalists, military historians, and military officers such as the British brigadier Nigel Aylwin Foster, who, having served in Iraq with the CPA, had been highly critical of the Americans' "cultural ineptitude." ("[I]f I could sum it up," Aylwin Foster said at the time, "I never saw such a good bunch of people inadvertently piss off so many people.") On the ground, the coalition relied increasingly on people like the remarkable Emma Sky, an Oxford-educated Middle East expert who had lived in the region for years, and Lieutenant Colonel Nycki Brooks, who had "encyclopedic knowledge" of Iraq's groups and subgroups and who was minutely aware of which tribal leaders were connected to whom.

As in Tal Afar and Ramadi, the U.S. military no longer sequestered its troops in safe-zone FOBs, nor did it simultaneously try to kill everyone who had ever joined or supported the insurgency. On the contrary, U.S. troops were sent to live among the local people in Baghdad, "rather than raiding into the area from remote, secure bases." As Petraeus explained in a 2007 report to Robert Gates, the secretary of defense:

> By living among the population we reinforced the Awakening Movements already underway and further empowered local communities that decided to reject extremism. We came to more clearly recognize that sheiks and tribes have important roles to play as key organizing structures in Iraq's culture of honor.

Taking a page from the British, the United States pursued a variant of divide-and-conquer in order to beat back the insurgency. As McChrystal would later put it, they sought out "the groups just shy of the most extreme poles" and tried to separate them from "the irreconcilables"—the groups dead set on insurgency. "The key," wrote McChrystal, was "to feel for the fissures between the groups, and rip."

Experts today agree that merely deploying twenty thousand additional troops would not have been sufficient had American commanders not "stopped fighting Iraq's tribal structure and instead started to cooperate with it," building alliances with influential sheikhs and both Sunni and Shia local leaders.

Measured by any number of metrics, the new approach was an unprecedented success. In just over nine months, from the height of sectarian conflict in December 2006 to September 2007, civilian deaths fell by 45 percent in Iraq overall and almost 70 percent in Baghdad. Deaths caused by ethnosectarian violence fell by 55 percent countrywide and by 80 percent in Baghdad. Although coalition casualties rose in the first part of 2007, a tipping point occurred in July and the numbers fell precipitously afterward. As Petraeus testified before a skeptical Congress in September 2007, "in the past 8 months, we have considerably reduced the areas in which Al Qaeda enjoyed sanctuary. . . . The most significant development in the past six months likely has been the increasing emergence of tribes and local citizens rejecting Al Qaeda and other extremists."

What's really extraordinary is that we managed to achieve documentable success—regaining lost cities, drastically reducing both American and Iraqi civilian casualties, and bringing together formerly warring Sunnis and Shias to fight on the U.S. side—in the worst possible circumstances, when sectarian strife and anti-Americanism in Iraq were already raging. Fundamental mistakes made early on meant that even the most strategically brilliant group-conscious policies adopted three years later would always face an uphill battle. Undoing the effects of the draconian 2003 de-Baathification order, for example, proved impossible. It is sobering to imagine what success we might have had if we had entered the Iraq War with our eyes open to Iraq's complex tribal politics in the first place.

DEMOCRACY AND IRAQI TRIBAL POLITICS

It's often said that the surge was too little, too late. That may well be true, but another way to look at it is that the tribe-conscious gains finally being made on the military front were fatally sabotaged by our continuing, breathtaking tribe blindness on the political front.

The December 2005 national elections swept members of the Shia majority into control of the new Iraqi parliament. Harmonious multiethnic coalitions did not form. For prime minister, the United States ultimately threw its weight behind former dissident Nouri al-Maliki, who assumed office in 2006.

It is mind-boggling that when the U.S. government chose to back Maliki—vesting in him the hope of unifying the country—we paid such scant attention to the group affiliations into which he was born and raised. Unbelievably, we seemed not to notice or care that Maliki was a devout Shia who had spent his whole life hating and fighting Sunnis. Maliki's grandfather was a famous Shia revolutionary. His father was jailed by the Sunni Baath Party, and Maliki himself eventually fled after being sentenced to death by Saddam Hussein for belonging to a secret Shia organization. To this day, Maliki speaks openly about how Sunni Baathist officers in 1979 "arrested everyone who was connected to me," including two of his brothers, and executed sixty-seven people from his village.

Perhaps we had Nelson Mandela in mind—who rose above and forgave his former oppressors—but if anyone had thought about it for even a second, they wouldn't have been so surprised that once in power, Maliki began excluding, detaining, persecuting, and executing Sunnis. After the Obama administration took over and U.S. troops began withdrawing, Maliki shed all pretense of conciliation and pursued an increasingly brazen sectarian agenda. He forced Sunnis out of the political process, cracked down on peaceful Sunni protests, and imprisoned thousands of Sunnis indefinitely without trial. Even while President Obama was praising Maliki at the White House for "ensuring a strong, prosperous, inclusive and democratic Iraq," Shia militias were terrorizing Sunnis, forcing thousands out of their homes, and summarily executing seventy-two civilians in the Diyala province. As time went on, many Sunnis of all backgrounds came to believe that Maliki was a puppet of the (Shia) Iranian government, determined to perpetrate genocide against them.

Thus was born ISIS. Also known as ISIL, Daesh, or the Islamic State, ISIS is many things. A fantasy caliphate that rejects the nation-state. An al-Qaeda offshoot that has eclipsed its parent. An apocalyptic cult that rapes, enslaves, and immolates. But at its core, the Islamic State is also a movement founded, led, and populated by Sunnis who feel shut out, mistreated, and persecuted by the Shia-dominated government in Iraq.

Indeed, a key difference between ISIS and al-Qaeda—which are now rival terrorist organizations—is that the former explicitly targets Shias. ISIS's caliphate is openly Sunni, as devoted to killing Shia "apostates" as it is to killing Western "infidels." Before he was killed by U.S. strikes, al-Zarqawi (now regarded as the founder of the Islamic State) reportedly disgusted Osama bin Laden by insisting that all "Shiites should be executed." Bin Laden's mother was a Shia.

It's impossible to understand the stunning success of ISIS without understanding the ethnopolitical dynamics of postwar Iraq. Iraq's Sunni Arabs correctly perceived that democracy would disempower them and—whatever the ethnically blind U.S.-drafted Constitution might say—leave them at the mercy of the majority Shias. And it was the height of naïveté for the United States to expect that Iraq's Shias would put centuries of Sunni oppression and brutality behind them.

The fact is that while many, if not most, Sunni Iraqis hate ISIS, they often fear and hate the specter of Shia dominance more. Even affluent, well-educated Sunni doctors and professors often preferred ISIS to Maliki, who finally was forced out in 2014. According to veteran Middle East reporter Patrick Cockburn, "Mr. Maliki is not to blame for everything that has gone wrong in Iraq, but he played a central role in pushing the Sunni community into the arms of ISIS."

Sunnis continue to feel disenfranchised and marginalized under Maliki's successor, Haider al-Abadi. As late as 2016, according to a Carnegie Endowment report, some 25 percent of Iraq's Sunni Arabs "remain[ed] supportive of the Islamic State. In Mosul, the country's second-largest city, a majority of the population appear[ed] to support the Islamic State or to express indifference about the subject." Meanwhile, with the United States focused on defeating ISIS, the real beneficiary has been Shia-dominated Iran. The United States spent over $1 trillion on the war in Iraq; some 4,500 American lives were lost. Yet fourteen years after the United States toppled Saddam Hussein, Iran's power is ascendant, with Tehran now wielding more influence over Baghdad than Washington.

TRIUMPHALISM AND ETHNONATIONALISM
IN THE POST–COLD WAR ERA

Our failure in Iraq is part of a much larger pattern in post–Cold War American foreign policy. After the collapse of the former Soviet Union, a triumphal consensus swept U.S. policy making circles. Communism and authoritarianism had failed, so the correct policy combination had to be their exact opposite: markets and democracy. It was only natural that America—the world's greatest champion of free market democracy, not to mention the sole superpower left standing—would take the lead in spreading this winning formula.

It was a time of extraordinary bipartisan optimism. Republicans and Democrats alike saw markets and democracy as a universal prescription for the many ills of underdevelopment. Market capitalism was the most efficient economic system the world had ever known. Democracy was the fairest political system, and the most respectful of individual liberty. Working hand in hand, markets and democracy would transform the world into a community

95

of prosperous, peace-loving nations, and individuals into civic-minded citizens and consumers. In the process, ethnic hatred, religious zealotry, and other "backward" aspects of underdevelopment would be swept away. Thomas Friedman captured this view in his 1999 number one *New York Times* bestseller, *The Lexus and the Olive Tree*, quoting a Merrill Lynch ad: "'The spread of free markets and democracy around the world is permitting more people everywhere to turn their aspirations into achievements, . . . [erasing] not just geographical borders but also human ones.'" Globalization, wrote Friedman, "tends to turn all friends and enemies into 'competitors.'"

That's not what happened. Instead of global peace and prosperity, the decade between 1991 and 2001 saw the proliferation of ethnic conflict; intensifying nationalism, fundamentalism, and anti-Americanism; confiscations, expulsions, calls for renationalization; two genocides of magnitudes not seen since the Nazi Holocaust—and the greatest attack on American soil since Pearl Harbor.

Just as in the Cold War, during this decade of U.S. triumphalism, we failed to take into account the potency of tribal politics. Most important, we failed to see that democracy has ethnic, sectarian, and other group-dynamic ramifications. In many parts of the world, far from neutralizing tribal hatred, democracy catalyzes it.

Iraq and Yugoslavia exemplify a pattern that has played out repeatedly in the developing world. In countries with long-pent-up ethnic and religious divisions, especially where national identity is weak, rapid democratization often galvanizes group hatred.

Vote-seeking demagogues find that the best way to mobilize popular support is not by offering rational policy proposals but by appealing to ethnic identity, stoking historical grievances, and exploiting group fear and anger. As America celebrated the global spread of democracy in the 1990s, ethnonationalist slogans proliferated: "Georgia for the Georgians," "Eritreans Out of Ethiopia," "Kenya for Kenyans," "Whites should leave Bolivia," "Serbia for Serbs," "Croatia for Croats," "Hutu Power," and "Jews Out of Russia." All too often, poor majorities use their new political power to take revenge against resented minorities, while minorities, fearful of being targeted by the newly empowered majority, resort to violence of their own. None of this is rocket science. It's basic tribal politics.

The point is not that democracy is to *blame* for the rise of ISIS. On the contrary, if anything, the blame rests with the cruelly repressive dictatorship of Saddam Hussein, the long-suppressed Shia anger that now makes democratization so challenging, and the bloodcurdling ideology of radical Islam. The fact remains that in many postcolonial countries—with their long legacies of divide-and-rule, corruption, and autocracy—rapid democratization can have catastrophic consequences. Just as U.S. blindness to tribal politics helped create the Taliban in Afghanistan, so too it helped create ISIS.

CHAPTER FIVE

Terror Tribes

Insanity in individuals is something rare—but in groups . . .
it is the rule.

—FRIEDRICH NIETZSCHE

A striking fact about terrorists is that, unlike serial killers, they are not generally psychopaths. Most serial murderers, experts agree, exhibit traits consistent with diagnosable psychopathic personality disorders. By contrast, psychologists studying terrorism have struggled in vain for years to identify particular deviant or abnormal personality traits typical of terrorists.

For example, some studies purport to show that terrorists are "narcissistic" or "driven by depression" or suffer from low self-esteem or had abusive childhoods. One West German researcher found that "[t]he terrorist group represents an outlet for archaic aggressive tendencies, frequently rooted in youthful conflicts with stepfathers." A nineteenth-century commentator hypothesized that "vitamin deficiencies" were linked to terrorist violence; more recently, a psychiatrist has suggested that "faulty ear functioning may be common among terrorists." Yet another expert postulated that terrorists tend to come from "societies where fantasies of cleanliness are prevalent."

In fact, all these claims have now been rejected, each batted down with a torrent of counterexamples. There is simply no reliable evidence that people who join terrorist organizations or engage in terrorists acts have unusually troubled childhoods or deviant personalities. On the contrary, suicide bombers and other terrorists are often described by stunned friends and acquaintances as "lovely," "friendly," "very personable," "a nice guy." Indeed, there is now consensus among researchers that "terrorists are essentially normal individuals."

The problem with attempts to identify "typical terrorist traits" or "the terrorist personality" is that they focus on the individual. But terrorism is above all a *group* phenomenon: it's a murderous expression of tribal politics. To understand how group dynamics can so twist an individual's psyche, it's helpful to start with some basic group psychology.

THE PSYCHOLOGY OF GROUPS

Groups not only shape who we are and what we do. They can also distort our perception of objective facts. Muzafer Sherif's now-classic Robbers Cave experiment offered an early demonstration. In the 1950s, twenty-two boys around the age of eleven were brought to a deserted camp in Oklahoma for three weeks and divided into two roughly similar cohorts, who immediately named themselves the Eagles and Rattlers.

For the first week, the two groups were kept completely separate, but in the second stage they were asked to compete in a series of physical games like baseball and tug-of-war. Intense group rivalry—replete with name calling, flag burning, and nighttime raids—immediately flared. At this point, the researchers conducted an experiment. A bean-collecting contest was held, after which each boy handed the beans he had gathered to the counselor to be counted. The counselor then pretended to pour each boy's beans onto a projector screen, instead pouring the same dummy set of beans onto the screen each time. The boys from both groups then estimated how many beans they thought each boy had collected by looking at the screen. Though the number of beans on the projector remained exactly the same, the boys consistently overestimated the performance of their own group members compared to the performance of out-group members.

Can intelligence or education overcome these distortive tendencies? It appears that just the opposite is true. In one recent study, Dan Kahan of Yale Law School and his coauthors took a pool of more than a thousand subjects, testing them first for their political leanings and their "numeracy" (basically, math skills plus their ability to analyze data and draw valid inferences). He then gave all the subjects a tricky problem requiring analysis of (fictional) quantitative data. Some subjects were asked a politically neutral question: whether a new skin cream made a rash better or worse. They were shown a table with numbers that would allow them to evaluate the claim. Predictably, subjects with stronger numeracy skills tended to come up with the right answer more often.

Other subjects, however, were given the exact same numbers but were asked whether a gun ban increased or decreased crime. Subjects who saw these numbers demonstrated political bias. Those with liberal, Democratic leanings tended to conclude that the gun ban decreased crime; those with conservative, Republican leanings tended to conclude that the gun ban increased crime.

But here's the kicker: those with stronger numeracy skills demonstrated *more* bias. They were *more* likely to err in the direction of their political predispositions, possibly because of their superior ability to manipulate data. In other words, Kahan found that the *smarter* you are with numbers, the *more* likely you are to manipulate evidence to conform to your group's core beliefs. This finding has now been replicated for several different hot-button factual controversies—for example, climate change—and extended beyond numeracy. The better informed people are, and the better educated, the more polarized they tend to be on politically controversial factual issues, and the more stubbornly they manipulate new facts to support their tribe's worldview.

Another way group membership affects our judgment is through pressure to conform. In Solomon Asch's landmark 1951 study, subjects were seated at a table with six confederates—fake participants who were actually part of the experiment team. The participants were shown a card with a line on it. Then they were shown another card with three very different lines and asked to point to the one that was the same length as the first line. The answer should have been obvious. But after watching the six plants choose a patently wrong answer, 75 percent of the real subjects went along with the others and picked the wrong line too.

Stanford University professor Robb Willer extended the Asch conformity analysis to investigate how incorrect information can be propagated, even when in-group members know it's bogus. To foster in-group bonds, Willer created the illusion that subjects were part of a group with a knack for sophisticated wine tasting (by reporting overblown credentials for the other members). Participants were asked to taste two wines that were actually from the same bottle. Subjects were then placed at solo computer stations. Each was told that they would be the fifth out of six subjects to rate the wines. Each got to see the first four responses, which were not actually from their peers but created by a computer. All of the computer ratings insisted that one of the identical wines was far inferior to the other. Over half the subjects conformed to social pressure, agreeing with these fake ratings. The subjects then received a final fake response—a "deviant" one that actually spoke the truth (finding the two wines indistinguishable). Subjects were then asked to judge the wine-rating abilities of what they thought were the other group members.

The results were fascinating. When *privately* asked to rank their fellow wine tasters, the conforming subjects revealed that they actually favored the "deviant"—suggesting that in reality they too had found the wines indistinguishable. But when asked to *publicly* express their views, the subjects punished the "deviant" by ranking him lower. In other words, the subjects publicly enforced a group-consensus norm they didn't actually agree with. As Willer points out, this type of conformity is especially dangerous because, "through a cascade of self-reinforcing social pressure," false realities can be accepted as true, while truth tellers are punished and individuals become wedded to their own hypocrisy. These cascades can "trap a population into worshipping a naked emperor, without the possibility of a child breaking the spell."

Group identification can powerfully reinforce these conformity effects. In experiments similar to Asch's landmark study, subjects have been found to conform much more when presented with judgments said to come from members of an in-group, and much less when judgments are said to come from out-group members. And it's not just that people tend to think what their fellow tribe members think. They will do what their fellow tribe members do—even to the point of savagery.

In the words of Gustave Le Bon, the nineteenth-century French social psychologist who essentially invented crowd psychology, an individual who is part of a group "descends several rungs in the ladder of civilisation." By himself, a person "may be a cultivated individual"; in a group, "[h]e possesses the spontaneity, the violence, the ferocity, and also the enthusiasm and heroism of primitive beings." An individual who acts together with others in a group acquires "a sentiment of invincible power which allows him to yield to instincts which, had he been alone, he would perforce have kept under restraint."

Fanaticism fueled by the disinhibiting effects of group identity almost certainly has a physiological basis, although we are just beginning to understand it. Describing young male ISIS fighters racing by on trucks, "black flags waving," fists clenched, exhilarated "from the slaughter of infidels," psychologist and neuroscientist Ian Robertson writes that the militants are experiencing "a biochemical high from a combination of the bonding hormone oxytocin and the dominance hormone testosterone. Much more than cocaine or alcohol, these natural drugs lift mood, induce optimism and energise aggressive action on the part of the group." Group bonding, Robertson notes, increases oxytocin levels, which spurs "a greater tendency to demonise and de-humanise the out-group" and which physiologically "anaesthetizes" the empathy one might otherwise feel. "It is groups," Robertson concludes, "which are capable of savagery, much more than any individual alone."

This is the darkest side of the tribal instinct: the ease with which we dehumanize outsiders and the satisfaction we derive from doing so. Strong group affiliations cause people to regard out-group members as "all alike" (an out-group homogeneity effect), to characterize them with negative traits or dangerous proclivities, and to view them as less than human. Individuals are also much more likely to attribute human emotions (like admiration, sorrow, or disillusion) to in-group members, while seeing only "primary," more animal emotions (like anger, surprise, fear) in out-group members. These effects have been found to exist between Belgians (in-group) and Arabs (out-group); whites (in-group) and blacks (out-group); and Canadians (in-group) and Afghans (out-group).

Most disturbingly, such effects appear, sometimes in extreme form, in young children. Consider two recent studies about in-group and out-group attitudes of Arab and Jewish kids in Israel. In the first, Jewish children were asked to draw both a "typical Jewish" man and a "typical Arab" man. The researchers found that even among preschoolers, Arabs were portrayed more negatively and as "significantly more aggressive" than Jews. Likewise, in a 2011 study, Arab high school students in Israel were asked for their reactions to fictitious incidents involving the accidental (non-war-related) deaths of either an Arab or Jewish child, for example due to electrocution or a biking accident. Roughly 64 percent of the subjects expressed sadness about the death of the Arab child, whereas only 5 percent expressed sadness about the death of the Jewish child. Indeed, almost 70 percent said they felt "happy" or "very happy" about the Jewish child's death.

THE BANALIZATION OF EVIL

Islam Yaken grew up in an upper-middle-class family in Cairo. He graduated from a private high school and Ain Shams University. Old friends remember him as "funny but respectful" and recall that his dreams were ordinary: to build his own business as a fitness trainer and "get a hot girlfriend." Yaken worked hard, offering fitness lessons at local gyms and posting online exercise videos. "Every guy dreams of having a six-pack so he can take his shirt off at the beach or at the pool and have people check him out," he told his YouTube followers. But Yaken struggled. He couldn't land a steady job in Egypt's depressed economy; his business foundered.

In 2012, after losing a close friend in a motorcycle accident, he met an ultraconservative sheikh. Previously unreligious, Yaken grew a beard and became intensely devout, refusing to talk to women and forcing himself, out of shame and anger, not to look at them. When a coup forced the Muslim Brotherhood out of power, Yaken became disillusioned with Egypt's political system and left for Syria without telling his friends or family. They learned of his transformation when his Twitter feed began broadcasting grue-some photos of decapitated heads in a basket, rants about the glory of ISIS—and workout videos for jihadists. Now a "poster boy" (and personal trainer) for ISIS, Yaken has been pictured on horseback with a machine gun and scimitar. In a ghastly way, ISIS allowed Yaken to realize his career ambitions and lifted him to a status and stature he lacked in Egypt.

Members of terrorist groups don't become killers and beheaders overnight. They are typically drawn in through a gradual process of socialization, indoctrination, and radicalization—with group identity and dynamics playing a critical role at every juncture.

Jejoen Bontinck, a Belgian who converted to Islam in his teens, is one of the thousands of Europeans who left comfortable homes to join ISIS in Syria. Like Yaken, Jejoen seemed like an ordinary teenager but "fell down in a black hole" after he was eliminated from a reality television contest (in which he danced like Michael Jackson), then dumped by his girlfriend. Enter Sharia4Belgium, a radical Islamist group based in Antwerp committed to turning Belgium into an Islamic state. (There's also Sharia4Holland and Islam4UK.) Led by a militant preacher, Fouad Belkacem, with ties to ISIS, Sharia4Belgium gave Jejoen an instant tribe (mem-bers of the group call one another "brothers"), a sense of impor-tance and duty, role models to admire, and enemies to hate.

Over twenty-four intensive weeks, Jejoen and his new brothers listened to archived lectures by a "martyred" imam that reduced the world to Muslims versus infidels and watched videos that portrayed jihadists fighting in Afghanistan and Chechnya as "selfless heroes defending Islam against corrupt crusaders." On one occasion, they watched a video of a beheading. They discussed where they wanted to fight in the future, perhaps Libya or Somalia. "You sit for months in a group in which jihad is considered quite normal," Jejoen later recalled. The recruits also received martial arts training, kickboxing lessons, and a lecture on "the methodology to overthrow the regimes," all of which gave them a sense of empowerment, control, and self-esteem. The last four weeks of the program were devoted to the importance of loyalty to fellow Muslims.

Along with a few of his brothers, Jejoen eventually made his way to the small town of Kafr Hamra in Syria, just outside Aleppo, where aspiring European jihadists were housed in a walled villa with an indoor swimming pool—or, if they were really lucky, in a place apparently seized from a Syrian government official called "the palace," which had a rooftop pool and an orchard the size of a football field. The leader of Jejoen's team was another Belgian, Houssien Elouassaki, who at twenty-one was essentially the training camp's second-in-command for Europeans. "It is something incredible," said Houssien's brother in a wiretapped telephone call. "He is the youngest emir in the world."

For disaffected young Muslims like Yaken, Jejoen, and Houssien, becoming a jihadi is a big step up: from anonymous nobody to righteous warrior who commands respect, wields power, has an opportunity to rise—and, not least, is attractive to women.

There's no doubt about it: Brand Caliphate made itself cool

and surprisingly effective with young Muslim women. ISIS has been a shrewd marketer, filling its social media with images of confident, strapping warriors carrying AK-47s—the jihadist equivalent of Abercrombie models. Hundreds of Western women have traveled to Syria and Iraq to become the wives of ISIS fighters. ISIS wives stood guard as their husbands raped captive Yazidi (non-Muslim) girls held as sex slaves. For many young Muslim women in the UK and Europe, ISIS managed to make terrorism hip. "In this world," as one Middle East reporter put it, "the counterculture is conservative. Islam is punk rock. The head scarf is liberating. Beards are sexy."

More than any other terrorist organization in recent history, ISIS—which became "the world's richest terrorist group" in 2014 and at one point was making millions of dollars a day from oil, taxation, and extortion—has offered young, alienated Muslims a sense of excitement and romance, a link to a grand history, and a chance to be part of a winning team. As one fighter in northern Syria put it, "We have here mujahideen from Russia, America, the Philippines, China, Germany, Belgium, Sudan, India and Yemen and other places. They are here because this [is] what the Prophet said and promised, the Grand Battle is happening."

Like the caliphates of yore, ISIS has "court poets," including the celebrity poetess Ahlam al-Nasr, who married the Vienna-born ISIS bigwig Abu Usama al-Gharib to great social media fanfare, making them the "it" couple of terrorism—a "jihadi power couple." Originally from Syria, al-Nasr sided with the 2011 demonstrations against President Assad, and many of her poems vividly capture group pain:

> *Their bullets shattered our brains like an*
> > *earthquake,*
> > > *even strong bones cracked then broke.*
> *They drilled our throats and scattered*
> > *our limbs—*
> > > *it was like an anatomy lesson!*
> *They hosed the streets as blood still*
> > *ran*
> > > *like streams crashing down from the*
> > > > *clouds.*

After ISIS captured Mosul, al-Nasr published a triumphant poem, in traditional Arabic meter, which spread online like wildfire:

> *Ask Mosul, city of Islam, about the*
> > *lions—*
> > > *how their fierce struggle brought*
> > > *liberation.*
> *The land of glory has shed its humiliation*
> > *and defeat*
> > > *and put on the raiment of splendor.*

Known as the "Poetess of the Islamic State," al-Nasr is clearly gifted; her mother, a former law professor, recalls that al-Nasr "was born with a dictionary in her mouth." She palpably feels and empathizes deeply; her elegies to fallen mujahedin are filled with aching beauty. But the tribe she has chosen is ISIS—she wrote a thirty-page essay defending the caliphate's decision to burn the Jordanian pilot Moaz al-Kasasbeh alive.

Very few people, no matter how angry, impoverished, or degraded, actually engage in terrorist activity. For most of us, it is incomprehensible that seemingly normal, likeable young men and women, often from loving families, could blow themselves up or participate gleefully in gruesome beheadings. How could a poet of deep sensibility rhapsodize burning a man alive?

The tribal instinct makes this behavior intelligible. In its darkest manifestations, tribalism desensitizes by dehumanizing. It can distort reality on a massive scale, by motivating people to see the world in a way that favors their group commitments. Through the pressure to conform, group identity induces people to do things they never would have considered on their own. Individual responsibility is merged into and corrupted by group identity, and people become capable of engaging in and celebrating atrocious acts of brutality.

THE PUZZLE OF POVERTY

It's difficult to avoid the sense that poverty must play a role in producing terrorism. Indeed, it's often said—for example, by Secretary of State John Kerry in 2014—that poverty is "the root cause of terrorism." But many terrorist leaders have come from relatively privileged backgrounds—Osama bin Laden is said to have inherited $25 million, and ISIS leader Abu Bakr al-Baghdadi has a Ph.D. Moreover, numerous studies have purportedly "disproven" the link between poverty and extremism—by showing, for example, that low per capita national income is not associated with terrorism and that individual poverty does not predict the likelihood of engaging in terrorist acts.

What these studies overlook is the critical importance of tribal politics and group identity. Of course poverty doesn't always lead to violence. The key to understanding extremism lies not in poverty as such, but in *group inequality*.

Every major terrorist movement of the last several decades—from the Tamil Tigers of Sri Lanka to Chechen separatists in Russia to Nigeria's Boko Haram to the militant Islamic movements of the Middle East—arose in conditions of group inequality, group disempowerment, group humiliation, and group hatred. Poverty alone does not create terrorism. But when stark inequalities track deep, preexisting racial, ethnic, religious, or sectarian divides, intense feelings of injustice, resentment, and frustration will become widespread, catalyzed by all the group-psychological phenomena just explored. These are the breeding-ground conditions of terrorist violence.

Once we take group identity and tribal politics into consideration, it becomes unsurprising that the leaders of terrorist organizations are sometimes well-off and well-educated. The point is that they are well-off and well-educated *members of frustrated, humiliated, economically and politically marginalized groups*. Extremist organizations—like all organizations—will often be led by the better situated, more ambitious, charismatic, and talented members of these groups. That's just how group dynamics work.

Thus the key to contemporary Islamic terrorism lies in the proliferation not merely of fundamentalist Muslim teachings but of the belief that Muslims, as a group, are being attacked, humiliated, and persecuted by an evil Western enemy. Osama bin Laden was a central figure in spreading this sentiment. He was a master of political tribalism. Inspired by Sayyid Qutb—an Egyptian poet often described as the founder of modern Islamic fundamentalism—bin Laden recast the conflict. It was no longer just about Israel. Instead, he chose as al-Qaeda's archenemy the United States, the most powerful country in the world, "the head of the snake," the "Great Satan." He famously called on every Muslim in every country to kill Americans whenever possible:

> [T]he United States has been occupying the lands of Islam in the holiest of places, the Arabian Peninsula, plundering its riches, dictating to its rulers, humiliating its people, terrorizing its neighbors. . . . [W]e issue the following fatwa to all Muslims: The ruling to kill the Americans and their allies—civilians and military—is an individual duty for every Muslim who can do it in any country in which it is possible to do it. . . .

Bin Laden created the ultimate global us-versus-them, asking Muslims to see themselves in a pitched historical battle to the death with the infidels.

To this, ISIS added the dream of a restored caliphate,

creating a direct tie to Islam's glorious imperial past, as well as layers of intra-Islamic group conflict. First, ISIS pitted itself against al-Qaeda. After an al-Qaeda leader mocked ISIS members as "simpletons who have deluded themselves with their announcement of the caliphate," an ISIS spokesman responded: "All who try to sever the ranks will have their heads severed." More fundamentally, ISIS invoked the ancient schism between Sunnis and Shias, calling for all Shias to be put to death.

Nevertheless, the core message of ISIS remains the invocation of Muslim "humiliation" and a worldwide call to Muslims to join in Islam's glorious rebirth after centuries of oppression. In 2014, three years after bin Laden was killed, the "Caliph" of the Islamic State, Abu Bakr al-Baghdadi, declared:

> [T]he time has come for those generations that were drowning in oceans of disgrace, being nursed on the milk of humiliation, and being ruled by the vilest of all people, after their long slumber in the darkness of neglect—the time has come for them to rise.

Similarly, ISIS propaganda on the Internet (translated into English, French, and German) calls triumphantly for Sunni Muslims to "gather around your khalifah, so that you may return as you once were for ages, kings of the [E]arth and knights of war."

Against a backdrop of stark group inequality, the most successful extremist groups offer their members precisely what existing societal institutions do not: a tribe, a sense of belonging and purpose, an enemy to hate and kill, and a chance to reverse the group polarity, turning humiliation into superiority and triumph. This is the formula that al-Qaeda and ISIS have exploited.

They aren't merely propounding a religious ideology. They offer their members status and power through group identity: being a warrior of Allah, with a heroic mission, whether defeating the Great Satan or restoring an Islamic caliphate. As terrorism expert Scott Atran puts it, "what inspires . . . is not so much the Qur'an or religious teachings"; jihadis "almost never kill and die just for the Cause, but also for each other: for their group, whose cause makes their imagined family of genetic strangers—their brotherhood, fatherland, motherland, homeland, totem, or tribe."

ISIS may be on the verge of defeat, but the conditions that allowed it to rise remain very much alive. Consider this statement from a Muslim father living in Ceuta, Spain, during the Iraq War:

> The Spanish authorities treat us like we were all criminals. Our people have been here for hundreds, maybe thousands, of years, but even the Hindus get better treatment. We are always looking for work. . . . [Y]ou can't help but feel the suffering of your people, in Palestine, in Iraq, in Afghanistan. . . . I swear, if George Bush were here in front of my son, I would shoot him and gladly die. And if I had the means, I would strap a bomb on myself and blow up American soldiers in Iraq even if my own son, whom I love more than life, were to grow up without a father. But I have no means to get there.

Millions of Muslims all over the world—in Europe, in Africa, in the Middle East—feel victimized, threatened, and impoverished by Western enemies, whether America, Europe, Israel, Christianity, or Western civilization as a whole. To some extent, these feelings are beyond reach: they are the predictable distortions of group psychology, exaggerated and pounded home by demagogic leaders, by imams, and by echo-chamber social media. But to some extent, these feelings are self-fulfilling prophecies. As populist anti-Muslim sentiments rise in Europe and America, fueled by terrorist killings, Muslims in some places will in fact be more targeted, more marginalized, more socially isolated. As long as this cycle continues, Islamic terror organizations, new or old, will find a ready audience for their barbaric group appeals.

CHAPTER SIX

Venezuela

[A] trumpet tootles. Block-letter words pop up on the screen: "humanity," "struggle," "socialism.". . . And then comes a close-up of the show's host and star, Hugo Chávez, president of Venezuela, usually dressed in all red. . . . It is the only television show in the world in which a head of state regularly invites cameras to follow him as he governs.

—RACHEL NOLAN, *describing the Venezuelan reality TV show* Aló Presidente

Venezuela is a tragic mess, and U.S. foreign policy there for the last twenty years has been completely ineffective. Once a staunch U.S. ally with the world's largest proven oil reserves, Venezuela has been a thorn in America's side since 1998, when Hugo Chávez rose to power. As we haplessly funded his opposition to the tune of hundreds of millions of dollars, Chávez simply turned to Russia and China, allowing our rivals to gain important footholds in the region. For two decades, Chávez's defiance of the United States—he called President George W. Bush the "devil"—and immense popularity helped fuel the rise of similar anti-U.S., left-wing movements elsewhere in Latin America.

To be fair, Venezuela was not foremost on Washington's agenda in the 2000s—with 9/11 and two wars preoccupying U.S. foreign policy—but in Venezuela too we undermined our own interests, turning vast numbers against us, through our blindness to the tribal identities that mattered most and the simmering eth-nonationalist resentment that Chávez harnessed and gave voice to.

BEAUTY AS A WINDOW INTO
VENEZUELA'S TRIBAL POLITICS

Latin Americans are obsessed with beauty pageants, and nowhere is this more true than in Venezuela, which has had more interna-tional beauty queens than any other country. Indeed, it's often said that beauty is Venezuela's second-largest industry after oil. Every year, two thirds of the country's population of 30 million tune in to the Miss Venezuela contest. Thousands of Venezuelan girls as young as four are enrolled in beauty academies. The beauty obsession can push Venezuelan girls to unimaginable ex-tremes. At sixteen, some have their intestines shortened to absorb less food; others have plastic mesh sewn into their tongues to make it painful to eat.

Beauty queens in Venezuela carry outsize importance. Irene Sáez, a Miss Venezuela who went on to win Miss Universe, be-came mayor of Chacao, the "Beverly Hills" of Caracas, then a state governor, then a presidential candidate in 1998. Her rival was a former army paratrooper whom the world had not yet heard of: Hugo Chávez.

Up to that point, every Miss Venezuela had been light skinned with European features, bearing little resemblance to Venezuela's darker-skinned masses. Sáez was a six-foot-one-inch strawberry blonde with green eyes. She looked very much like the country-club elite who had dominated Venezuela for generations, but nothing like the vast majority of the country's population.

By contrast, Chávez did look like them. He had, in his own words, a "big mouth" and "curly hair." "I'm so proud to have this mouth and this hair," he added, "because it's African." In 1998, it was inconceivable that a person with Chávez's complexion and "African" features could become Miss Venezuela or the country's president. At the same time, it was taboo to even mention these racial realities. Chávez's stunning victory shattered both the barrier and the taboo.

After sweeping to power, Chávez disbanded Venezuela's Congress and Supreme Court, nationalized hundreds of companies, and seized control of the country's oil sector. Although his regime was beset by political instability and his policies led to billions of dollars in capital flight, Chávez was reelected in 2000 and served as president for another thirteen years, with some spectacular successes, including dramatic declines in illiteracy and infant mortality. Chavez was even able to score victories in the United States: in 2005, with the cooperation of former Massachusetts congressman Joseph Kennedy II, Chávez began providing millions of gallons of free oil to poor Americans.

Today, however, Venezuela is in chaos, on the verge of a

humanitarian crisis, with criminal elements apparently controlling large sectors of the state. Hunger is rampant. Grief-stricken parents are giving away their babies because they can't afford to feed them. The country has one of the highest murder rates in the world (recent victims include another former Miss Venezuela).

How could Chávez—an ex-convict with a penchant for bizarre ideation (he once suggested that capitalism might have killed life on Mars)—have risen to power? How could he keep winning elections even as the country seemingly lurched from crisis to crisis?

These questions baffled U.S. policy makers throughout the 2000s. Washington completely misunderstood the Chávez phenomenon. Although it had been a decade since the collapse of the Soviet Union, the United States reverted to a Cold War mentality and saw Chávez solely as an anticapitalist thug-buffoon who, along with his friend and ally, Fidel Castro, was threatening to spread communism throughout Latin America. In Washington's eyes, such a regime had to be antidemocratic; its popular support couldn't be genuine or deep or sustainable.

But Chávez was very much the product of democracy— democracy under conditions of inequality, deeply buried racial tensions, and a market-dominant minority. Whether because of ideological blinkers or self-delusion, the United States stubbornly underestimated Chávez's popularity, failing to grasp the seismic shifts in the region's tribal politics that he epitomized. The United States saw a dictator; Venezuelans from the poor barrios saw, at long last, a president who looked like and spoke for them.

From a tribal politics point of view, Chávez's rise is simple to explain. He was a product of a battle between Venezuela's dominant "white" minority and its long-degraded, poorer, less-educated, darker-skinned indigenous- and African-blooded masses. Even today, partisan finger pointers in the United States have little understanding of the origins of the autocratic havoc now engulfing the country.

"PIGMENTOCRACY" AND THE MYTH OF
RACIAL DEMOCRACY

All over Latin America, it's often said that "there is no racism," because everyone, high and low, is "mixed-blooded." Instead of black or white, "everyone is a *mestizo*."

The reality is far more complex. Latin American society is fundamentally *pigmentocratic:* characterized by a social spectrum with taller, lighter-skinned, European-blooded elites at one end; shorter, darker, indigenous-blooded masses at the other end; and a great deal of "passing" in between. The roots of pigmentocracy are traceable to the colonial era.

Unlike their British counterparts in, say, India or Malaysia, the Spanish colonialists freely and prolifically procreated with indigenous women. From the outset, Spanish and Portuguese chroniclers waxed enthusiastic about the charms of Amerindian women, who were "beautiful, and not a little lascivious, and fond of the Spaniards" by one account and "[v]ery handsome and great lovers, affectionate and with ardent bodies" by another. In an important sense, "the Spanish Conquest of the Americas was a conquest of women. The Spaniards obtained the Indian girls both by force and by peaceful means"—sometimes as tokens of friendship from Indian leaders. Intermarriage, concubinage, and polygamy were common.

Although this "racial mixing" might suggest a readiness among Latin America's colonizers to transcend ethnic boundaries and skin color, in reality it was nothing of the sort. On the contrary, what emerged was an invidious social system known as the Society of Castes (*sociedad de castas*), in which individuals were classified in accordance with their racial "purity," with whites occupying the highest stratum.

The names of the specific *castas* that emerged in Spanish America varied across different regions and changed over the years. The following list is illustrative of eighteenth-century New Spain:

1. Spaniard and Indian beget mestizo
2. Mestizo and Spanish woman beget castizo
3. Castizo woman and Spaniard beget Spaniard
4. Spanish woman and Negro beget mulatto
5. Spaniard and mulatto woman beget morisco
6. Morisco woman and Spaniard beget albino
7. Spaniard and albino woman beget torna atrás
8. Indian and torna atrás beget lobo
9. Lobo and Indian woman beget zambaigo
10. Zambaigo and Indian woman beget cambujo
11. Cambujo and mulatto woman beget albarazado
12. Albarazado and mulatto woman beget barcino
13. Barcino and mulatto woman beget coyote
14. Coyote woman and Indian beget chamiso

15. Chamiso woman and mestizo beget coyote mestizo
16. Coyote mestizo and mulatto woman beget ahí te estás

That the Spaniards were supposed to be "pure-blooded" is, to say the least, ironic. Among the numerous groups that, by the Middle Ages, had inhabited and commingled with one another on Iberian soil were Celts, Greeks, Phoenicians, Carthaginians, Romans, Visigoths, Jews, Arabs, Berbers, and Gypsies.

Nevertheless, with the exception of countries like Chile and Uruguay (where indigenous people were largely extinguished almost immediately), disdain among a "pure white" Spanish elite for the "colored" masses is a deeply ingrained feature of the history of every modern Latin American country. In Mexico, mixed-blooded mestizos were for years prohibited from owning land or joining the clergy. In Peru, even intellectuals believed that "the Indian is not now, nor can he ever be, anything but a machine." In Chile, victory in the War of the Pacific (1879–83) was often attributed to the "whiteness" of the Chileans, as compared with the defeated "Indians" of Bolivia and Peru. In Argentina, a popular writer wrote in 1903 that mestizos and mulattos were both "impure, atavistically anti-Christian; they are like the two heads of a fabulous hydra that surrounds, constricts, and strangles with its giant spiral a beautiful, pale virgin, Spanish America."

In Venezuela, there was an added layer of complexity and racism due to the importation of roughly one hundred thousand slaves from Africa between the sixteenth and nineteenth centuries. Indeed, according to one historian, more than half of Venezuela's population was black when the country declared independence in

1811. Over the centuries, Venezuela's elites blamed all of the country's social ills on "the constant mixing of whites, Indians, and blacks" and repeatedly and actively encouraged immigration from Europe in order to "whiten" Venezuela. After World War II, substantial numbers of immigrants arrived from Spain, Portugal, Italy, Germany, and other countries. This postwar influx from Europe "slowed the longstanding tendency in the country toward racial mixing."

Nevertheless, throughout the twentieth century, a national myth—promoted by the country's intellectuals and elites—perpetuated the idea that Venezuela was a "racial democracy" in which racism and discrimination did not exist. As late as 1997, a prominent Venezuelan businessman and columnist wrote:

> [I]n Venezuela we complain about a lot of things that we think are wrong. But we have some things that should serve as an example to other countries. One is that race is not important in judging a person. In Venezuela racial discrimination is not a factor either in employment or in social or intellectual realms. . . . Prejudice against someone because of the color of his skin does not exist. This is not an obstacle here as it is in other places.

As elsewhere in Latin America, this myth of color blindness and "everyone is a mestizo" conveniently hid the fact that wealth was overwhelmingly concentrated in white hands while the country's impoverished underclass, representing a full 80 percent of the population, consisted primarily of darker-skinned Venezuelans with more indigenous and African ancestry. At the same time, the myth suppressed the mobilization of the country's poor along ethnic or racial lines.

Thus on the eve of the 1998 presidential election, even as Venezuela's elite proudly declared that their country was free of racism, a small minority of cosmopolitan "whites"—including descendants of the original Spanish colonizers as well as more recent European immigrants—dominated Venezuela economically, politically, and socially.

This domination was at its most visible in the country's beauty pageants. Whiteness was equated with perfection. The blond Sáez—the Miss Venezuela who lost to Chávez—was described by the media as "the most perfect woman in the history of all the beauty pageants of the universe." Conversely, any sign of African or Indian heritage—including broader noses, fuller mouths, or *pelo malo* (bad hair), the derogatory term for tightly curled black hair—was considered ugly. (Hair straightening is another extremely profitable industry in Venezuela.) Many black, indigenous, and darker-skinned Venezuelans internalized this Eurocentric standard of beauty.

PRESIDENT HUGO CHÁVEZ

It probably never occurred to Venezuela's white elite that they actually might lose power. It probably never occurred to the U.S. foreign establishment either, since these elites were basically their only points of contact. After all, they controlled not only the country's oil sector but the media, banks, foreign investment networks, all the most valuable land, and the most lucrative businesses. As elsewhere in Latin America, this minority was also very closely knit. As one Venezuelan put it, "In Venezuela there are more boards of directors than there are directors."

But in 1998, the Venezuelan people—exercising their democratic power—elected Hugo Chávez as president in a landslide victory, to the horror of the United States. Chávez reversed the vector of Venezuelan racism. Instead of being embarrassed by his mixed origins, Chávez defiantly called himself "the Indian from Barinas" and reveled in his indigenous and African features, once gloating to an interviewer, "Hate against me has a lot to do with racism." By combining ethnicity with populism and class appeals, Chávez galvanized Venezuela's destitute majority, most of whom, like Chávez, are mixed-blooded, with "thick mouths" and visibly darker skin than most of the nation's elite. "He is one of us," cried cheering washerwomen, maids, and peasants. "We've never had another president like that before."

For all the talk of color-blind racial democracy, Venezuela's elite couldn't help themselves. They called Chávez "El Negro" (The Black) and *ese mono* (that monkey). Political graffiti like "Death to the Monkey Chávez!" began to appear on the walls of upper- and middle-class neighborhoods. In one political cartoon he was depicted as an ape. But Chávez used all this to his advantage. He fashioned himself as the champion of Venezuela's oppressed. Once in office, he passed a new constitution guaranteeing for the first time cultural and economic rights for indigenous populations. His government also passed a Law Against Racial

Discrimination, a remarkable step in a country where the mere existence of race, let alone racism, had long been denied.

Commentators disagree slightly about whether Chávez created racial consciousness in Venezuela—by repeatedly sending the message that "[t]he rich people are racist and they hate you"—or whether he embraced an already existing "movement demanding that race be taken seriously." Regardless, what differentiated Chávez from other politicians was, in the words of Moisés Naím (a former Venezuelan minister of trade and industry and later editor of *Foreign Policy*), "his enthusiastic willingness to tap into collective anger and social resentments that other politicians failed to see, refused to stoke, or more likely, had a vested interest in not exacerbating." Deliberately fomenting class conflict and lacing it with ethnic and racial resentment, Chávez "broke with the tradition of multiclass political parties and the illusion of social harmony that prevailed in Venezuela for four decades."

Like all demagogues, Chávez was a master at tribal politics. "Oligarchs tremble," he campaigned to great, agitated crowds, referring to Venezuela's "rotten" elites. He also attacked foreign investors, calling them "squealing pigs" and rich "degenerates." Chávez swept to electoral victory not by offering a well-thought-out economic policy. Rather, in Naím's words, he "cater[ed] to the emotional needs of a deeply demoralized nation," employing an "inchoate but very effective folksy mixture of Bolivarian soundbites, Christianity, collectivist utopianism, baseball and indigenous cosmogony, peppered with diatribes against oligarchs, neoliberalism, foreign conspiracies, and globalization."

Chávez was the first president not to invite the winner of the

Miss Venezuela pageant to the presidential palace after her crowning. He also ordered that two oil tankers named after former white Miss Venezuelas—the *Maritza Sayalero* and the *Pilín León*—be named *Negra Hipólita* and *Negra Matea,* two legendary black women who, according to lore, raised Simón Bolívar. The Chávez regime also saw Venezuela crown its first nonwhite Miss Venezuela.

BACKLASH BY VENEZUELA'S ELITE

Chávez's nationalization and antibusiness policies upended the economy. Fearful of confiscation, Venezuela's wealthy elites withdrew more than $8 billion, transferring most of it to overseas banks. But the real battleground between Chávez and the Venezuelan elite was the national oil company, PDVSA, which generates about 95 percent of the country's export earnings and represents the nation's lifeblood.

Although technically state owned, PDVSA was famous for being efficiently run by members of the business elite—"oligarchs," in Chávez's view. In March 2002, Chávez fired PDVSA's president, General Guaicaipuro Lameda, widely respected by foreign investors for his professional steering of the oil behemoth. In Lameda's place, Chávez installed a left-wing academic with little business experience.

In April 2002, only a few weeks later, a coup deposed Chávez, who was taken by force to a military base. Astonishingly, the Bush administration hailed the coup as "a victory for democracy." If, as is rumored, the United States was behind the coup, the move was a massive moral and strategic mistake. If instead, as the Bush administration insisted, it had no connection to the coup and genuinely believed that Chávez's ouster was a democratic triumph, this was an astounding display of blindness to the realities of Venezuela's tribal politics.

The coup was a classic effort led by a market-dominant minority to retaliate against a democratically elected government threatening their wealth and power. Although supported at first by trade union leaders and skilled labor, the regime that briefly uprooted Chávez "looked like it had come from the country club." Interim president Pedro Carmona, a wealthy white, was head of the country's largest business association. Union representatives were completely excluded from positions of authority. "All of them oligarchs," scoffed a dark-skinned street vendor. "Couldn't they have appointed one person like us?"

To the dismay of the Bush administration—and the embarrassment of major U.S. newspapers like the *New York Times* and the *Chicago Tribune,* which initially supported Chávez's "resignation"— a popular uprising returned Chávez to power with stunning speed. Not thousands, but millions, of Chávez supporters, mostly poor from the barrios, surrounded the presidential palace, and within forty-eight hours, Chávez was back in office. Except for the United States, every democratic country in the western hemisphere, even those at odds with Chávez, had condemned the coup. By appearing to support the abortive overthrow of a democratically elected leader, and calling it a victory for democracy, the United States committed a serious misstep. We looked not only, as the BBC put it, "rather stupid," but hypocritical, and our influence in the region declined sharply.

But the battle was not over; it would be a fight to the death. In December 2002, strikes broke out, shutting down oil production and bringing the entire economy to a grinding halt. In the United States, strikes are usually instigated by blue-collar workers seeking higher wages. Venezuela's strikes, however, were spearheaded by the country's wealthy business elite, along with other anti-Chávez groups. I explained this in a January 2003 op-ed in the *New York Times*, while making the larger point that democracy in conditions of extreme inequality can "create political and economic instability," leading to the election of populist, anti-free-market leaders. In addition, I pointed out:

> There is also an ethnic dimension to Venezuela's crisis. Along with roughly 80 percent of Venezuela's population, Mr. Chávez is a "pardo"—a term with both class and ethnic overtones that refers loosely to brown-skinned people of Amerindian or African ancestry. But Venezuela's economy has always been controlled by a tiny minority of cosmopolitan whites. . . .

I was completely unprepared for what happened next. I began receiving a deluge of vicious hate e-mails—at a rate of about a hundred a minute—all from Venezuelans. A number of things stood out. First, they were all in English, suggesting that they were written by relatively privileged Venezuelans; many of the writers were affiliated with businesses or universities and had U.S. connections. Second, they virtually all insisted that Chávez was an antidemocratic force, rarely mentioning that he had been democratically elected. Finally, they were adamant that anti-Chávez opposition had nothing to do with race, because racism did not exist in Venezuela. Here are a few relatively moderate samples:

> As a Venezuelan I was appalled at Dr. Amy Chua's superficial and biased treatment of the Venezuelan situation in her January 7 article Power to the Privileged. . . . Class hatred and racism have never been a real issue in Venezuela. . . . Venezuela is a social and racial melting pot that has allowed children from humble backgrounds to move up in the world, get a good education, job or political position. . . . Also, this melting pot has produced some of the most beautiful women in the world, who consistently earn Miss Universe and Miss World titles.

> Race has never been an "issue" in Venezuela. The fact that Chávez—whom you describe as a "pardo" (which he is not by the way) may have a darker colour of his skin does not at all constitute—and has never constituted—a social prejudice in Venezuelan social behaviour. . . . So Professor Chua you don't have the slightest idea of what you are talking about. HOWEVER Chávez himself has openly spread the issue of the colour of his skin in order to justify his dictatorial behaviour. And you have fallen for it.

Having grown up in Venezuela and lived there for 30 years, I can attest that racial lines are almost non-existent. Blacks and "pardos" have today the same opportunities and life style as Caucasians.

And literally hundreds more like this. The e-mail campaign seemed to be well organized. As if following a protocol, most of them copied my dean, the president of Yale, and every member of my faculty (not to mention Hillary Clinton and the head of the United Nations). As it happened, I had just started teaching at Yale Law School, and many of my brand-new colleagues came up to me with strange looks on their faces to ask what was going on. I also received death threats, including one that said, "Venezuelans will get you in Chicago," where I was scheduled to give a talk (the venue provided bodyguards). When I gave a talk at the University of Pennsylvania, Venezuelans protested the lecture.

Today, the story line has changed. Venezuela's glaring racial inequities are now widely acknowledged, as is the fact that Chávez's popularity was based in significant part on his ability to turn Indian and African heritage into a source of pride, identity, and mobilization against a long-dominant white elite. (Chávez was not the only Latin American leader to play the ethnic card. Similarly ethnically tinged populist movements swept Alejandro Toledo to victory in Peru and Evo Morales to the presidency in Bolivia.)

Chávez was reelected in a landslide in 2006, then again in 2012. However else his legacy may be judged, Chávez undoubtedly delivered to his poor constituents. As of 2012, Chávez had cut poverty "by half, and extreme poverty by 70 percent." College enrollment doubled, and millions had access to health care for the first time. As Brazil's president Lula said that year, "A victory for Chávez is . . . a victory for the people of Venezuela." Although Chávez was the beneficiary of high oil prices for many years—it's often said that Venezuela's leaders' fortunes rise and fall with the price of oil—the fact remains that by many metrics, Venezuela was more democratic under Chávez than before he came to power.

At the same time, there is also no doubt that Chávez was a strongman with autocratic leanings and that his achievements exacted an enormous economic cost. By 2006, government expenditures were exceeding government revenues. To stay afloat, Chávez borrowed more than $55 billion from China and Russia. As inflation soared, Chávez imposed price controls, which, according to many, disincentivized manufacturing and started the country on the road to today's disastrous shortages. Oil production, drained of expertise and foreign investment, fell sharply, crippled by operational failures.

Nevertheless, Chávez maintained surprising popularity right up until his death, which was met with massive grief among "Chavistas" and Venezuela's underclass. Chávez had won the hearts of the poor. His embrace of a long-neglected, long-spurned swath of Venezuela endeared him to them, and they were willing to look past his shortcomings.

One of the most extraordinary features of Chávez's presidency was his reality TV show, *Aló Presidente* (*Hello President*), which aired every Sunday at 11:00 A.M. and went on for as long as Chávez wanted, usually four to eight hours. Utterly unprecedented and shocking at the time, Chávez's persona—part entertainer, part head of state—may seem strangely familiar to Americans today. The conceit was that the Venezuelan people should get to see "the revolution" unfolding, so every week Chávez would appear live, sometimes on the street, sometimes in front of an audience in the presidential palace, and talk, joke, sing, issue decrees, or order people to jail. Occasionally, he interviewed other heads of state, Oprah style. Because he made actual policy on the show, often without any warning, it was imperative for his cabinet members to watch in order to keep current. And when he would point to a building and declare, "*Exprópiese!*" (Expropriate it!), the live audience would burst into applause.

In 2010, Chávez joined Twitter and was immensely successful, using his account to post missives ranging from insults directed at other countries to what he had eaten for lunch ("Just ate a tremendous bowl of fish soup"). He once gave a nineteen-year-old woman an apartment for becoming his three-millionth follower. Outrageous and unfiltered, he tweeted about everything from trips ("Hey how's it going . . . I'm off to Brazil") to revolution ("We will be victorious!") to his gastrointestinal problems ("Hello Tums"). Loathed by the elite, he was, until his death, a man of the people.

Chávez died suddenly of colon cancer in 2013—a little more than a year after he suggested that the U.S. government might be secretly infecting Latin America's left-wing leaders with cancer cells. Chávez's vice president and successor, Nicolás Maduro, tried to continue Chávez's policies, but without Chávez's charisma or shrewdness. Venezuela's crisis turned into a full-blown collapse when global oil prices plummeted in 2014, plunging Venezuela into a state of mass hunger and rampant crime. In 2016, inflation hit 800 percent. Shortages of basic staples like milk, rice, meat, and toilet paper have triggered protests across the country, met by the government with deadly force.

Today, Venezuela is practically a failed state. While Maduro claims the "Chavista" mantle, it does not appear that he has popular support, with even many diehard Chávez supporters demanding that he step down, denouncing him for "destroy[ing] Chávez's good name." His July 2017 creation of a new "constituent assembly"—filled with supporters, including his son and his wife—was widely viewed as an anti-democratic bid to consolidate autocratic power and stifle dissent. Moreover, according to Naím, Maduro is increasingly a "puppet" for Cuba, military strongmen, and drug traffickers, who wield the real power over the country's crumbling state.

When democracy does battle against a market-dominant minority—as it did in Venezuela throughout the Chávez era—the consequences can ultimately be catastrophic. In the worst cases, both the economy and democracy can be ravaged. Sadly, this worst-case scenario appears to be playing out in Venezuela today.

CHAPTER SEVEN

Inequality and the Tribal Chasm in America

What a chimera then is man! What a novelty, what a monster, what a chaos, what a contradiction, what a prodigy! Judge of all things, feeble earthworm, repository of truth, sewer of uncertainty and error, the glory and the scum of the universe.
—BLAISE PASCAL

Professing to be wise, they became fools. . . .
—ROMANS 1:22

The Middle East, Southeast Asia, and Latin America may seem worlds away from the United States, but America is not immune to the forces of tribal politics tearing those regions apart.

We all have a vague sense that inequality lies at the heart of our country's deep divides. But exactly how is poorly understood. It turns out that in America, there's a chasm between the tribal identities of the country's haves and have-nots—a chasm of the same kind wreaking political havoc in many developing and non-Western countries.

In America as in Venezuela, great swaths of the country have come to regard the "establishment"—the political and economic elite—as foreign and even threatening to them. In America as in Venezuela, a highly improbable candidate with no political experience swept to the presidency by attacking that establishment and leading what was widely called a revolution.

The difference, of course, is that Hugo Chávez's revolution was Socialist, and Donald Trump's decidedly was not. Populism in America is not anticapitalist. America's have-nots don't hate wealth—many of them want it, or want their children to have a shot at it, even if they think the system is "rigged" against them. Whether black, white, or Latino, poor and working-class Americans hunger for the old-fashioned American Dream. Hence the endless popularity of shows like *American Idol, The Voice, The Apprentice, Empire, The Sopranos, Who Wants to Be a Millionaire, Shark Tank,* and *Duck Dynasty*. When the American Dream eludes them—even when it mocks them, or spits in their faces—they would sooner turn on the establishment, or on the law, or on immigrants and other outsiders, or even on reason, than turn on the dream itself.

In America, it's the progressive elites who have taken it upon themselves to expose the American Dream as false. This is their form of tribalism. A jarring amount of upper-income progressive activism serves as a vehicle for elite group identity formation. But this form of progressive tribalism didn't work in 2016. As David Leonhardt put it in an essay called "How Democrats Can Get Their Mojo Back," whites without college degrees "shifted sharply to Donald Trump," and blacks without college degrees "affected the result by staying home in larger numbers. Both decisions . . . stemmed in part from alienation."

Yes, inequality is fracturing our nation. But just as America's foreign policy establishment repeatedly fails to understand the group realities that matter most to people abroad, America's elites have been blind to—or dismissive of—the group identities that matter most to ordinary Americans. If we want to understand our current political turmoil, we need to open our eyes to the vastly different group identities of America's rich and poor.

THE OCCUPY MOVEMENT

A City University of New York (CUNY) study of the participants at a major Occupy rally on May 1, 2012, found that about one-quarter were students. Of the nonstudents, 76 percent had a bachelor's degree, and of this group, more than half had postgraduate degrees. The participants were also disproportionately affluent; more than half had incomes of $75,000 or more. Only about 8 percent earned less than $25,000, compared to almost 30 percent of New Yorkers as a whole. In a different study of Occupy protesters in New York's Zuccotti Park, veteran Democratic Party pollster Douglas Schoen concluded, "Our research shows clearly that the movement doesn't represent unemployed America. . . . The vast majority of demonstrators are actually employed."

Yet another poll, which surveyed more than five thousand visitors to the occupywallst.org Web site, found that 90.1

percent had more than a high school education, and 81.2 percent were white (only 1.6 percent were black). While other surveys show considerably more racial and ethnic diversity, there is consensus that Occupiers were disproportionately young, white, and highly educated, which helps explain the movement's oft-noted technological savvy.

Also striking, Occupy participants were unusually politically active—much more so than the American population as a whole. According to the CUNY study, 94 percent of those surveyed had previously participated in another political protest, and 42 percent said that they "had previously participated in 30 or more such events during their lifetimes." Nearly 50 percent were also active in other organizations, including immigrant rights groups, women's rights groups, and antiwar organizations. As the CUNY study concluded, "[Occupy Wall Street] was not a spontaneous movement that appeared out of nowhere. It was carefully planned by a group of experienced political activists."

Other anti-inequality groups in America have similar attributes. Take, for example, The Other 98%, which describes itself as "a non-profit organization and a grassroots network of concerned people that shines a light on economic injustice, undue corporate influence and threats to democracy. We work to kick corporate lobbyists out of DC, hold elected officials accountable, and make America work . . . for the other 98% of us." The team of six talented leaders featured on their Web site includes a former Wall Street analyst; a former Web designer for Bank of America; two graduates of Bard College, a highly selective liberal arts school; a veteran affinity group organizer; and a former Greenpeace worker who "has had the great fortune to be integrally involved in powerful peaceful actions all over the world: from the high seas with the Rainbow Warrior to the streets of Seattle," and who now "works from his home-office on a sleepy little island in the Puget Sound where he and his wife Genevieve homeschool their 8 year old twins."

Occupy Wall Street was, in the words of one of its creators, Micah White, a "failure." White might have overstated it; the Occupy movement brought inequality to the forefront of public debate, and many attribute to Occupy the attention given in the 2016 presidential campaign to "Wall Street greed," student debt, and increasing the minimum wage. But as journalist George Packer put it, "Occupy Wall Street flashed across the sky and flared out, more a meme than a movement."

The most common theories for why the Occupy movement failed include the absence of a strong, visible leader, the lack of a concrete affirmative agenda, and the diffuseness of online activism. All those factors likely played a role, but what's often missed—and arguably more important—is the fact that Occupy attracted so few members from the many disadvantaged groups it purported to be fighting for.

Imagine if the suffragette movement hadn't included large numbers of women, or if the civil rights movement included very few African Americans, or if the gay rights movement included very few gays. Internal coherence gave all these movements an authentic and potent group identity that helped them persevere in the face of setbacks to eventually achieve significant results. By contrast, the participants of Occupy were not the hungry or exploited, but rather relatively privileged self-identified activists. Which is why when the next big thing to protest came along, Occupy's participants moved on. (Sometimes they didn't even have to move on physically, just virtually. As White put it in June 2015, "Social media has a negative side . . . [people started] to feel more comfortable posting on Twitter and Facebook than going to an Occupy event.")

This is not to say that Occupy wasn't a real movement, with a real group identity capable of mobilizing and galvanizing its members. Many young and relatively privileged Americans today are disillusioned with and frustrated by the world they are entering. As Michael Ellick put it, "You have generations of people graduating from high school and college who are in debt for careers that don't exist anymore, were educated into a world that doesn't exist anymore." Occupy offered a meaningful tribe to such people. It gave members a sense of belonging and status. Protestors from Zuccotti Park to Oakland felt themselves part of a larger movement taking on a big, bad enemy; its motto was "We kick the ass of the ruling class." But Occupy gave this sense of belonging and status almost exclusively to the well educated and relatively privileged.

It's not just that the poor didn't participate in Occupy. More often than not, they affirmatively dislike activist movements—more irony still. In the words of a writer from working-class America, "Many lower class Americans view protesters as disreputable and unhelpful, as 'professional activists' who are entirely disconnected from the working class because they've never experienced struggle in their own personal lives, and who protest mainly to find personal validation." In a related context, Nigerian American novelist Teju Cole once tweeted, "The White Savior Industrial Complex is not about justice. It is about having a big emotional experience that validates privilege."

In contrast to the extremely politically active Occupy participants, America's poor are far less politically engaged. They are starkly less likely to work on political campaigns, contact elected officials, or vote. In part, this is because historically marginalized communities tend to distrust strangers and large organizations they see as controlling the levers of power from afar. It's hard to get excited about politics and elections when no matter which party comes into power, your life never changes.

In addition, low-income Americans seem to be withdrawing from traditional communal and civic activities. In his 2015 bestseller, *Our Kids*, Robert Putnam shows that the poor in America are less likely to join athletic leagues, youth groups, and volunteer organizations, leaving them with far fewer social connections and networks. Consistent with Charles Murray's observations in *Coming Apart*, Putnam also finds that church attendance among the poor and working class is declining, most strikingly among the young. On the basis of this evidence, Putnam concludes that among America's have-nots, "we have witnessed . . . a giant swing toward the individualist." But this is not the right conclusion.

America's underclasses are intensely tribal. To begin with,

many among America's lower classes are deeply patriotic, even if they feel they're losing their country to distant elites who know nothing about them. The ranks of America's police and armed forces, two organizations famous for group loyalty, are filled predominantly with nonelites. Beyond this is a whole world of other group affiliations. It's just that the groups that America's have-nots belong to are often ones that elites view as antisocial, irrational, or even contemptible, if they even know about them at all.

SOVEREIGN CITIZENS

In 2014, a survey was taken of hundreds of officials from law enforcement agencies around the country. Whom did these officials identify as the single greatest threat to their communities? Not Islamic extremists or violent street gangs, but a bizarre antigovernment group known as the sovereign citizens. Although the movement dates back to the 1980s, its numbers began to increase dramatically after the 2008 recession, and experts attribute the movement's rapid growth to high unemployment and economic dislocation. Gavin Long, who shot six policemen in Baton Rouge in 2016, three fatally, was a sovereign citizen—evidently one of many African American members unaware of the movement's white supremacist origins.

With an estimated three hundred thousand followers, the movement is based on an elaborate conspiracy theory. Some of its central beliefs include:

1. At some point in American history, the legal system set up by our Founding Fathers was secretly replaced by an illegitimate government. We know this to be true because of the gold fringe that adorns flags in courtrooms.

2. The illegitimate government currently in power induces Americans to enter into "contracts," which turn them into federal slaves. These "contracts" can be formed, for example, by applying for a Social Security number.

3. The U.S. government uses every newborn's birth certificate to establish a secret corporate trust in the baby's name, which is then used to siphon off future earnings into a secret bank account. Fortunately, sovereign citizens can access the secret bank account through a series of highly complicated legal maneuvers.

4. The creation of the newborn's corporate trust establishes two entities: a corporate shell person and the natural person. We know this because most government documents, like driver's licenses and tax bills, use all-capital letters to spell names.

5. It is possible to avoid being tricked by the illegitimate government by clearly identifying oneself as a natural person as opposed to the corporate shell. This might be done, for example, by specifying, "I am Spencer Todd, representative of SPENCER TODD ©."

6. Through correct formatting of legal documents, sovereign citizens can separate the natural (free) person from the corporate (enslaved) legal entity, liberating themselves from government jurisdiction. Thus, a sovereign could avoid paying tax bills or cable TV bills addressed to JOHN SMITH by claiming that JOHN SMITH is a separate legal entity.

7. The only governmental authority that is actually legitimate in America today is the county sheriff.

Sovereign citizens specialize in "paper terrorism." Sovereigns involved in even minor disputes—for instance, contesting dog-licensing fees—deliberately inundate courts with filings. Sovereign filings in tax cases often exceed a thousand pages, overwhelming prosecutors, public defenders, and judges not only with the volume of filings but with "the nonsensical language the documents are written in."

Richard Posner, one of the most distinguished judges in the country (now retired), presided in 2015 over the criminal trial of a sovereign citizen. After a deluge of motions, Judge Posner summarized the defendant's arguments:

He also asserts "Lack of Jurisdiction over the Person (contracted Artificial Subject vs Natural Borne)"—whatever that means. He also asserts that "Queen of England, entered into a Treaty with the Federal Government For the

Taxing of Alcoholic beverages and cigarettes sold in America. The Treaty is called—The Stamp Act and in this Act, the Queen ordained that her Subject, the American people, are Exonerated of all other Federal Taxes. So the Federal Income Tax and the State Income Taxes Levied against all Americans is Contrary to an International Treaty and against the Sovereign Orders of the Queen."

Judge Posner responded as follows:

The Stamp Act was enacted by the Parliament of Great Britain in 1765. It did not relieve Americans of any taxes; on the contrary, it imposed a comprehensive tax on the use of paper by Americans. The Act was not a treaty between Britain and the federal government of the United States, for there was no United States; there were just the 13 British colonies that 11 years later declared independence from Great Britain. There were no federal taxes that the Act could have relieved Americans from having to pay. The sovereign of Britain at the time was a King, not a Queen; the King's wife (Princess Charlotte of Mecklenburg-Strelitz) was Great Britain's Queen but had no governmental authority.

As absurd as sovereign citizens' beliefs sound, the psychological appeal of the movement is easy to understand. Far from being nobodies, sovereigns see what's *really* going on. Like America's Founding Fathers (to whom they compare themselves), they are revolutionaries waging war against a tyrannical government. They flock to exclusive seminars and conferences where they bond and strategize with like-minded visionaries. The Washitaw Nation, an African American subgroup of the movement, claims a particularly noble provenance. According to one of its recent leaders—who calls herself Empress Verdiacee "Tiari" Washitaw-Turner Goston El-Bey—members of the Washitaw Nation fall outside federal authority because they are the descendants of the "Ancient Ones," blacks who occupied North America tens of thousands of years before the Europeans arrived.

To top it all off, sovereign citizens offer their members the alluring possibility of hitting pay dirt—of eventually, through legal maneuvers yet to be honed, tapping into the giant secret bank account. As the Southern Poverty Law Center put it, "sovereigns believe that if they can find just the right combination of words, punctuation, paper, ink color and timing, they can have anything they want—freedom from taxes, unlimited wealth, and life without licenses, fees or laws."

Conspiracy theories are strangely common all over the world. But there's something distinctly American about sovereign citizens, and the group's existence tells us a lot about America's class divide. Its members are among America's most disadvantaged—unemployed, in debt, with little or no opportunity to rise—just the kind of people Occupy was trying to help. But sovereigns are not against inequality. They are not opposed to wealth; on the contrary, they want to get it for themselves. Moreover, they are deeply suspicious of the establishment. They believe the entire government is involved in a labyrinthine scheme to keep them down, to deny them the American Dream.

STREET GANGS AND NARCO-SAINTS

It's a searing indictment of America that so many enterprising urban youth end up joining the Crips, Bloods, Sureños, Asian Boyz, or another of America's twenty-seven thousand street gangs, often engaged in drug trafficking or other criminal activity. Few groups are more tribal than gangs, which in the United States frequently have a racial or ethnic identity, whether African American, Haitian, Cambodian, Dominican, Somali, Vietnamese, or Salvadoran (like the famously violent Mara Salvatrucha, better known as MS-13).

As reflected in gang names like All About Cash, Cash Ave, and Cash Money Boys, gang members are often fixated on acquiring money any way they can, in order to afford flashy cars and the latest fashions. Many are also ambitious, willing to hustle, take risks, and sacrifice for a chance to rise in the hierarchy. In a sense, street gangs offer doomed versions of the American Dream. Most active gang members end up in prison or dead by the age of twenty. But for all too many disaffected, unemployed, often minority young men "with few skills and a contempt for low-wage jobs," street gangs offer exactly what the legitimate system doesn't: status, a strong tribe, and their best—perhaps only—shot at real upward mobility.

Also connected to drug trafficking is a very different group pop-ular among America's poor, especially those of Hispanic de-scent: the cult of Nuestra Señora de la Santa Muerte (Our Lady of the Holy Death).

If you walk around San Francisco's Mission District, or Melrose Avenue in Central Los Angeles, or Mid-City in New Or-leans, you'll see cheap storefronts with female skeletons in the windows—life-size skeletons, clad in long black, white, or red robes and usually holding scythes. These are worship houses or in-store altars for followers of a faith that started in Mexico but has now spread into every American city with a significant His-panic population. Santa Muerte is, in religious studies professor Andrew Chesnut's words, "the fastest growing religious move-ment in the entire Americas."

A syncretic blend of Catholic and Mesoamerican traditions, Santa Muerte is "Mexico's saint of delinquents and outcasts," as *Vice* put it, fantastically popular among petty thieves, prostitutes, gang members, smugglers, and drug dealers, who tattoo her im-age on their necks, arms, and backs. Because she doesn't share the Catholic Church's opposition to homosexuality, Santa Muerte is also the patron saint of many members of the LGBT community, including transgender sex workers. "She's the saint who doesn't discriminate, so she accepts all comers," says Chesnut. Although most of her devotees are not drug traffickers, she is known as a "narco-saint," who assists smugglers and is far more understand-ing than the Virgin Mary. As Chesnut explains, "[Y]ou can ask her for anything—to bless a shipment of crystal meth, for example." (Santa Muerte was featured in the first scene of season three of *Breaking Bad*, when a sketch of Heisenberg was pinned to her statue.)

In the last ten years, the growth of the cult has been "meteoric." The skeleton saint—also known as the Bony Lady or Skinny Girl—now has some 10 to 12 million devotees, who pray to her on Facebook and leave cigars, shots of rum, Barbie dolls, and ashtrays as offerings at her shrines. NBC recently covered her presence in Miami, and in Houston a grassroots movement works to raise money to build her a permanent church.

Santa Muerte is just one of many narco-saints. Another, especially popular in northern Mexico and Southern California, is the legendary bandit Jesús Malverde, also known as the "angel of the poor" or the "saint of the drug dealers." (Malverde was also featured on *Breaking Bad*, in the form of a bust on a DEA agent's desk in a season two episode.)

Malverde's cult is based in Mexico's northwestern coastal state of Sinaloa, home to the powerful Sinaloa drug cartel, which engineered the prison escape of drug kingpin Joaquín "El Chapo" Guzmán. The destination of hundreds of pilgrims each year, Malverde's shrine in the capital city of Culiacán is filled with photos and plaques. Inscriptions include "Thank you Malverde for saving me from drugs" and "Thank you Malverde for not having to lose my arm and leg." There are also desperate letters, like this one from Los Angeles: "Dear holy and miraculous Malverde . . . I'm writing this letter so that you'll help me with a problem I have with some friends I had, so that they won't look for me anymore.

Make them forget the problems we had. Make them please leave my parents and my sister and me in peace."

Narco-saint cults may strike elites as irrational or ridiculous, but they respond to the distinctive plight and marginalized status of the less well-off, offering them a group affiliation responsive to their needs and sense of exclusion. In the words of a Mexican American lawyer, "Most Mexican-Americans today live in deep social isolation. I'm talking about the overwhelming majority: those with poor education, poor housing, poor wages. There's a clear distrust of U.S. politics, a perception that only a few control the country, with the rest of Americans being used as labor." Narco-saint cults are not dangerous in the way that the sovereign citizens or street gangs are, but they are dangerous in another way: they testify to the growing number of alienated poor Americans who are retreating into ethnically insular communities with little sense of connection to the country's institutions or its civic life.

The have-not groups discussed so far are outside mainstream American culture; they are so illicit or socially marginal that they have virtually no political influence. But other groups popular with lower-income Americans are very different. Some of them may be equally unknown to America's elites, but they are much more politically salient—indeed, closely related to the rise of Donald Trump.

THE PROSPERITY GOSPEL

There are sixty-five megachurches in America with more than 10,000 weekly attendees, and almost half of these preach the prosperity gospel. The average prosperity church has 8,500 members. The celebrity pastor Joel Osteen has a congregation of 35,000 at the Lakewood Church in Houston and draws 7 million viewers weekly to his televised sermons. Not far behind, the African American televangelist Creflo Dollar preaches to 30,000 at the World Changers Church he founded in Georgia.

While most elites have never heard of the prosperity gospel, Donald Trump used it to his advantage. On the 2016 campaign trail, prosperity gospel televangelist Mark Burns praised Trump and introduced him with these rousing words (a strange twist on Barack Obama's): "There is no black person, there is no white person, there is no yellow person, there is no red person, there's only green people! Green is money! Green are jobs!!"

The prosperity gospel, which is Christian but cuts across denominations, preaches that being rich is divine. Given that Jesus said, according to the Gospel of Matthew, "You cannot serve both God and money" and "It is easier for a camel to go through an eye of a needle than for a rich man to enter the kingdom of God," the theological underpinnings of the prosperity gospel are a little murky—but prosperity preachers have been quite creative.

According to some, despite appearances, Jesus himself was rich. As evidence, they point to the circumstances of his birth. "As soon as Jesus arrived," noted Dollar (who owns two Rolls-Royces and a private jet), the "anointing to prosper acted like a magnet, drawing wise men with gifts of gold, frankincense, and myrrh. . . . *Those were not cheap gifts. . . . Prosperity attached itself to baby Jesus immediately,* and that same gift to prosper has been given to us as heirs of Christ." Similarly, on the popular *Believer's Voice of Victory* television show, prosperity author John Avanzini observed that Jesus had a nice house ("big enough to have company stay the night with Him") and wore designer clothes ("You didn't get the stuff he wore off the rack . . . this was custom stuff").

Other prosperity movement leaders focus on the Old Testament. "[A]ccording to Deuteronomy," explained the influential prosperity pastor Kenneth Hagin, poverty was a punishment God brought on people "if they disobeyed Him." After all, in the Garden of Eden, God "surrounded Adam and Eve with every material blessing they could possibly need." After the Fall, it was Satan who inflicted misery on mankind. Jesus' death and Resurrection redeemed humanity not just from sin but from disease and poverty as well. As the African American pastor Leroy Thompson explained, "He took your place in *poverty* so you could take His place in *prosperity*."

One of the most distinctive features of prosperity services is openly praying for money. In her book *Blessed,* Kate Bowler describes a Sunday service at the Victorious Faith Center, an African American church in North Carolina. It was normally the pastor who riveted the crowd with his fiery sermons, but on this occasion, his wife rose unexpectedly from her seat in the front row and faced the congregation:

Faith requires action, she declared with surprising volume. . . . Her small figure seemed to grow as the room got more excited. . . . "MONEY!" she shouted, the congregation calling out with her. "Cometh unto me . . ."—she paused in anticipation—"NOW!" With that, the first lady began to dance. . . . [S]ome 80 believers, young and old, threw off their inhibitions and joined her. The murmur rose to a din as people began to call out their needs . . . tears streamed down as people remembered what they desired or the losses that they hoped to replace. "Money cometh unto me NOW!" voices called again.

With its blatant emphasis on getting rich, the prosperity gospel has many detractors. Few of its followers attend elite universities in the Northeast, where one is much more likely to find the children of millionaires claiming to be deeply antimaterialistic. But the prosperity gospel holds enormous appeal for have-nots and have-lesses—and it is especially popular with disadvantaged minorities.

For the struggling, the prosperity gospel offers hope, direction, and a community of similarly situated peers—unlike the unrepresentative anti-inequality protest groups. At the same time, it offers the less well off a more dignified self-image. As Bowler puts it, the teachings of the prosperity gospel "lift believers' chins and square their shoulders." Osteen preaches that his congregants are not "victims" but "victors." Creflo Dollar teaches that even the poor control their own destinies. Rather than thinking of themselves as society's oppressed—or as part of the 99 percent, or even simply as have-nots—prosperity adherents see themselves as the favored, the optimistic, the blessed.

NASCAR NATION

Sports are always tribal. But whereas football, baseball, and basketball are popular across the social spectrum, NASCAR—with 75 million fans, the second-most-attended sport after the NFL—takes open pride in its white, working-class origins.

According to NASCAR lore, stock-car racing was started by Appalachian moonshiners trying to transport bootleg whiskey while evading law enforcement. Although the demographics of its fan base are rapidly evolving—today 40 percent of NASCAR fans are women—the "NASCAR Nation" holds tightly to its image as stereotypically white, masculine, Southern, and rural. Its fan base remains overwhelmingly Republican, and racing-speak is filled with macho idioms like "If it ain't rubbin' it ain't racin'," "Gentlemen, let's get it on," "Boys, have at it," and, of course, "Gentlemen, start your engines."

NASCAR is all about tribalism. Fans are loyal not just to a manufacturer (Chevrolet, Ford, Dodge, or Toyota) and a driver, but also to their corporate sponsors, which include big names like Goodyear, Home Depot, McDonald's, Geico, Miller, Mountain Dew, and Burger King. A recent study showed that NASCAR fans are more brand loyal than the fans of any other sport and that they feel they are contributing to their team when they buy sponsored products. "I have an Interstate battery in three of my vehicles that I own now," said one NASCAR fan. "Got to drink Budweiser. If you ain't drinking Budweiser, you don't belong here." Fans are three times more likely to buy a product sponsored by their NASCAR team than an unsponsored product, and this applies to everything from cell phones to breakfast foods. "I have a Nextel phone, so you know I'm a big supporter. I use Tide," said one fan. "Anything you see out there, I'm using. I eat Cheerios."

Fan devotion to NASCAR is so intense that it's often compared to a religion. Sociologists who have studied stock-car culture in America refer to the "NASCAR congregation," worshipping the "Gospel of NASCAR," and the "pilgrimages" that fans make, arriving in their RVs the Friday before the race and staying through the weekend. An "important theme," concluded one researcher, summarizing numerous fan interviews, "was that of *belonging.*"

Part of the group experience of NASCAR is the sheer physical intensity of attending a stadium event with a quarter of a million other human beings roaring for their drivers as cars hurtle by at more than two hundred miles per hour. "You can't even hear yourself think," one fan put it. "That's why NASCAR's slogan is 'feel the thunder.' If you haven't been there, you can't understand." The "fans scream at one another above the roar, some of them screaming in pure joy."

At the moment, NASCAR is struggling with its group identity. Its wealthy owner and CEO, Brian France, has been trying to broaden the NASCAR base by reaching out to women and minorities, as well as wealthier Americans. Nevertheless, at NASCAR races, there continues to be a proud assertion of a distinctive regional and cultural identity. Indeed, at the Daytona International Speedway in June 2015, NASCAR fans defied a request not to fly Confederate flags after the Charleston church massacre. "Spotting a Confederate flag [was] easier than finding a souvenir shop, restroom or beer stand," Fox News reported. "My family is from Alabama and we've been going to Talladega forever," explained a fan. "It isn't a Confederate thing so much as a NASCAR thing. That's why I fly it."

At the same time, NASCAR events are extremely patriotic, with American flags waving and proclamations about "the greatest nation on Earth." Of course, it's precisely the merging of these two identities that makes the NASCAR experience so appealing to some and so repugnant to others: the idea that NASCAR's America is the "true" America.

WORLD WRESTLING ENTERTAINMENT (WWE) AND THE TRUMP PHENOMENON

Like adherents of the prosperity gospel, the NASCAR Nation tends to love Donald Trump and see in him the America they stand for; indeed, Brian France endorsed him for president. But the "sport" most illuminating of Trump's startling political success—and of the class dimension behind that phenomenon—is not NASCAR. It's professional wrestling.

WWE is perhaps the single best example of the cultural divide between America's haves and have-nots. For elites, WWE is so unfathomably alien and appalling—gaudy, fake, bombastic, violent, and hypermasculine—it's not just an object of ridicule but the subject of voyeuristic academic study. When Roland Barthes (a darling of poststructuralism and famed scholar of semiotics) wrote about the "world of wrestling" in his landmark work *Mythologies,* he launched a cottage academic industry devoted to analyzing— in increasingly abstruse terms—the appeal and meaning of professional wrestling.

Left intellectuals are fascinated, even obsessed in a horrified way, with the "phenomenology" of watching professional wrestling. Do working-class Americans understand they are watching something fake? Do they simply suspend disbelief? Or is it possible that some of them are duped into thinking they are watching an actual contest? Cultural theorists have written about how professional wrestling elides the distinction between real and fictive; how it performs narratives about modern romance; how it represents a modern form of melodrama; how it allows lower- and working-class viewers to play out the drama of good versus evil, might versus right.

In contrast to speculating about the phenomenon of professional wrestling, Donald Trump actually has participated. He once entered the ring, taking on WWE founder Vince McMahon in a mock showdown that ended in a victorious Trump shaving McMahon's head—an exhibition that, in one *Huffington Post* writer's words, was "both mesmerizing and gross." Trump is in the WWE Hall of Fame—inducted in 2013—and is listed on its Web site as a "WWE Superstar." Trump's connection to wrestling did not end when he won the White House. Among President Trump's first cabinet-level nominees was the former CEO of WWE (and wife of its founder), Linda McMahon, whom he chose to head the

Small Business Administration. And far from being abashed by his own time in the ring, in July 2017 Trump proudly tweeted a video clip from the McMahon match, showing himself pummeling a figure with a CNN logo superimposed on its head.

The parallels between the Trump phenomenon and WWE are unmistakable. Although WWE has a significant black and Latino working class following as well, the prototypical WWE fan is white, male, single, working class, and, according to some experts, disaffected. Geographically, professional wrestling is especially popular in America's former industrial heartland and the South— and has practically no fanbase in multicultural California. It's no surprise, then, that the WWE audience resembles the coalition of voters who buoyed Trump's candidacy.

Nor is it a coincidence that coastal elites, including the media, find Trump and WWE equally repulsive. In a *New York Times* op-ed, Gail Collins described Linda McMahon as "[a] political novice who made her fortune building up an entertainment business that specialized in blood, seminaked women and scripted subplots featuring rape, adultery and familial violence . . . [and whose] family yacht is named Sexy Bitch." By contrast, Trump said of his cabinet pick, "Linda has a tremendous background and is widely recognized as one of the country's top female executives advising businesses around the globe."

To understand Trump's relationship to the WWE and his appeal to its audience is to see a microcosm of the 2016 election. For Trump's supporters, as in *WrestleMania*, showmanship and symbols are often what matter. Where progressives saw an uncivilized brute bloviating about his sexual prowess, lying on cue, and viciously dressing down his opponents, Trump supporters saw something familiar and playfully spectacular. In Trump's world, as in the wrestling world, absurd "alternative facts" are not falsehoods but story lines, fueling an entertainment-driven narrative. Through this lens, Trump is a hero in the mold of Hulk Hogan or Stone Cold Steve Austin: a domineering titan promising to vanquish the forces of evil, to crusade against political correctness, to make aggressive masculinity fashionable again. Riffing off political analyst Salena Zito's famous statement that the press took Trump "literally, but not seriously," whereas his supporters took him "seriously, but not literally," Trump donor—and, briefly White House communications director—Anthony Scaramucci put it this way: "don't take him literally, take him symbolically."

AMERICA'S TWO WHITE TRIBES

To many on the left, anyone who even mentions economic factors as having contributed to Trump's election is either racist or, at a minimum, perpetuating and enabling racism. As a *Vox* article put it, "As this election fades into the distance . . . we'll spin a collective fairy tale about how a neglected group of white Americans who themselves were victims simply wanted change and used their votes to demand it. . . . There will be a push to 'understand' them, and this will be presented as the mature and moral thing to do. . . . And when that happens—when the deep bigotry that fueled the result is forgotten or explained away—racism will win yet again."

But to see the divisiveness in today's America—and the forces that brought about Trump's election—as solely about racism, while ignoring the role of inequality, misses too much of the picture. Even putting economics aside, it misses the role played by white-against-white resentment and antagonism.

Consider the following from a 2016 *National Review* op-ed about the "white working class":

> [N]obody did this to them. They failed themselves. . . . [T]ake an honest look at the welfare dependency, the drug and alcohol addiction, the family anarchy—which is to say, the whelping of human children with all the respect and wisdom of a stray dog—[and] you will come to an awful realization. . . .
>
> Nothing happened to them. . . . There wasn't a war or a famine. . . . Even the economic changes of the past few decades do very little to explain the dysfunction and negligence—and the incomprehensible malice—of poor white America. . . .
>
> The truth about these dysfunctional, downscale communities is that *they deserve to die*. Economically, they are negative assets. Morally, they are indefensible. . . . The white American underclass is in thrall to a vicious, selfish culture whose main products are misery and used heroin needles.

Especially in our age of political correctness, it's hard to imagine this kind of language being applied to any other group. The truth is that white Americans often hold their biggest disdain for other white Americans—the ones on the opposite side of the cultural divide. In January 2017, Silicon Valley executive Melinda Byerley created a stir when she tweeted out her explanation for why "we"—referring to people like herself, "who won't sacrifice tolerance or diversity"—don't want to live in middle America: "[N]o educated person wants to live in a shithole with stupid people"—especially "violent, racist, and/or misogynistic ones."

The antipathy and disdain are mutual. Trump supporters in the country's heartland see liberals as smug, elitist, hypocritical, condescending, and pampered. Many genuinely believe that liberals "hate America." The number one *New York Times* bestselling author Ann Coulter has accused liberals of "treason." In her words, "Liberals hate America, they hate 'flag-wavers,' they hate abortion opponents, they hate all religious groups except Islam (post 9/11). Even Islamic terrorists don't hate America likes liberals do."

In other words, white America is itself divided. Indeed, there is now so little interaction, commonality, and intermarriage between rural/heartland/working-class whites and urban/coastal whites that the difference between them is practically what social scientists would consider an "ethnic" difference. They think of themselves as belonging to distinct and opposing political tribes. As Appalachian writer J. D. Vance puts it in *Hillbilly Elegy,* "I may be white, but I do not identify with the WASPs of the Northeast. Instead, I identify with the millions of working-class white Americans of Scots-Irish descent who have no college degree . . . [whose] ancestors were day laborers in the Southern slave economy, sharecroppers after that, coal miners after that."

Tribalism in America propelled Donald Trump to the White House. If we want to understand this tribalism, we have to acknowledge the impact of inequality and the wedge it has driven between America's whites. "Coastal elites" have become a kind of market-dominant minority from the point of view of America's heartland, and, as we've seen all over the developing world, market-dominant minorities invariably end up producing democratic backlash.

CHAPTER EIGHT

Democracy and Political Tribalism in America

There is nothing which I dread so much as a division of the republic into two great parties, each arranged under its leader, and concerting measures in opposition to each other. This, in my humble apprehension, is to be dreaded as the greatest political evil under our Constitution.

—JOHN ADAMS,
letter to Jonathan Jackson (1780)

America is woven of many strands; I would recognize them and let it so remain. . . . Our fate is to become one, and yet many—This is not prophecy, but description.

—RALPH ELLISON, *Invisible Man*

At the core of American political tribalism, however, is race. This has always been true, but the present moment is especially fraught. We are on the verge of an unprecedented demographic transformation, which will place intense strain on the social fabric.

America is a super-group—the only one among the major powers of the world. We have forged a national identity that transcends tribal politics—an identity that does not belong to any subgroup, that is strong and capacious enough to hold together an incredibly diverse population, making us all American. This status was hard-won; it is precious.

The destructive, fracturing tribalism that is seizing American politics puts this in jeopardy. The United States is in no immediate danger of actually breaking up, unlike the United Kingdom and the European Union. But America is in danger of losing something even more important: who we are.

The Left believes that right-wing tribalism—bigotry, racism—is tearing the country apart. The Right believes that left-wing tribalism—identity politics, political correctness—is tearing the country apart. They are both right.

THE BROWNING OF AMERICA

For the first time in U.S. history, white Americans are about to lose their status as the country's majority.

In 1965, whites were still a dominant majority in America (84 percent), with the rest of the population mostly African American. But since then, there has been an immigration explosion; over the last fifty years, nearly 59 million immigrants have arrived in the United States (legally or illegally), the largest wave of immigration in U.S. history. Unlike previous waves, these immigrants have been largely from Asia and Latin America. Between 1965 and

2015, the Asian population in America grew exponentially, from 1.3 million to 18 million, as did the Hispanic population, from 8 million to almost 57 million. As a result, the complexion of America is "browning."

Already, non-Hispanic whites are a minority in America's two most populous states, Texas and California. They are also a minority in New Mexico; Hawaii; Washington, DC; and hundreds of counties across the country. By 2020, more than half of all American children under the age of eighteen are expected to be nonwhite. According to Pew Foundation projections, whites will cease to be a majority in America by 2055. The U.S. Census predicts that this will happen by 2044.

To be sure, the "browning of America" is not set in stone. The current projections for when America will become majority-minority depend on certain assumptions that may not hold. For example, the Census typically categorizes multiracial, multiethnic children as minority, but many of them might self-identify as white. And with Asians outpacing Hispanics as the largest group of new immigrants, perhaps "browning" is already outdated and "beiging" is more apt, raising different fears, connotations, and dynamics.

The fact remains—it's going to happen. Whether in 2044, 2055, or later, non-Hispanic "whites," as we understand the term, will cease to be a majority in America for the first time.

How whites in America feel about this is extremely hard to measure. To begin with, some white Americans, especially in the country's many multicultural pockets, may genuinely welcome America's changing complexion. In 1998, President Bill Clinton said the following in a speech at Portland State University:

In a little more than fifty years, there will be no majority race in the United States. No other nation in history has gone through demographic change of this magnitude in so short a time. . . . [N]ew immigrants are energizing our culture and broadening our vision of the world. They are renewing our most basic values and reminding us all of what it truly means to be an American.

Many activists and academics would go much further and agree with the radical (white) historian Noel Ignatiev that there is "nothing positive about white identity" or that the browning of America is a long-overdue corrective to what activist author William Wimsatt calls "the sickness of race in America."

But if there's one axiom of political tribalism, it's that dominant groups do not give up their power easily, and America is unlikely to be an exception. Indeed, U.S. history offers sobering evidence. While a white minority in America is unprecedented at the national level, it's not at the state level. After the Civil War, newly emancipated blacks suddenly eclipsed whites in the voting population in a number of Southern states, including Alabama, Florida, Georgia, Louisiana, Mississippi, and South Carolina. In all these states, whites were terrified by the prospect of black majority rule. With blacks "in a large majority," Southern politicians warned, "we will have black governors, black legislatures, black juries, black everything. . . . We will be completely exterminated, and the land . . . will go back into a wilderness and become another Africa or St. Domingo."

Southern whites responded to this threat by ushering in the

period known as Jim Crow. (There were even, as late as the twentieth century, delegations from the American South to South Africa to learn "tips" on how to disenfranchise and subjugate a black majority.) Through property and literacy qualifications, poll taxes, racially motivated redistricting, intimidation, and outright lynching, all the Southern states were highly successful in preventing blacks from exercising the suffrage. In Louisiana, for example, the number of registered black voters fell from 130,334 in 1896 to only 1,342 in 1904.

Of course, that was a long time ago, in an America that might seem gone with the wind—before *Brown v. Board of Education,* before the Civil Rights Act of 1964, before the Voting Rights Act of 1965, before affirmative action, before the appointment of America's first black Supreme Court justice, before the rise of political correctness, before the election of America's first African American president.

But such progress can be a two-edged sword. Many believe that the gains and successes of blacks make some whites, especially lower-income whites, feel threatened.

"WHITELASH"

It may seem absurd to some, but two thirds of white working-class Americans feel "that discrimination against whites is as big a problem today as discrimination against blacks and other minorities." (Interestingly, 29 percent of black Americans agreed with this statement.) Indeed, a significant number of white Americans believe that "there is more racism against them than there is against black Americans"—even though "by nearly any metric . . . statistics continue to indicate drastically poorer outcomes for Black than White Americans."

Strong evidence suggests that white anxiety—about being displaced, being outnumbered, being discriminated against—has fueled recent conservative populist politics in America. Stanford sociologist Robb Willer and his colleagues conducted a series of survey-based experiments to test the "decline of whiteness" as an explanation for the rise of the Tea Party. In one experiment, Willer found that white survey participants shown a picture of President Obama with an artificially darkened skin tone were more likely to report they supported the Tea Party than those shown a picture with Obama's skin tone artificially lightened. In another experiment, Willer found that participants who were told "whites remain the largest ethnic group in the U.S." were less likely to report their support for the Tea Party than those who were told "minorities [are] expected to surpass whites in number by 2042."

According to numerous studies, similar dynamics fueled the 2016 presidential election. A *Wall Street Journal* analysis found that Donald Trump had especially strong support in counties "most unsettled by rapid demographic change"—i.e., by the recent influx of nonwhite immigrants into previously heavily white populations in small-town Iowa, Indiana, Illinois, Minnesota, and Wisconsin. A postelection survey by the Public Religion Research Institute, which was reported in the *Atlantic,* found that "52 percent of Trump voters said that they feel like the country has changed so much, they often feel like strangers in their own land."

White anxiety about antiwhite discrimination cuts across party lines. According to a 2016 Pew study, about half of Republicans believe there is a lot or some discrimination against whites, but so do nearly 30 percent of Democrats. Even so, a striking YouGov/ *Huffington Post* survey conducted in December 2016 found that Trump voters were five times more likely to believe that "average Americans"—a term psychological research has shown is "implicitly synonymous" with "white Americans"—aren't getting their fair share in society than they were to believe that "blacks" aren't getting their fair share. Indeed, according to political scientist Michael Tesler, "perceptions that whites are currently treated unfairly relative to minorities appeared to be an unusually strong predictor of support for Donald Trump in the general election."

There is in fact some justification for these feelings of white marginalization—at least among a certain segment of the white population. Poor and working-class whites have among the highest rates of unemployment and addiction. Life expectancy is declining for whites without a high school degree—something true of almost no other demographic, including high school dropouts from other racial groups. Educational prospects for poor white children are extremely bleak. Private tutors and one-thousand-dollar SAT courses are completely cost prohibitive to poor or even working-class people—and poor whites don't benefit from affirmative action. Whereas most elite colleges do special outreach for racial minorities, they rarely send scouts to the backwoods of Kentucky. Out of roughly two hundred students in the Yale Law School class of 2019, there appears to be exactly one poor white—or three, if we include students from families living just above the federal poverty line. Administrators have described this class as the "most diverse" in the school's history.

It is simply a fact that the "diversity" policies at the most selective American universities and in some sectors of the economy have had a disparate adverse impact on whites. Relative to their population percentage, working-class whites, and particularly white Christians from conservative states, are often the most underrepresented group at America's elite universities. White employees increasingly feel victimized by prodiversity promotion policies that they see as discriminating against them—and the United States Supreme Court has agreed, striking down as illegal a particularly bald-faced attempt by the city of New Haven, Connecticut, to invalidate promotions for white firefighters in order to promote more minorities.

While whites generally are still extremely disproportionately represented in the U.S. Senate, the media, and the corporate world, working-class whites are decidedly not. Between 1999 and 2008, only 13 of the 783 members of Congress who served had spent more than a quarter of their adulthood in blue-collar jobs. As political scientist Nick Carnes writes, "Although women and racial minorities were still underrepresented at the end of the twentieth century, their gains during the postwar period sharply contrasted [with] the stable underrepresentation of working-class people, who made up between 50% and 60% of the nation during the last hundred years but who constituted 2% or less of the legislators who served in each Congress during that time."

The result of all this is that working-class whites have among the lowest upward mobility rates in the nation. Not surprisingly, when surveyed about the prospects of children today, whites were overwhelmingly more pessimistic than Latinos and blacks. Just 24 percent of whites believed the next generation would be better off financially or the same as their parents, compared to 49 percent of blacks and 62 percent of Latinos.

Beyond their economic anxiety, many whites feel an intense cultural anxiety. America's culture wars are nothing if not a fight for the right to define our national identity—and it's a bitter, race-inflected battle. After Beyoncé channeled Black Lives Matter at the 2016 Super Bowl, half the country deified her while the other half accused her of "cop killer entertainment." At the 2017 Oscars, the question of whether Best Picture would go to *La La Land* (a throwback musical that some criticize for "whitesplaining" jazz) or *Moonlight* seemed to have massive implications—as did the gaffe that initially gave the award to the former by mistake. White male heroes like John Wayne have given way to the clueless white male, who doesn't even realize how racist he is, and is regularly made into television sport (as on *Saturday Night Live*). For tens of millions of white Americans today, mainstream popular culture displays an un-Christian, minority-glorifying, LGBTQ America they can't and don't want to recognize as their country—an America that seems to exclude them, to treat them as the enemy.

All this was roiling below the 2016 presidential campaign. As Van Jones put it on election night, Trump's victory was in part a "whitelash."

THREATENED IN AMERICA

To state the obvious, whites are not the only group that feels threatened in America today. Indeed, for many minorities the very idea that whites could feel threatened is disingenuous and infuriating. The whole premise of the Black Lives Matter movement is that our country is and has been since its founding built on unceasing violence, abuse, and terror against black Americans, that ours is a country where, as writer Ta-Nehisi Coates wrote in his "Letter to My Son," black Americans are routinely murdered while going about the routine business of life: "choked to death for selling cigarettes," "shot for seeking help," and "shot down for browsing in a department store."

Whites may feel threatened, but they do not face mass, disproportionate incarceration. As author and civil rights lawyer Michelle Alexander has observed, "The United States imprisons a larger percentage of its black population than South Africa did at the height of apartheid." In Washington, DC, an estimated "three out of four young black men (and nearly all those in the poorest neighborhoods) can expect to serve time in prison." White parents in America do not live in fear, as many black parents do, that their children will be gunned down without cause by the police.

Jim Crow may officially be over, but attempts to disenfranchise blacks continue. In 2016, a federal appellate court found that the North Carolina legislature had deliberately targeted black voters in its voter identification requirements as well as in provisions restricting same-day registration, out-of-precinct provisional voting, and early voting—provisions enacted only after the legislature had collected data on racial voting patterns. The restrictions, ruled the court, "target African Americans with almost surgical precision." Similar measures were struck down in Texas.

Daily life, as psychologist Beverly Tatum has shown, differs materially for people of color in America, starting at an early age. White three-year-olds are never asked why their skin looks "so dirty." Whites are generally not followed around in stores or asked for identification when no one else is questioned. They are not passed over by taxi drivers or subjected to constant media images of people who look like them in handcuffs. Whites do not have to see people react to them by clutching their purses and crossing the street and are not regularly subjected to police brutality. "I hope none of them ask about my spring break," says the protagonist of Angie Thomas's bestselling novel *The Hate U Give*. "They went to Taipei, the Bahamas, Harry Potter World. I stayed in the hood and saw a cop kill my friend." If many whites feel anxiety in today's America, many blacks feel an existential threat that seems never to end.

Muslim Americans too feel threatened in today's United States. The day after the 2016 presidential election, Omer Aziz described in a *New Republic* essay how he and his Muslim American friends reacted to Trump's win: "We felt in the deepest chambers of our being that America had betrayed us, had repudiated who we were. In a matter of minutes, the shining city on the hill became an armed citadel determined to oppose our existence. . . . [A]s people who come from the edges of society, we know what the face of white terror looks like and what Trump's victory means for our future. There is no silver lining."

Mexican Americans feel threatened; the president of their country swept to power with anti-Mexican rhetoric. Reports abound of indiscriminate raids and detentions by ICE agents, and many live in fear that they or someone they love will be rounded up and deported.

Women in America—not all, but many—feel threatened. They fear that overt sexism will not only be normalized but made fashionable again in the name of anti–political correctness. They fear that America may be entering a new era of sexual predation, sexual harassment, and sexual assault. Gay and transgender Americans feel threatened. They fear that a new conservative Supreme Court will undo hard-fought gains and that they will be subject to renewed hostility, stigma, and discrimination. Progressives in general feel threatened, under siege by what they see as a white-male-dominated, reactionary administration intent on destroying their vision of a tolerant, open, multicultural America.

Finally—even though they won—Trump supporters feel threatened, under constant, vitriolic attack from liberal America. In a survey of Eastern Washington State residents, one small-business owner who voted for Trump said, "Citizens can be afraid to speak out on real issues for fear of being called Racist, Homophobic, Xenophobic, etc. when they are none of those things." Another said, "I saw a YouTube video from the University of Chicago where students and some educators had made a piñata of President Trump and were telling the children to hit it and knock it down and when they did, the adults told them to rip it apart. What kind of message is that sending to young children?" And in the words of a former Democrat who voted twice for Bill Clinton but for Trump in 2016: "I feel like we are in some kind of civil war right now. . . . The Democratic Party has changed so much that I don't recognize it anymore. . . . They are scarier to me than these Islamic terrorists."

Thus we find ourselves in an unprecedented moment of pervasive tribal anxiety. For two hundred years, whites in America represented an undisputed politically, economically, and culturally dominant majority. When a political tribe is so overwhelmingly dominant, it can persecute with impunity, but it can also be more generous. It can afford to be more universalist, more enlightened, more inclusive, like the WASP elites of the 1960s who opened up the Ivy League colleges to more Jews, blacks, and other minorities—in part because it seemed like the right thing to do.

Today, no group in America feels comfortably dominant. Every group feels attacked, pitted against other groups not just for jobs and spoils but for the right to define the nation's identity. In these conditions, democracy devolves into zero-sum group competition—pure political tribalism.

IDENTITY POLITICS, LEFT AND RIGHT

In a sense, American politics has always been identity politics. If we define "identity politics" broadly, to include cultural and social movements based on group identities, then slavery and Jim Crow were forms of identity politics for white Americans, just as the suffragette movement at the turn of the twentieth century was for women.

Nevertheless, at different times in the past, both the American Left and the American Right have stood for group-transcending values. Neither does today.

Fifty years ago, the rhetoric of pro–civil rights, Great Society liberals was, in its dominant voices, expressly group transcending, framed in the language of national unity and equal opportunity. Introducing the bill that eventually became the Civil Rights Act of 1964, John F. Kennedy famously said: "This is one country. It has become one country because all of us and all the people who came here had an equal chance to develop their talents. We cannot say to ten percent of the population that you can't have that right; that your children cannot have the chance to develop whatever talents they have." In his most famous speech, Dr. Martin Luther King Jr. proclaimed: "When the architects of our republic wrote the magnificent words of the Constitution and the Declaration of Independence, they were signing a promissory note to which every American was to fall heir. This note was a promise that all men—yes, black men as well as white men—would be guaranteed the unalienable Rights of Life, Liberty, and the pursuit of Happiness." While more radical black power movements, led by activists like Malcolm X, Stokely Carmichael, and the Nation of Islam's Elijah Muhammad, espoused a more overtly racial, pro-black, or even antiwhite agenda, King's ideals—the ideals that captured the imagination and hearts of the public and led to real change—transcended group divides and called for an America in which skin color didn't matter.

Leading liberal philosophical movements of that era were similarly group blind and universalist in character. John Rawls's enormously influential *A Theory of Justice,* published in 1971, called on people to imagine themselves in an "original position," behind a "veil of ignorance," in which they could decide on their society's basic principles without regard to "race, gender, religious affiliation, [or] wealth." At roughly the same time, the idea of universal human rights proliferated, advancing the dignity of every individual as the foundation of a just international order. As Will Kymlicka would later point out, the international human rights movement deliberately elevated individual rights as opposed to group rights: "Rather than protecting vulnerable groups directly, through special rights for the members of designated groups, cultural minorities would be protected indirectly, by guaranteeing basic civil and political rights to all individuals regardless of group membership."

Thus, although the Left was always concerned with the oppression of minorities and the rights of disadvantaged groups, the dominant ideals in this period tended to be group blind, often cosmopolitan, with many calling for transcending not just ethnic, racial, and gender barriers but national boundaries as well.

Meanwhile, leading conservatives also began championing group blindness, although in a much more nationalist, patriotic register. Ronald Reagan, who would become the demigod of this movement, emphasized both American exceptionalism as a "city upon a hill" and the values of rugged individualism, embracing equality of opportunity through free markets. While explicitly rejecting racism, and even claiming the legacy of Martin Luther

King Jr., Reagan also rejected affirmative action and mandatory minority hiring: "We are committed to a society in which all men and women have equal opportunities to succeed, and so we oppose the use of quotas," Reagan explained. "We want a color-blind society. A society, that in the words of Dr. King, judges people not by the color of their skin, but by the content of their character."

To be sure, many on the left claim that the Right's rhetoric of color blindness was always disingenuous. They cite, for example, Reagan's famous denunciation of "welfare queens" as a term loaded with disparaging racial overtones. Nevertheless, Reagan raised a flag of color blindness around which the American Right would rally for decades to come. Thus in 2013, when President Obama said that "Trayvon [Martin] could have been me thirty-five years ago," Fox News radio host Todd Starnes was quick to label the president "Race-Baiter in Chief," and Newt Gingrich called the speech "disgraceful."

Perhaps in reaction to Reaganism, in the 1980s and 1990s, a new movement began to unfold on the left—a movement emphasizing group consciousness, group identity, and group claims. Many on the left had become acutely aware that color blindness was being used by conservatives to oppose policies intended to redress historical wrongs and persisting racial inequities. Many also began to notice that the leading liberal figures in America, whether in law, government, or academia, were predominantly white men and that the neutral "group-blind" invisible hand of the market wasn't doing much to correct longstanding imbalances. With the collapse of the Soviet Union, the anticapitalist economic preoccupations of the old Left began to take a backseat to a new way of understanding oppression: the politics of redistribution was replaced by a "politics of recognition." Modern identity politics was born.

As Oberlin professor Sonia Kruks writes, "[W]hat makes identity politics a significant departure from earlier, pre-identarian [movements] is its demand for recognition on the basis of the very grounds on which recognition has previously been denied: it is *qua* women, *qua* blacks, *qua* lesbians that groups demand recognition. . . . The demand is not for inclusion within the fold of 'universal humankind' . . . nor is it for respect 'in spite of' one's differences. Rather, what is demanded is respect for oneself *as* different."

But identity politics, with its group-based rhetoric, did not initially become the mainstream position of the Democratic Party. In the 1992 campaign, Bill Clinton famously repudiated Sister Souljah, a singer and activist who had said in justification of violence in Los Angeles, "If black people kill black people every day, why not have a week and kill white people?" Said Clinton: "If you took the words *white* and *black*, and you reversed them, you might think David Duke was giving that speech." At the 2004 Democratic National Convention, Barack Obama famously declared, "There's not a black America and white America and Latino America and Asian America; there's the United States of America."

THE NEW TRIBAL LEFT

A decade and a half later, we are very far from Obama's America. Indeed, for today's Left, group blindness is the ultimate sin, because it masks the reality of group hierarchies and oppression in America. As writer Catherine Crooke puts it:

America has always channeled its politics and its power through hierarchies of identity. . . . European America acquired its land through the genocide of American Indians. It grew rich thanks to the importation and forced labor of enslaved blacks, who on the one hand became undeniably part of the American family through widespread sexual coercion, and on the other hand were legally and socially excluded from the American political community for generations. . . . In light of these realities, to insist upon a singular America is to deny the impact of violent marginalizations past and present. Progressives reject the whitewashing of the lived experiences of non-white or non-male Americans . . .

It's indisputable that whites, and specifically white male Protestants, dominated America for most of its history, often violently, and that this legacy persists. Thus, for the Left, identity politics is a means to "confront rather than obscure the uglier aspects of American history and society."

But in recent years, whether because of growing strength or

growing frustration with the lack of progress, the Left has upped the ante. A shift in tone, rhetoric, and logic has moved identity politics away from inclusion—which had always been the Left's watchword—toward exclusion and division. For much of the Left today, anyone who speaks in favor of group blindness is on the other side, indifferent to or even guilty of oppression. For some, especially on college campuses, anyone who doesn't swallow the antioppression orthodoxy hook, line, and sinker—anyone who doesn't acknowledge "white supremacy" in America—is a racist. When liberal icon Bernie Sanders told supporters, "It's not good enough for somebody to say, 'Hey, I'm a Latina, vote for me,'" Quentin James, the National Black Americans Director for the Ready for Hillary PAC, retorted that Sanders's "comments regarding identity politics suggest he may be a white supremacist, too."

Once identity politics gains momentum, it inevitably subdivides, giving rise to ever-proliferating group identities demanding recognition. One of the most important concepts in left-academic circles today is "intersectionality," which understands oppression as operating on multiple axes simultaneously. Thus Columbia law professor Kimberlé Crenshaw, who coined the term over twenty-five years ago, has explored how the claims of black women were often excluded from both feminist and antiracist movements because the experiences of black women did not reflect the typical "women's experience" or "black experience." Similarly, political activist Linda Sarsour has pointed out that while equal pay for women is an important issue, "look at the ratio of what white women get paid versus black women and Latina women."

Pathbreaking in the 1990s, intersectionality has in recent years been misinterpreted and used in ways not originally intended, becoming, as Crenshaw put it in 2017, "basically identity politics on steroids," dividing people into ever more specific subgroups created by overlapping racial, ethnic, gender, and sexual orientation categories. Today, there is an ever-expanding vocabulary of identity on the left. Facebook now lists more than fifty gender designations from which users can choose, from genderqueer to intersex to pangender. Or take the acronym LGBTQ. Originally LGB, variants over the years have ranged from GLBT to LGBTI to LGBTQQIAAP as preferred terminology shifted and identity groups quarreled about who should be included and who should come first.

Because the Left is always trying to outleft the last Left, the result can be a zero-sum competition over which group is the least privileged, an "Oppression Olympics" often fragmenting progressives and setting them against each other.

All these dynamics were on display at the Women's March of January 21, 2017, when a staggering 4.2 million people gathered in solidarity at events around the country, with an estimated crowd of almost 500,000 in DC alone. In many ways, the march was a stupendous success, an expression of progressive unity. The *New Yorker* reported that the "crowds on Saturday were so enormous, so radiant with love and dissent, that" the "coming together" of all marginalized groups "seemed possible."

Below the surface, however, political-tribe tensions plagued the march. The original name of the march, the "Million Woman March," was also the name of an important 1997 protest for black women's unity. Black women quickly accused the organizers of appropriation. On Facebook, one critic wrote: "I take issue with white feminists taking the name of something that Black people started to address our struggles. That's appropriation. . . . I will not even consider supporting this until the organizers are intersectional, original and come up with a different name." Another critic lambasted the organizers as racist: "This is the perfect example of how white supremacy disguised as white feminism can be incredibly damaging to Black bodies, Black culture and Black herstory."

Acknowledging these criticisms, the organizers changed the name of the march and brought on nonwhite activists as cochairs. But tensions continued. Many black women felt used, especially in light of the glaring fact that 53 percent of white women had voted for Trump. Others chose not to participate in the march, because "they didn't want to be apart [sic] of a mass mobilization of white women." And on the march's Facebook page, one black activist encouraged white women to assume a more passive role in the fight, to listen and learn from those who had already been engaged in the struggle: "You don't just get to join because now you're scared, too. I was born scared." ShiShi Rose, a Brooklyn blogger, wrote, "Now is the time for you to be listening more, talking less. You should be reading our books and understanding the roots of racism and white supremacy. You should be drowning yourselves in our poetry."

Predictably, these criticisms ignited backlash from some white women, who began "to feel not very welcome" and didn't understand why women of color had to be "so divisive." Some who had planned to fly to DC decided not to go. One fifty-year-old South

Carolinian woman, who had been excited to bring her daughters, canceled her trip after reading online posts. "This is a women's march," she said. "We're supposed to be allies in equal pay, marriage, adoption. Why is it now about, 'White women don't understand black women'?" Others responded angrily to the organizers' online request that white women "understand their privilege, and acknowledge the struggle that women of color face." "Fuck You is my immediate reaction," one white woman wrote. "You're no better than trump voters," wrote another.

Although inclusivity is presumably still the ultimate goal, the contemporary Left is pointedly exclusionary. During a Black Lives Matter protest at the DNC held in Philadelphia in July 2016, a protest leader announced that "this is a black and brown resistance march," asking white allies to "appropriately take [their] place in the back of this march." The war on "cultural appropriation" is rooted in the belief that groups have exclusive rights to their own histories, symbols, and traditions. A prototypical example of cultural appropriation would be a white person wearing a sombrero and a fake mustache to a Halloween party, but some on the Left today would also consider it an offensive act of privilege for, say, a straight white man to write a novel featuring a gay Latina. Transgressions are called out daily on social media; no one is immune. Beyoncé was criticized for wearing what looked like a traditional Indian bridal outfit; Amy Schumer, in turn, was criticized for making a parody of Beyoncé's "Formation," a song about black female pride and empowerment. Students at Oberlin complained of a vendor's "history of blurring the line between culinary diversity and cultural appropriation by modifying the recipes without respect for certain Asian countries' cuisines." And a student op-ed at Louisiana State University claimed that white women styling their eyebrows to look thicker—like "a lot of ethnic women"—was "a prime example of the cultural appropriation in the country."

Not everyone on the Left is happy with the direction that identity politics has taken. Many are dismayed by the focus on cultural appropriation. As a progressive Mexican American law student put it, "If we allowed ourselves to be hurt by a costume, how could we manage the trauma of an eviction notice?" He added: "Liberals have cried wolf too many times. If everything is racist and sexist, nothing is. When Trump, the real wolf, came along, no one listened."

THE NEW TRIBAL RIGHT

Meanwhile, identity politics has seized the Right, too, in an about-face from its longtime rhetoric of color blindness. Political scientist Samuel P. Huntington was a pivotal figure in this shift. His controversial 1996 bestseller *The Clash of Civilizations* framed Islamic culture as inimical to Western values; his even more controversial 2004 bestseller *Who Are We?* warned of the threat to "Anglo-Protestant culture" posed by large-scale Hispanic immigration. Viewed by many as shocking at the time, the us-versus-them, anti-Muslim, anti-immigrant sentiments that Huntington expressed were bread and butter for conservatives on the 2016 campaign trail.

Candidate Trump famously called for "a total and complete shutdown of Muslims entering the United States," described illegal Mexican immigrants as "rapists," and referred disparagingly to an Indiana-born federal judge as "Mexican," accusing the judge of having "an inherent conflict of interest" rendering him unfit to preside over a suit against Trump. (Making the argument that Trump used identity politics to win the White House is like shooting fish in a barrel.) Michael Flynn, who served briefly as Trump's national security adviser, asserted in August 2016 that Islamism "is a vicious cancer inside the body of 1.7 billion people on this planet and it has to be excised." Senator Marco Rubio compared the war with Islam to America's "war with Nazis." Even moderate Republicans like Jeb Bush advocated for a religious test to allow Christian refugees to enter the country preferentially.

At the same time, we are also seeing on the right—particularly the alt-right—political tribalism directed against minorities perceived as "too successful." At the "Unite the Right" rally in Charlottesville, Virginia, David Duke warned a raucous crowd that "the American media and the American political system" are "dominated" by "a tiny minority—the Jewish Zionist minority." Steve Bannon, Trump's former White House chief strategist, has complained that America's "[e]ngineering schools are all full of people from South Asia, and East Asia. . . . They've come in here to take these jobs" while Americans "can't get engineering degrees . . . [and] can't get a job." Bannon has also warned: "Two-thirds or three-quarters of the CEOs in Silicon Valley are from South Asia or from Asia . . . A country is more than an economy. We're a civic society." The "two-thirds or three-quarters" figure asserted by Bannon is a wild exaggeration—and reminiscent of the kind of targeting of market-dominant minorities common in the developing world.

This brings us to the most striking feature of today's right-wing political tribalism: the white identity politics that has mobilized around the idea of whites as an endangered, discriminated-against group. In part this development carries forward a long tradition of white tribalism in America. But white identity politics has also gotten a tremendous recent boost from the Left, whose relentless berating, shaming, and bullying might have done more damage than good. One Trump voter claimed that "maybe I'm just so sick of being called a bigot that my anger at the authoritarian left has pushed me to support this seriously flawed man." "The Democratic party," said Bill Maher, "made the white working man feel like your problems aren't real because you're 'mansplaining' and check your privilege. You know, if your life sucks, your problems are real." When blacks blame today's whites for slavery or ask for reparations, many white Americans feel as though they are being attacked for the sins of other generations.

Or consider this blog post in the *American Conservative*, worth quoting at length because of the light it sheds:

> I'm a white guy. I'm a well-educated intellectual who enjoys small arthouse movies, coffeehouses and classic blues. If you didn't know any better, you'd probably mistake me for a lefty urban hipster.
>
> And yet. I find some of the alt-right stuff exerts a pull even on me. Even though I'm smart and informed enough to see through it. It's seductive because I am not a person

with any power or privilege, and yet I am constantly bombarded with messages telling me that I'm a cancer, I'm a problem, everything is my fault.

I am very lower middle class. I've never owned a new car, and do my own home repairs as much as I can to save money. I cut my own grass, wash my own dishes, buy my clothes from Walmart. I have no clue how I will ever be able to retire. But oh, brother, to hear the media tell it, I am just drowning in unearned power and privilege, and America will be a much brighter, more loving, more peaceful nation when I finally just keel over and die.

Trust me: After all that, some of the alt-right stuff feels like a warm, soothing bath. A "safe space," if you will. I recoil from the uglier stuff, but some of it—the "hey, white guys are actually okay, you know! Be proud of yourself, white man!" stuff is really VERY seductive, and it is only with some intellectual effort that I can resist the pull. . . . If it's a struggle for someone like me to resist the pull, I imagine it's probably impossible for someone with less education or cultural exposure.

If the Left's exclusionary identity politics is ironic in light of the Left's ostensible demands for inclusivity, equally ironic is the emergence of a "white" identity politics on the right. For decades, the Right has claimed to be a bastion of individualism, a place where those who rejected the divisive identity politics of the Left found a home. For this reason, conservatives typically paint the emergence of white identity as having been forced on them by the tactics of the Left. As one political commentator puts it:

> Most on the right still perceive racial groupings of any kind as anathema. They still view individualism as one of America's greatest strengths and still view as disreputable political movements that organize around racial identities. . . . At the same time, many feel that society has come to glorify all things non-white, demonize all things white, and that if they do not fight back no one will. In short, feeling as though they are under perpetual attack for the color of their skin, many on the right have become defiant of their whiteness, allowing it into their individual politics in ways they have not for generations.

At its core, the problem is simple but fundamental. While black Americans, Asian Americans, Hispanic Americans, Jewish Americans, and many others are allowed—indeed, encouraged—to feel solidarity and take pride in their racial or ethnic identity, white Americans have for the last several decades been told they must never, ever do so. People want to see their own tribe as exceptional, as something to be deeply proud of; that's what the tribal instinct is all about. For decades now, nonwhites in the United States have been encouraged to indulge their tribal instincts in just this way, but, at least publicly, American whites have not. On the contrary, if anything, they have been told that their white identity is something no one should take pride in. "I get it," says Christian

Lander, creator of the popular satirical blog *Stuff White People Like*, "as a straight white male, I'm the worst thing on Earth."

But the tribal instinct is not so easy to suppress. As Vassar professor Hua Hsu put it in an *Atlantic* essay called "The End of White America?," the "result is a racial pride that dares not speak its name, and that defines itself through cultural cues instead." In combination with the profound demographic transformation now taking place in America, this suppressed urge on the part of many white Americans—to feel solidarity and pride in their group identity, as others are allowed to do—has created an especially fraught set of tribal dynamics in the United States today.

ETHNONATIONALISM LITE

In early 2017, a *Foreign Policy* headline proclaimed, "The GOP Is America's Party of White Nationalism." Trump is an "ethnonationalist president," declared a columnist in *Vice*, with Muslims, "migrants from Latin America," and "all non-whites" now "subordinate and unwelcome." "White Nationalism is upon us," wrote Jamelle Bouie in *Slate*.

It is a stunning and frightening fact that an openly white nationalist movement exists in America today with a prominence, or at least a brazenness, hard to imagine only a few years ago. The leader of this movement, the well-educated and articulate Richard Spencer, has gone out of his way to be incendiary, invoking Nazi symbolism, opposing interracial marriage, donning a "fashy" (fascist) haircut, and calling for an all-white "ethno-state" to be achieved through "ethnic cleansing." Although Spencer has said that this ethnic cleansing would be "peaceful," in November 2016 he told a *Washington Post* reporter, "Look, maybe it will be horribly bloody and terrible. That's a possibility with everything." Many hear echoes of Spencer's rhetoric in statements from some of Trump's closest advisers, including Stephen Miller and the now ousted Steve Bannon.

And it's not just rhetoric. In February 2017, a white navy veteran gunned down two Indian American engineers in Kansas, shouting, "Get out of my country." A few weeks later, an Indian-born U.S. citizen was murdered right outside his home in South Carolina, and in Washington State, a white gunman shot a Sikh American in the arm, telling him, "Go back to your country, terrorist." In May 2017, a knife-wielding man yelling anti-Muslim epithets on a Portland commuter train fatally stabbed two people who tried to subdue him. In the first three months of 2017, mosques were "targets of threats, vandalism, or arson" on thirty-five occasions.

Nevertheless, it would be absurd to attribute Spencer's white nationalist views to the half of American voters who supported Donald Trump. White nationalism of this kind would require expelling or exterminating between a third and half of America's population, and to suggest that 62 million Americans endorse this is preposterous—just more partisan vitriol. An August 2017 NPR/ PBS Marist poll showed that only 4 percent of Americans support white nationalism. Indeed, according to the Pew Foundation, a majority of *Republicans* (56 percent) say it is "neither good nor bad" that "in the next 25 to 30 years African Americans, Latinos, and people of Asian descent will make up a majority of the population."

But those who believe that we are in "an ethnonationalist moment" in America are not entirely wrong. A kind of "ethnonationalism lite" is widespread among white Americans today. It does not dream of an all-white America; it opposes racism and celebrates tolerance and exults in the image of America as a "nation of immigrants." But it is nostalgic for a time when minorities were not so loud, so demanding, so numerous—a time when minorities were more grateful.

This demand for gratitude is well expressed by Internet sensation Tomi Lahren, the controversial twenty-five-year-old conservative political commentator who recently became a Fox News contributor. Like many of the most visible pro-Trump female talking heads, Lahren is white, blond, and attractive. Here's part of what Lahren said in a viral video takedown of Colin Kaepernick—the former 49ers quarterback who refused to stand for the national anthem:

> Colin, I support the First Amendment. I support your right to freedom of speech and expression. Go for it, bud. It's this country, the country that you have so much disdain for that allows you the right to speak your mind. It protects your right to be a whiny, indulgent, attention-seeking crybaby. It also protects my right to shred you for it.
>
> See, the national anthem and our flag, they are not symbols of black America, white America, brown America, or purple America, for that matter. There are patriots of every race that have fought and died for this country, and we honor the flag and sing the anthem as a reminder. And

Colin, if this country disgusts you so much, *leave*. I guarantee there are thousands and thousands of people around the world that would gladly take your spot . . .

A mind-boggling 66 million people have viewed this video. Lahren obviously resonates with huge numbers of white Americans when she criticizes minorities for blaming whites without recognizing how much America, and specifically how much white America, has "done" for them. "Do you know how many of our ancestors fought in the Civil War to free your ancestors?" Lahren has said on another occasion. "The bloodiest war in U.S. history was over what was right, and it was largely white people fighting it."

It is easy to see why Lahren is so popular. She celebrates America as a great, moral, and exceptional nation, with a moral and exceptional Constitution. She ignores everything bad that white America has ever done. She even credits whites with freeing the slaves without mentioning who enslaved them in the first place.

To ask for gratitude from minorities is to ask for a kind of subservience—gratitude is what's owed to a benefactor; it implies a debt—while also asserting an ownership of the country's past: *We built this land of opportunity and invited you in, and now we're being demonized for its imperfections.*

Many Americans want to celebrate the country's history and greatness without having to dredge up its racist past every single time. They want to be able to take pride in the Founding Fathers without always having to apologize for slavery, the Trail of Tears, or segregation. They love the story of America as a land of freedom and opportunity—but they are starting to fear that when minorities become a majority in America, the story will change. History books will be rewritten to depict America as a land of oppression, racism, and imperialism. Beloved classics like *Little House on the Prairie* and *Anne of Green Gables* will be banned for promulgating white supremacy, the Jefferson Memorial will be torn down, and the Oscar for Best Picture will go only to movies like *12 Years a Slave*. America will be cast as a nation, in Ta-Nehisi Coates's words, of "majoritarian pigs."

Whites who believe that minorities hold these views of America necessarily look with anxiety on the prospect of minorities becoming a majority. Their love of country becomes tied up, even if unconsciously, with the idea of whites remaining in control of the nation's politics, culture, and identity.

But how can minorities be filled with gratitude when in their view Americans elected a president who, as Toni Morrison puts it, "questioned whether Barack Obama was born in the United States," "seemed to condone the beating of a Black Lives Matter protester at a campaign rally," and made white nationalism possible again? If Lahren, with her 66 million views, is going to remind minorities of how much whites have done for them, how can minorities not respond, as Coates has, that America is a land where it is not only "traditional to destroy the black body—*it is heritage*"?

We're not only in a zero-sum game. We're in a vicious circle. Is there any way out?

Epilogue

Despite everything, I sense a shift in America.

It could just be congenital optimism on my part. Or it could be because I'm the daughter of immigrants and my view of America will always be shaped by how they see the country and taught me to see it.

But for whatever reason, I see something new happening. You'd never know it from cable news or social media, but all over the country there are signs of people trying to cross divides and break out of their political tribes.

In small-town Utica, New York, Bosnian Muslims and Unitarian Christians made it a point to watch the Super Bowl together, wanting to understand one another as "human beings first." Neighbors in Hackettstown, New Jersey, organized a Meetup to "Make America Relate Again," for everyone in the community "regardless of how you voted in the last election" to socialize "in a non-politicized way," because "we are all Americans. And approaching each other with compassion is the only way we will be able to heal the deep rifts that divide us." Silicon Valley's Ro Khanna is hammering away at the tech industry to seek out talent in America's heartland, to expand operations there, and to "approach the rest of the nation with more humility." Van Jones, visibly upset on election night, famously sat down for dinner with a family of Trump voters in blue-collar Ohio a month later, pleading with them, "Help me understand." His CNN colleague, the African American comedian W. Kamau Bell, books gigs at noncoastal universities like Appalachian State, and actually interviewed Richard Spencer at Alabama's Auburn University for Bell's documentary series *United Shades of America*. The University of Minnesota has established a fellowship called "Crossing the Divide," for "emerging journalists" to travel across the country over a three-month period, with the goal of shedding light on not only "the divisions that are pulling the country apart, but how communities are trying to bridge the differences."

Individually, any single example will seem trivial, and it's hard to prove they represent a trend. There are certainly powerful voices opposed to conciliation, insisting, as Charles Blow has, that "[t]he Trump phenomenon is devoid of compassion, and we must be closed to compromise." Nevertheless, if you look beyond the headlines, and listen past the loudest partisans, you'll find something quite remarkable. All over the country, ordinary Americans are making heartfelt efforts to "reach across the aisle," "understand the other side," and "empathize with each other's humanity."

This may all seem pie-in-the-sky—or like a Band-Aid for bullet wounds—but a prodigious body of evidence shows that when individuals from different groups actually get to know one another as human beings, tremendous progress can be made.

This phenomenon was first analyzed by Gordon W. Allport in

his 1954 book, *The Nature of Prejudice*. By looking at the racial integration of merchant marines, police departments, and housing projects, Allport found that face-to-face contact between members of different groups can dismantle prejudices, build common ground, and even change lives. In the last sixty years, the same basic findings have been replicated all over the world, from England to Italy to Sri Lanka, with respect to all forms of group prejudice, from ethnicity to sexual orientation to mental illness.

The U.S. military may be the best example. When President Harry Truman first issued Executive Order 9981 to integrate the U.S. armed forces, popular opinion was strongly against him; nearly two thirds of white servicemen opposed desegregation of the military, and the American public agreed by a similar margin. Internal opposition was so widespread that the army dragged its feet and ignored their commander in chief's order for as long as possible, hoping Dewey would best him in the 1948 election.

Truman won, of course, and integration efforts proceeded. And in 1951, in the midst of the Korean War, researchers published a study on the effectiveness of desegregated units. To the surprise of many, they discovered that "cooperation in integrated units was equal or superior to that of all-White units." As Conrad Crane, director of the U.S. Army Military History Institute, recounted, "When your life depends on your buddy, the color of their skin tends to become less important; it's how good they are."

This proved true in Vietnam as well. Karl Marlantes, a marine lieutenant, recalls being on a remote jungle hilltop in Vietnam in 1968 and being asked by Ray Delgado, "an 18-year old Hispanic kid from Texas," if he wanted to try a tamale from a care package that Ray's mother had sent him. Marlantes said, "Sure," but found the tamale very tough to eat.

"Lieutenant," Ray finally said. "You take the corn husk off."

I was from a logging town on the Oregon coast. I'd heard of tamales, but I'd never seen one. Until I joined my company of Marines in Vietnam, I'd never even talked to a Mexican.

In Marlantes's view, "not everything about the war was negative. . . . I saw how it threw together young men from diverse racial and ethnic backgrounds and forced them to trust one another with their lives. . . . If I was pinned down by enemy fire and I needed an M-79 man, I'd scream for Thompson, because he was the best. I didn't even think about what color Thompson was."

For Marlantes and many others, the experience of interacting, living, and working with members of other ethnic and racial groups had a profound effect:

White guys had to listen to soul music and black guys had to listen to country music. We didn't fear one another. And the experience stuck with us. Hundreds of thousands of young men came home from Vietnam with different ideas about race—some for the worse, but most for the better. Racism wasn't solved in Vietnam, but I believe it was where our country finally learned that it just might be possible for us all to get along.

A more recent example is the astonishing transformation in Americans' opinions about same-sex marriage. As recently as 1988, support in the United States for same-sex marriage was just 11 percent; today, 62 percent support it. Many factors contributed to this shift, but one of the most important was simple. In 2013, 75 percent of Americans reported having "a friend, relative, or coworker who has revealed to them that he or she is gay"—up from only 24 percent in 1985. Justice Ruth Bader Ginsburg—whose votes on the Supreme Court helped bring about marriage equality—described this change in a 2014 interview: "Once [gay] people began to say who they were," she said, "you found that it was your next-door neighbor or it could be your child, and we found people we admired."

It's crucial to emphasize that mere exposure to people from different tribes is not sufficient. On the contrary, studies show that minimal or superficial exposure to out-group members can actually worsen group division. One study by Harvard professor Ryan Enos found that simply being exposed to two men speaking Spanish on a train led commuters—most of whom were white and liberal—to have significantly more conservative attitudes on immigration. Unsurprisingly, negative interactions with people from other groups also increase group hostility. So merely putting members of different groups in the same space is not enough and indeed can aggravate political tribalism.

Instead, what is needed is one-on-one human engagement, which is hard precisely because of how divided we are. But anything worth achieving is difficult. When people from different tribes see one another as human beings who at the end of the day want the same things—kindness, dignity, security for loved ones—hearts can change. As a Coptic priest in New York put it, "[H]umility is a mediator. It will always be the shortest distance between you and another person."

Speaking of distances between people, Yale University, where I've taught for fifteen years, has, along with other liberal colleges, been much mocked and decried of late, and in some ways I understand why. Over the last several years, I have sometimes watched with dismay as a tiny but highly vocal handful of students use their privileged positions not to foster the free exchange of ideas but to shame and punish—almost invariably at no cost to themselves—tearing apart the student community and driving dissenters underground, where resentment only festers. But I have also seen with my own eyes over and over the very best of America, practically miracles.

I've taught a seminar where the daughter of an undocumented worker from Mexico and the son of a cop from New Hampshire started off hating each other and ended up loving each other. I've watched as a Holocaust survivor's granddaughter and an organizer of the anti-Israeli boycott movement struggled to understand each other, and ultimately agreed to disagree, without friendship, but without venom—baby steps. I've seen a former Navy SEAL and a human rights activist bond over Trivial Pursuit. I've seen a talented black poet—who spent eight years in prison because of a carjacking he did at sixteen before coming to Yale—win the admiration and awe of opponents of Black Lives Matter with his grace and empathy.

B ut even this is not enough. Remaining a super-group requires something more. It's not enough that we view one another as fellow human beings; we need to view one another as fellow Americans. And for that we need to collectively find a national identity capacious enough to resonate with, and hold together as one people, Americans of all sorts—old and young, immigrant and native born, urban and rural, descendants of slaves as well as descendants of slave owners.

It's not clear whether this is possible in our time of rage. A political meme popular among Trump supporters during the 2016 election cycle showed European immigrants from the early twentieth century with the following text overlaid: "THEY CAME TO TAKE PART IN THE AMERICAN DREAM. EUROPEAN CHRISTIANS BUILT THIS NATION. THEY DIDN'T COME TO BITCH, COLLECT WELFARE, WAGE JIHAD, AND REPLACE THE AMERICAN CONSTITUTION WITH SHARIA LAW." This is tribalism. It creates within America a virtuous Us and a demonized Them. To put it mildly, this vision of the American Dream isn't going to be acceptable for half the country—nor is it intended to be.

But the same can be said of the other side. A progressive headline after the 2016 election read "'WHITE WORKING CLASS' NARRATIVE IS NOTHING BUT A RACIST DOG WHISTLE"—a widely held view. A political blog post titled "America: Land of the Oppressed, Home of the Cowards" asserts that "America is neither the land of the free nor the home of the brave. It is the land of oppression [for] everyone other than rich, white, Christian males." According to the filmmaker Michael Moore, the United States is "a nation founded on genocide and on the backs of slaves." And Toni Morrison, one of America's most beloved novelists, wrote, "Unlike any nation in Europe, the United States holds whiteness as the unifying force." Sadly, there's a grain of truth to what Moore and Morrison say. But if America is nothing more than a land of oppression, founded on nothing more than genocide and white supremacy, it's hard to see why America is worth fighting for.

Today's purveyors of political tribalism, on both left and right, may think they are defending American values, but in fact they are playing with poison. America will cease to be America—and will no longer be a super-group—if we define our national identity in terms of "whiteness," "Anglo-Protestant culture," "European Christianity," or any other terms not inclusive of all religions and ethnicities. But it will also cease to be America if enough of us come to believe that our country and its ideals are a fraud. There is a world of difference between saying that America has failed to live up to its own ideals, with egregious injustice persisting today, and saying that the principles supposedly uniting us are just smoke screens to disguise oppression.

The peril we face as a nation today is not only that America might fail to live up to its promise, but that Americans might stop believing in that promise or the need to fight for it. The increasing belief on the left that this promise was always a lie, or on the right that it has always been true—and has already been achieved— are two sides of the same coin.

A few months after the 2016 election, a student said to me one of the most remarkable things I've ever heard. Giovanni came from the humblest origins. As a child, he lived with his Mexican American family in an old taco truck before they moved up to an eighteen-hundred-dollar motor home. He told me about a retired white couple from rural Louisiana, whom I'll call Walter and Lee Ann Jones, who lived in the same Texas trailer park as Giovanni's family. According to Giovanni, the Joneses were extremely kind from day one: "Walter helped us set up the taco truck and would bring my sister and me sweets from the local food pantry, where he volunteered to haul food with his pickup truck. Multiple Thanksgivings, Walter ensured my family had a turkey and sides to cook, which he also brought from the pantry. Walter also loved guns and made it known that he would protect us if anyone caused any trouble. 'There's a lot of bad people here, but I dare them to try and mess with you. They will regret it.'"

But a decade later, during the 2016 election cycle, Giovanni realized, based on a number of social media posts made by the Joneses, that Walter and Lee Ann held strongly racist attitudes. In Giovanni's view, however, the Joneses exemplify "a critical paradox that progressives often overlook or dismiss, to their own detriment." Despite their racist attitudes toward "faceless brown people generally," the Joneses "treat my family with nothing but love and respect, despite our Mexican descent and immigrant status. In fact, the Joneses even consider my sister and me to be their adoptive-grandkids. Furthermore, the food pantry where Walter volunteered primarily served the black community. On multiple occasions, I observed first-hand the joy it brought Walter to help these communities."

I found Giovanni's story striking first because he was talking about racism in a way that is completely taboo among progressives (a group he identifies with). Among progressives, once someone is deemed racist, that's it. You can't talk to him, you can't compromise, and you certainly can't suggest that he might be a decent person just because he's nice to a few minorities. (Liberal eyes start rolling as soon as the "racist" mentions his "black friends.") I also found the story striking because of a further insight Giovanni offered: the Joneses didn't think of themselves as racists. In their minds, "the countless iterations of treating minorities with decency and kindness is undeniable evidence that they are not racist." As a result, when liberals call them "bigots," they feel unjustly attacked, creating a chasm of anger. "When the conviction that they are morally blameless clashes with liberal outrage, it drives a wedge between elite progressives and the working-class people they ostensibly desire to help."

Finally, I found the story remarkable because it reflected a generosity in scarce supply these days. In case it's not clear, the Joneses were Trump supporters, whereas Giovanni viewed Trump as a deep, visceral threat to his family and his community. Yet he was willing to reach across the tribal divide, out of a belief in a shared humanity and a sense of coming from the same place, the same America—in Giovanni's case, a trailer park in Texas where people helped one another get by.

If we're to come together as a nation, we all need to elevate ourselves. We need to find a way to talk to each other if we're to have any chance of bridging divides. We need to allow ourselves to see our tribal adversaries as fellow Americans, engaged in a common enterprise.

Those who are worried about terrorism should be able to express that worry without being branded an Islamophobe. Those who view America's seismic demographic changes and massive influx of immigrants with anxiety should be able to express that anxiety without being branded a racist. Transformational population change *is* dislocating, and diversity has costs. But we've been through this before. Over and over, throughout American history, waves of new immigrants have come to our shores, always met with suspicion and fear that the nation's character will be endangered, its streets made unsafe, its values lost. Every time, we've overcome this fear, prospered, and grown stronger.

With every wave of immigration in the past, American freedom and openness have triumphed. Will we, telling ourselves "*These* immigrants are different," be the weak link, the first generation to fail? Will we forget who we are?

At the same time, those committed to exposing the grotesque injustices of America's past and present—they are right too, and doing us all a service. No country can be great if it can't be honest, and America, in particular, with its resounding constitutional principles, needs to be held to its own standards or fall under the weight of hypocrisy. But other generations seeking justice have done so for the promise of America. Even as James Baldwin lacerated the "collection of myths to which white Americans cling: that their ancestors were all freedom-loving heroes," he made clear that his dream was to "achieve our country," "to make America what America must become," for "great men have done great things here, and will again." Martin Luther King Jr. wrote that African Americans sitting at whites-only lunch counters were "standing up for the best in the American dream." At a service honoring Dr. King, President Barack Obama said of the leaders of the civil rights movement, "[A]s much as our Government and our political parties had betrayed them in the past, as much as our Nation itself had betrayed its own ideals . . . [t]hey didn't give up on this country. . . . Imperfect as it was, they continued to believe in the promise of democracy, in America's constant ability to remake itself, to perfect this Union."

In the blockbuster Broadway hit play *Hamilton,* Lin-Manuel Miranda brilliantly used an all-minority cast to portray America's Founding Fathers. This was a radical—and radically patriotic—move.

Hamilton doesn't deny American racism or injustice. On the contrary, the pointed casting draws attention to those historically excluded from center stage in the nation's creation, and reminds us that America's ideals always far exceeded its reality. But the play is also a reminder that this country's history is built on principles that transcend their time. It testifies to the aspiration that every American, regardless of ethnicity or race, can embrace the nation's history and identity as his or her own. It gives voice to an America that is not rooted in blood or parentage, that is open to people of all different ethnicities, and that allows—indeed, gains strength from allowing—all those subgroup identities to flourish. It speaks for the idea of America as a super-group.

What holds the United States together is the American Dream. But it must be a version of the dream that recognizes past failure instead of denying it. Failures are part and parcel of the story line of a country founded on hope, a country where there's always more to be done.

Dreams are not real, but they can be made so. The American Dream is a promise of freedom and hope for every individual on these shores. But it is also a call on all of us to make true the myths we tell ourselves about what America has always been. More than anyone else, Langston Hughes was the poet of this dream. In his 1935 poem "Let America Be America Again," he writes:

Let America be the dream the dreamers dreamed—
Let it be that great strong land of love.

But then a second voice enters:

(It never was America to me.)

The first voice replies:

Say, who are you that mumbles in the dark?

And the second answers:

I am the poor white, fooled and pushed apart,
I am the Negro bearing slavery's scars.

I am the red man driven from the land,
I am the immigrant clutching the hope I seek—
And finding only the same old stupid plan
Of dog eat dog, of mighty crush the weak.

But far from concluding with defeat, Hughes offers a prayer and an affirmation:

O, let America be America again—
The land that never has been yet—
And yet must be—the land where every *man is free. . . .*

O, yes,
I say it plain,
America never was America to me,
And yet I swear this oath—
America will be!

Acknowledgments

I am deeply indebted to two extraordinary women: my agent, Tina Bennett, and my editor, Ann Godoff. I have no idea how I got so lucky. Many thanks also to Casey Denis, Sarah Hutson, and the rest of the fabulous team at Penguin.

This book reflects the invaluable help of numerous Yale Law School students. In particular, I would like to thank Bill Powell for reading the manuscript in its entirety and offering fabulous critiques and edits, as well as Yusef Al-Jarani, Joe Chatham, Aislinn Klos, Taonga Leslie, and Giovanni Sanchez for their critical insights and editorial help. This book would not have been possible without the dozens, in some cases hundreds, of hours of outstanding research assistance provided by Jeanine Alvarez, Eric Brooks, Eric Chung, Greg Cui, Meredith Foster, Matteo Godi, Jordan Goldberg, Kim Jackson, Dan Listwa, Josh Macey, Alex Mahler-Haug, Brian McGrail, David Miller, Adeel Mohammadi, Andy Mun, Matt Nguyen, Wazhma Sadat, Spencer Todd, Alex Wang, Sarah Weiner, Rachel Wilf, Ryan Yeh, and Nathaniel Zelinsky. I am also grateful to the following students for their assistance on particular chapters: Danielle Abada, Sam Adkisson, Laith Aqel, Leslie Arffa, Omer Aziz, Denisha Bacchus, Janine Balekjdian, Bianca Bamgbade, Emily Barreca, Andrea Basaraba, Jordan Blashek, Humza Bokhari, Hal Boyd, Sam Breidbart,

John Brinkerhoff, Matt Butler, Luis Calderon Gomez, Katie Choi, Matt Chou, Michael Chung, Ali Cooper-Ponte, Catherine Crooke, Colleen Culbertson, Samir Doshi, Rhea Fernandes, Shikka Garg, Mario Gazzola, Pardis Gheibi, Ben Hand, Amber Koonce, Josh Handelsman, Rhoda Hassan, Yasin Hegazy, Jordan Hirsch, Julia Hu, Eri Kalu, Stephen Karp, Louis Katz, Amber Koonce, Aaron Korthuis, Hilary Ledwell, Yena Lee, Elizabeth Leiserson, Brandon Levin, Aaron Levine, Miranda Li, Ellis Liang, Alina Lindblom, Athie Livas, Webb Lyons, Danielle Marryshow, Heath Mayo, Emma McDermott, Andrew Miller, Nick Molina, Blake Neal, Iulia Padeanu, Jenna Pavalec, Aaron Roper, Theo Rostow, Eugene Rusyn, Ram Sachs, Bella Schapiro, Joe Schottenfeld, Alex Schultz, Reema Shah, Max Siegel, Javier Sinha, Sean Song, Mitzi Steiner, Tori Stilwell, Paul Strauch, Styna Tao, Brandon Thomas, Todd Venook, Julia Wang, Michael Weaver, Zoe Weinberg, Helen White, Ethan Wong, Ben Woodring, Tian Tian Xin, Alice Xiang, Bo-Shan Xiang, Alyssa Yamamoto, Victor Yu, Danyang Zhao, and David Zhou.

Julian Aiken, Lora Johns, Sarah Kraus, Michael VanderHeijden, and many others on the Yale Law School Library staff awed me with their energy and resourcefulness; I cannot thank them enough for their patience and indulgence. Rosanna Gonsiewski was also fabulous and indispensable.

Many thanks to my brilliant colleagues Tony Kronman, Daniel Markovits, and John Witt for their incisive comments; Andrew Chesnut, Mina Cikara, Jay Van Bavel, and Robb Willer for reviewing chapters; and Sophia and Lulu Chua-Rubenfeld for their conceptual and editing help.

As always, my greatest debt is to my husband, Jed Rubenfeld, who for thirty years now has read every word I've written. I continue to be the fortunate beneficiary of his generosity and genius.

Notes

Introduction

1 **monks and friars:** For an erudite discussion of group dynamics among Benedictine and Franciscan monks, see Ulrich L. Lehner, *Enlightened Monks: The German Benedictines 1740–1803* (New York: Oxford University Press, 2011), especially 2, 32, 40–41.

1 **instinct to exclude:** See Matthew J. Hornsey and Jolanda Jetten, "The Individual within the Group: Balancing the Need to Belong with the Need to Be Different," *Personality and Social Psychology Review* 8 (2004): 248–64; Geoffrey J. Leonardelli and Marilynn B. Brewer, "Minority and Majority Discrimination: When and Why," *Journal of Experimental Social Psychology* 37, no. 6 (2001): 468–85; Marilynn B. Brewer, "When Contact Is Not Enough: Social Identity and Intergroup Cooperation," *International Journal of Intercultural Relations* 20, nos. 3/4 (1996): 291–303.

1 **They will seek:** See Yarrow Dunham, Andrew Scott Baron, and Susan Carey, "Consequences of 'Minimal' Group Affiliations in Children," *Child Development* 82, no. 3 (2011): 793, 797–802, 807–8; see also Henri Tajfel et al., "Social Categorization and Intergroup Behaviour," *European Journal of Social Psychology* 1, no. 2 (1971): 149–78.

1 **They will penalize:** See Dunham, Baron, and Carey, "Consequences of 'Minimal' Group Affiliations in Children," 797–801, 807–8; see also Muzafer Sherif et al., *The Robbers Cave Experiment: Intergroup Conflict and Cooperation* (Middletown, CT: Wesleyan University Press, 1988), 144–48.

2 **greatest and most humiliating:** See Joe Allen, *Vietnam: The (Last) War the U.S. Lost* (Chicago: Haymarket Books, 2008), 1; Louis B. Zimmer, *The Vietnam War Debate: Hans J. Morgenthau and the Attempt to Halt the Drift into Disaster* (Lanham, MD: Lexington Books, 2011), xv, 2.

2 **underestimated the extent**: See, e.g., Marilyn B. Young, *The Vietnam Wars, 1945–1990* (New York: HarperCollins, 1991), 24, 179–80; transcript of *The Fog of War: Eleven Lessons from the Life of Robert S. McNamara*, directed by Errol Morris (Hollywood, CA: Sony Pictures Classics, 2003), http://www.errolmorris.com/film/fow_transcript.html (Lesson 7); Fredrik

Logevall, *Embers of War: The Fall of an Empire and the Making of America's Vietnam* (New York: Random House, 2012), epilogue; Thomas Friedman, "ISIS and Vietnam," *New York Times*, October 28, 2014.

2 **resented 1 percent Chinese minority:** Amy Chua, *World on Fire: How Exporting Free Market Democracy Breeds Ethnic Hatred and Global Instability* (New York: Anchor Books, 2004), 33–34; Frank H. Golay et al., *Underdevelopment and Economic Nationalism in Southeast Asia* (Ithaca, NY: Cornell University Press, 1969), chapter 7; Tran Khanh, *The Ethnic Chinese and Economic Development in Vietnam* (Singapore: Institute of Southeast Asian Studies, 1993), 79–84; James S. Olson and Randy Roberts, *Where the Domino Fell: America and Vietnam, 1945–2010* (Malden, MA: Wiley-Blackwell, 2014), 47.

2 **70 to 80 percent:** Chua, *World on Fire*, 33–34; Golay et al., *Underdevelopment and Economic Nationalism in Southeast Asia*, chapter 7; Khanh, *The Ethnic Chinese and Economic Development in Vietnam*, 80–81; Pao-min Chang, *Beijing, Hanoi, and the Overseas Chinese* (Berkeley: Institute of East Asian Studies, 1982), 4, 16; Alexander Woodside, "Nationalism and Poverty in the Breakdown of Sino-Vietnamese Relations," *Pacific Affairs* 52, no. 3 (1979): 405.

2 **Vietnam's "capitalists" were:** Chua, *World on Fire*, 33–34; Li Tana, "In Search of the History of the Chinese in South Vietnam, 1945–75," in *The Chinese/Vietnamese Diaspora: Revisiting the Boat People*, ed. Yuk Wah Chan (Oxon, UK: Routledge, 2011), 53; Christopher Goscha, *Vietnam: A New History* (New York: Basic Books, 2016), 379–80.

3 **"We didn't probably understand fully":** Condoleezza Rice, interview by Bill Hemmer, Fox News, May 5, 2017, http://www.foxnews.com/us/2017/05/05/condoleezza-rice-discusses-north-korea-russia-with-bill-hemmer.html (at 22:50).

3 **American policy in Iraq:** Special Inspector General for Iraq Reconstruction, *Hard Lessons: The Iraq Reconstruction Experience* (Washington, DC: U.S. Government Printing Office, 2009), 11–12, 21, 274.

3 **A handful of critics:** For example, Ryan Crocker, who a decade later became ambassador to Iraq, cautioned that the overthrow of Saddam Hussein might trigger "violent clashes among Iraq's sects, tribes, and ethnic factions, possibly leading to the country's fragmentation." Special Inspector General for Iraq Reconstruction, *Hard Lessons*, 14; see also Conrad C. Crane and W. Andrew Terrill, "Reconstructing Iraq: Insights, Challenges, and Missions for Military Forces in a Post-Conflict Scenario" (Carlisle, PA: U.S. Army War College, Strategic Studies Institute, February 2003), v–vi, http://www.strategicstudiesinstitute.army.mil/pdffiles/PUB182.pdf; Robert D. Kaplan, "A Post-Saddam Scenario," *Atlantic*, November 2002.

3 **"everything" . . . "intensely anti-American":** Chua, *World on Fire*, Afterword to the Anchor Edition, 290–91.

4 **"I think protesting":** Essay by Blake Neal, February 3, 2017 (on file with author).

4   **enormously popular:** Hanna Rosin, "Did Christianity Cause the Crash?," *Atlantic*, December 2009.

4   **poor and working-class African and Hispanic:** Kate Bowler, *Blessed: A History of the American Prosperity Gospel* (Oxford: Oxford University Press, 2013), 111–13; Milmon F. Harrison, *Righteous Riches: The Word of Faith Movement in Contemporary African American Religion* (New York: Oxford University Press, 2005), 148–52; Emily Raboteau, "My Search for Creflo Dollar," *Salon,* January 6, 2013, http://www.salon.com/2013/01/06/my _search_for_creflo_dollar); Rosin, "Did Christianity Cause the Crash?"

4   **Three out of four:** Bowler, *Blessed*, 6.

4   **"In my opinion":** G. Sanchez, e-mail message to author, February 2, 2017.

5   **Right up until:** Michael M. Grynbaum, "As Race Tightened, News Anchors Seemed as Stunned as Anyone," *New York Times*, November 9, 2016; James B. Stewart, "Short-Term Reaction to Trump's Victory Is a Double Surprise to Wall Street Analysts," *Seattle Times*, November 12, 2016.

5   **Trump, in terms of taste:** Richard Thompson Ford, "The Ties That Blind," *New York Times*, February 10, 2017.

5   **Trump's base identifies:** J. D. Vance, "How Donald Trump Seduced America's White Working Class," *Guardian*, September 10, 2016; Stephen D. Reicher and S. Alexander Haslam, "Trump's Appeal: What Psychology Tells Us," *Scientific American*, March 1, 2017.

5   ***not* the same as:** Joan C. Williams, "What So Many People Don't Get About the U.S. Working Class," *Harvard Business Review,* November 10, 2016.

5–6 **difference between elites:** See Pierre Bourdieu, *Distinction: A Social Critique of the Judgment of Taste* (Cambridge, MA: Harvard University Press, 1984), 21–22; see also Paul Fussell, *Class: A Guide Through the American Status System* (New York: Touchstone, 1983).

6   **chrome bull testicles:** Many thanks to Bill Powell for alerting me to these "Truck Nuts," which are available on Amazon and, "believe it or not, a status symbol" at his high school.

6   **"supremacist," "regressive," "elitist,":** Linda Milazzo, "Newt Gingrich Declares, 'I Am Not a Citizen of the World!'" *Huffington Post*, July 10, 2009.

7   **"[I] have an unyielding":** President Barack Obama, speech at Grand Hall of Cairo University, June 4, 2009, http://www.theguardian.com/world /2009/jun/04/barack-obama-keynote-speech-egypt.

8   **For the first time:** Sandra L. Colby and Jennifer M. Ortman, *Projections of the Size and Composition of the U.S. Population: 2014 to 2060*, U.S. Census Bureau, March 2015, 9.

8   **"whites have replaced":** Evan Osnos, "The Fearful and the Frustrated," *New Yorker*, August 31, 2015 (quoting Michael I. Norton and Samuel R. Sommers, "Whites See Racism as a Zero-Sum Game That They Are Now Losing," *Perspectives on Psychological Science* 6, no. 3 (2011): 215–18).

8   **43 percent of black Americans:** "On Views of Race and Inequality, Blacks and Whites Are Worlds Apart," Pew Research Center, June 27, 2016,

http://www.pewsocialtrends.org/2016/06/27/on-views-of-race-and
-inequality-blacks-and-whites-are-worlds-apart.

8   hate crimes have increased 20 percent: Grant Smith and Daniel Trotta, "U.S. Hate Crimes up 20 Percent in 2016 Fueled by Election Campaign-Report," Reuters, March 13, 2017.

8   When groups feel: See Lincoln Quillian, "Prejudice as a Response to Perceived Group Threat: Population Composition and Anti-Immigrant and Racial Prejudice in Europe," *American Sociological Review* 60, no. 4 (1995): 605–7; Paul M. Sniderman et al., "Predisposing Factors and Situational Triggers: Exclusionary Reactions to Immigrant Minorities," *American Political Science Review* 98, no. 1 (2004): 47; Nyla R. Branscombe and Daniel L. Wann, "Collective Self-Esteem Consequences of Outgroup Derogation When a Valued Social Identity Is on Trial," *European Journal of Social Psychology* 24, no. 6 (1994): 641; Jolanda Jetten et al., "Rebels with a Cause: Group Identification as a Response to Perceived Discrimination from the Mainstream," *Personality and Social Psychology Bulletin* 27, no. 9 (2001): 1204–13; Michael T. Schmitt and Nyla R. Branscombe, "Meaning and Consequences of Perceived Discrimination in Advantaged and Privileged Social Groups," *European Review of Social Psychology* 12 (2002): 165–99.

9   "We all want to believe in progress": Brit Bennett, "I Don't Know What to Do with Good White People," Jezebel, December 17, 2014, http://jezebel.com/i-dont-know-what-to-do-with-good-white-people-1671201391.

10   Today, any of these acts: See Erich Hatala Matthes, "Cultural Appropriation Without Cultural Essentialism?," *Social Theory and Practice* 42, no. 2 (2016): 343–66; Kjerstin Johnson, "Don't Mess Up When You Dress Up: Cultural Appropriation and Costumes," *Bitch,* October 25, 2011.

10   "taking back" the country: Sean Illing, "Racists Love Trump—This Is What They Mean by 'Taking the Country Back'—Yet Another Poll Confirms Racial and Cultural Resentment Is Driving Trump's Rise," *Salon,* April 5, 2016, http://www.salon.com/2016/04/05/racists_love_trump_this_is_what_they_mean_by_taking_the_country_back_yet_another_poll_confirms_racial_and_cultural_resentment_is_driving_donald_trumps_rise.

10   "war on whites": Chris Massie, "Rep. Brooks: Dems' 'War on Whites' Behind Some Criticism of Sessions," CNN, January 12, 2017, http://www.cnn.com/2017/01/11/politics/kfile-mo-brooks-war-on-whites/index.html.

10   "My college-age daughter": Chris Bodenner, "'If You Want Identity Politics, Identity Politics Is What You Get,'" *Atlantic,* November 11, 2016, http://www.theatlantic.com/notes/2016/11/if-you-want-identity-politics-identity-politics-is-what-you-will-get/507437 (quoting "a Trump voter, Alan").

11   Most European and all East Asian: Jaroslav Krejčí and Vitězslav Velímský, "Ethnic and Political Nations in Europe," in *Ethnicity,* ed. John Hutchinson and Anthony D. Smith (Oxford: Oxford University Press,

1996), 211–21; Anthony D. Smith, *The Ethnic Origins of Nations* (Oxford: Blackwell, 1986), 148–49; Frank Dikötter, "The Discourse of Race in Twentieth-Century China," in *Race and Racism in Modern East Asia: Western and Eastern Constructions*, ed. Rotem Kowner and Walter Demel (Leiden, The Netherlands, Brill: 2013), 351, 367; Gi-Wook Shin, "Racist South Korea? Diverse but Not Tolerant of Diversity," in Kowner and Demel, *Race and Racism in Modern East Asia*, 369–71; Jean-Pierre Lehmann, "The Cultural Roots of Modern Japan," in Hutchinson and Smith, *Ethnicity*, 118, 120.

12 **world's first "tweeter-in-chief":** Samuel Burke, "Hugo Chávez Was First Tweeter-in-Chief," CNN, January 26, 2017, http://money.cnn.com/2017/01/26/technology/hugo-Chavez-first-twitter-president-venezuela-trump.

13 **"victory for democracy":** Juan Forero, "Uprising in Venezuela," *New York Times*, April 13, 2002; Chua, *World on Fire*, 144–45.

Chapter One: American Exceptionalism and the Sources of U.S. Group Blindness Abroad

15 **"America is God's Crucible":** Israel Zangwill, *The Melting Pot* (1908), act 1.

15 **"Daddy once told":** Angie Thomas, *The Hate U Give* (New York: Balzer + Bray, 2017), 196.

15 **minutely knowledgeable:** See, e.g., Omar Khalidi, "Ethnic Group Recruitment in the Indian Army: The Contrasting Cases of Sikhs, Muslims, Gurkhas and Others," *Pacific Affairs* 74, no. 4 (Winter 2001–2002): 530; David Omissi, "'Martial Races': Ethnicity and Security in Colonial India 1858–1939," *War & Society* 9, no. 1 (1991): 8–10, 18–19; Kaushik Roy, "The Construction of Regiments in the Indian Army: 1859–1913," *War in History* 8, no. 2 (2001): 129, 135, 137–39; Ukana B. Ikpe, "The Patrimonial State and Inter-Ethnic Conflicts in Nigeria," *Ethnic and Racial Studies* 32, no. 4 (2009): 685; Peter Richens, "The Economic Legacies of the 'Thin White Line': Indirect Rule and the Comparative Development of Sub-Saharan Africa," *African Economic History* 37 (2009): 37–38.

16 **deliberately pitting groups:** David Omissi, *The Sepoy and the Raj: The Indian Army, 1860–1940* (London: Macmillan Press, 1994), 9–10, 96; Zareer Masani, *Indian Tales of the Raj* (Berkeley: University of California Press, 1987), 23–24.

16 **some forty thousand British:** Amy Chua, *Day of Empire: How Hyperpowers Rise to Global Dominance—and Why They Fall* (New York: Doubleday, 2007), 214.

16 **practical necessity of:** See, e.g., J. C. Myers, "On Her Majesty's Ideological State Apparatus: Indirect Rule and Empire," *New Political Science* 27, no. 2 (2005): 147–60; Richens, "The Economic Legacies of the 'Thin White Line,'" 33–102.

16 **constructed its "empire":** See John Lewis Gaddis, *We Now Know: Rethinking Cold War History* (New York: Oxford University Press, 1997), 284 (most

"old" Cold War historians agree that "despite its anti-imperial traditions the United States constructed an empire after 1945," although they debate "whether this happened intentionally or by inadvertence"); see also Richard H. Immerman, *Empire for Liberty: A History of American Imperialism from Benjamin Franklin to Paul Wolfowitz* (Princeton, NJ: Princeton University Press, 2010), 2–4, 10, 13.

17 **"You cannot dedicate":** *The New York Times Current History: The European War*, vol. 3 (New York: New York Times Company, 1917), 441 (italics added).

17 **Native Americans . . . Mexican Americans:** Robert B. Porter, "The Demise of the Ongwehoweh and the Rise of the Native Americans: Redressing the Genocidal Act of Forcing American Citizenship upon Indigenous Peoples," *Harvard Blackletter Law Journal* 15 (1999): 123–24; Stephen Steinberg, "How Jewish Quotas Began," *Commentary* 52, no. 3 (1971): 67–76; Edwin E. Ferguson, "The California Alien Land Law and the Fourteenth Amendment," *California Law Review* 35 (1947): 61–73; Richard Delgado, "The Law of the Noose: A History of Latino Lynching," *Harvard Civil Rights–Civil Liberties Law Review* 44 (2009): 299–303.

17 **resegregation of the civil service:** Eric S. Yellin, *Racism in the Nation's Service: Government Workers and the Color Line in Woodrow Wilson's America* (Chapel Hill: University of North Carolina Press, 2013), 79–172; Kathleen L. Wolgemuth, "Woodrow Wilson and Federal Segregation," *Journal of Negro History* 44, no. 2 (1959): 158–73; Gordon J. Davis, "What Woodrow Wilson Cost My Grandfather," *New York Times*, November 24, 2015.

18 **long line of Yoruba kings:** Colin A. Palmer, "From Africa to the Americas: Ethnicity in the Early Black Communities," *Journal of World History* 6, no. 2 (1995), 224–25.

18 **Even now, immigrants:** Jack David Eller, *Culture and Diversity in the United States: So Many Ways to Be American* (New York: Routledge, 2015), 57.

18 **"savages that delight in war":** Michael Hunt, *Ideology and U.S. Foreign Policy* (New Haven, CT: Yale University Press, 1987), 46.

18 **566 federally recognized tribes:** "Federal and State Recognized Tribes," National Conference of State Legislatures, October 2016, accessed June 17, 2017, http://www.ncsl.org/research/state-tribal-institute/list-of-federal -and-state-recognized-tribes.aspx.

18 **"abused, conformist quasi-robots":** Wesley Yang, "Paper Tigers," *New York*, May 8, 2011.

18 **all "Gooks" to us:** Nguyen Cao Ky, *How We Lost the Vietnam War* (New York: First Cooper Square Press, 2002), 137–38.

19 **"strange mixture of blood":** Louis L. Snyder, *The New Nationalism* (Ithaca, NY: Cornell University Press, 1968), 266.

19 **extensive race slavery inside its borders:** In comparison to the nearly 4 million black slaves in the United States by the time of the Civil War (approximately 12.6 percent of the total population), the slave population in Europe was small. See "Census of 1860 Population-Effect on the

Representation of the Free and Slave States," *New York Times*, April 5, 1860. It is estimated that in the eighteenth century, the total slave population in England was between 14,000 and 15,000. See James Oldham, "New Light on Mansfield and Slavery," *Journal of British Studies* 27, no. 1 (1988): 47 n. 11. Estimates put the total black population, free or enslaved, in France at between 4,000 and 5,000. Samuel L. Chatman, "'There Are No Slaves in France': A Re-Examination of Slave Laws in Eighteenth Century France," *Journal of Negro History* 85 no. 3 (2000): 144. Similarly, the black population in The Netherlands at that time was just a few thousand with several hundred more scattered throughout Russia, Scandinavia, and Germany. Allison Blakeley, "Problems in Studying the Role of Blacks in Europe," *American Historical Association*, May 1997, https://www.historians .org/publications-and-directories/perspectives-on-history/may-1997 /problems-in-studying-the-role-of-blacks-in-europe. Europe's largest population of black slaves was in the Iberian Peninsula, with as many as 150,000 in the sixteenth century. Ibid. By the eighteenth century, however, that number diminished significantly; in the Spanish city of Cádiz, for example, the once sizable population of African slaves had decreased nearly to zero by the end of the eighteenth century. William D. Phillips, Jr., *Slavery in Medieval and Early Modern Iberia* (Philadelphia: University of Pennsylvania Press, 2014), 26. Canada's slave population was also small compared to that of the U.S.; it is estimated that there were no more than 4,200 slaves in total between 1671 and 1834, with only a third of those black and the rest aboriginal people. Marcel Trudel, *Canada's Forgotten Slaves: Two Hundred Years of Bondage*, trans. George Tombs (Montreal: Vehicule Press, 2013), 254–71.

19 **a British court ruled:** See Dinah Shelton, ed., *The Oxford Handbook of International Human Rights Law* (Oxford: Oxford University Press, 2013), 232 (discussing 1772 case of *Somerset v. Stewart*). While Lord Mansfield's decision in *Somerset v. Stewart* did not literally abolish slavery within the borders of England, it did severely undercut the institution's legal standing, precipitating its decline. See Oldham, "New Light on Mansfield and Slavery," 68.

19 **Great Britain abolished:** Geoffrey Care, *Migrants and the Courts: A Century of Trial and Error?* (London and New York: Routledge, 2016), 222 n. 26.

19 **"separate but equal" ... aftereffects of slavery:** See generally Michelle Alexander, *The New Jim Crow: Mass Incarceration in the Age of Color Blindness* (New York: The New Press, 2012); James Forman, Jr., *Locking Up Our Own: Crime and Punishment in Black America* (New York: Farrar, Straus and Giroux, 2017), epilogue; Chris Hayes, *A Colony in a Nation* (New York: W. W. Norton, 2017).

20 **47 million people:** United Nations, Department of Economic and Social Affairs, Population Division, *International Migrant Stock 2015*, accessed June 17, 2017, http://www.un.org/en/development/desa/population/mi gration/data/estimates2/estimates15.shtml (dataset in "Total international migrant stock").

20 **more than 140 countries:** Anna Brown and Renee Stepler, "Country of Birth: 2014," Statistical Portrait of the Foreign-Born Population in the United States, 2014, table 5 (Washington, DC: Pew Research Center), April 19, 2016, accessed April 14, 2017, http://www.pewhispanic.org /2016/04/19/statistical-portrait-of-the-foreign-born-population-in -the-united-states.

20 **19 percent . . . 12 million:** United Nations, Department of Economic and Social Affairs, Population Division, *International Migrant Stock 2015*.

20 **In 2014, Australia and Canada:** Organisation for Economic Co-operation and Development, *International Migration Outlook 2016* (Paris: OECD, 2016).

20 **As of 2015:** United Nations, Department of Economic and Social Affairs, Population Division, *International Migrant Stock 2015*.

21 **in 2008, "unthinkable":** Adam Nagourney, "Obama Elected President as Racial Barrier Falls," *New York Times*, November 4, 2008.

22 **have been super-group empires:** See generally Chua, *Day of Empire*, 192–232.

22 **92 percent:** "The Upper Han," *Economist*, November 19, 2016, https:// www.economist.com/news/briefing/21710264-worlds-rising-superpower -has-particular-vision-ethnicity-and-nationhood-has.

22 **the Muslim Uighurs:** Andrew Jacobs, "Xinjiang Seethes Under Chinese Crackdown," *New York Times*, January 2, 2016.

22 **Japan and Korea:** See Kosaku Yoshino, *Cultural Nationalism in Contemporary Japan: A Sociological Enquiry* (London: Routledge, 1992), 24–26; Gi-Wook Shin, *Ethnic Nationalism in Korea* (Stanford, CA: Stanford University Press, 2006), 4.

22 **most European nations:** See Alberto F. Alesina et al., "Fractionalization," *Journal of Economic Growth* 8, no. 2 (2003), 162–65, 184–89; Max Fisher, "A Revealing Map of the World's Most and Least Ethnically Diverse Countries," *Washington Post*, May 17, 2013.

23 **assimilate, at least publicly:** Robert F. Worth, "The Professor and the Jihadi," *New York Times*, April 5, 2017 (citing Olivier Roy and Gilles Keppel).

23 **"pure French" national identity:** "Marine Le Pen Rejects All That's Not 'Pure French,'" NBC News, December 23, 2016, http://www.nbcnews .com/video/marine-le-pen-rejects-all-that-s-not-pure-french-840325 187686.

23 **"ostentatious" displays of religion:** Justin Gest, "To Become 'French,' Abandon Who You Are," Reuters, January 16, 2015, http://blogs.reuters .com/great-debate/2015/01/16/to-become-french-leave-your-identity -behind.

23 **"is fundamentally compatible":** See Angelique Chrisafis, "French PM Calls for Ban on Islamic Headscarves at Universities," *Guardian*, April 13, 2016.

23 **"If you want":** "'Your Ancestors Were Gauls,' France's Sarkozy Tells Migrants," Reuters, September 20, 2016, http://www.reuters.com/article /us-france-election-sarkozy-idUSKCN11Q22Y.

23 **The "burkini ban":** Alissa J. Rubin, "French 'Burkini' Bans Provoke Backlash as Armed Police Confront Beachgoers," *New York Times*, August 24, 2016.

23 **stopped providing pork-free meals:** Romina McGuinness, "'You Eat or You Go' Muslims Furious as Mayor Scraps Pork-Free Option on School Dinner Menu," *Express* (UK), January 19, 2017; Angelique Chrisafis, "Pork or Nothing: How School Dinners Are Dividing France," *Guardian*, October 13, 2015.

24 **hostile to the nation:** See Worth, "The Professor and the Jihadi."

24 **is surprisingly weak:** See Frank Bechhofer and David McCrone, ed., *National Identity, Nationalism and Constitutional Change* (London: Palgrave Macmillan, 2009), 1–2, 200–201; Mark Easton, "How British Is Britain?," BBC, September 30, 2013, http://www.bbc.com/news/uk-24302914.

24 **linked to "Englishness":** See A. Maurice Low, "Nationalism in the British Empire," *American Political Science Review* 10, no. 2 (May 1916): 223–34. For an interesting analysis of the use of the British Royal Navy as a somewhat successful national unifying force, see Alex Law, "Of Navies and Navels: Britain as a Mental Island," *Geografiska Annaler: Series B, Human Geography* (special issue, *Islands: Objects of Representation*) 87, no. 4 (2005): 267–77; see also Amelia Hadfield-Amkhan, *British Foreign Policy, National Identity, and Neoclassical Realism* (Lanham, MD: Rowman & Littlefield Publishers, 2010), 101–34.

24 **84 percent of the total population:** Office for National Statistics, *2011 Census: Population Estimates for the United Kingdom, March 2011*, accessed June 17, 2017, http://www.ons.gov.uk/peoplepopulationandcommunity /populationandmigration/populationestimates/bulletins/2011census populationestimatesfortheunitedkingdom/2012-12-17.

24 **anathema in polite circles:** Andrew Gamble and Tony Wright, ed., *Britishness: Perspectives on the British Question* (West Sussex, UK: Wiley-Blackwell, 2009), 4, 143.

24 **Scottish independence was:** Steven Erlanger and Alan Cowell, "Scotland Rejects Independence from United Kingdom," *New York Times*, September 18, 2014.

24 **Little England movement:** See, e.g., Nick Clegg, "Where Would You Rather Live—Great Britain or Little England?," *Guardian*, April 21, 2014; Mark Leonard, "What Would a UK Outside the EU Look Like?," *Guardian*, October 5, 2015; see also Jessica Elgot, "English Patriotism on the Rise, Research Shows," *Guardian*, January 10, 2017.

24 **Britain has no restrictions:** "The Islamic Veil Across Europe," BBC, January 31, 2017, http://www.bbc.com/news/world-europe-13038095.

24 **To the dismay:** Nicola Woolcock, "Pork Is Removed from School Menus Across London Borough," *Times* (UK), February 13, 2015; Dan Hyde, "Schools Stop Serving Pork for Religious Reasons," *Telegraph* (UK), February 12, 2015; Julie Henry, "Bangers Ban in Hundreds of Schools," *Telegraph* (UK), June 17, 2012.

25 **called "cultural separatism":** David Cameron (as the leader of the Conservative Party), 2007 speech on Islam and Muslims, London, June 5, 2007, http://www.ukpol.co.uk/david-cameron-2007-speech-on-islam-and -muslims.

25 **"[America] does succeed":** Ibid.

25 **"feel little sense":** Clive Crook, "Britain, Its Muslims, and the War on Terror," *Atlantic*, August 2005.

25 **Second- and third-generation:** Cameron, 2007 speech on Islam and Muslims.

25 **growth of homegrown jihadis:** Robert Leiken, "Britain Finally Faces Up to Its Homegrown Jihadist Problem," *Wall Street Journal*, September 7, 2014.

25 **Manchester suicide bomber:** Martin Evans et al., "Everything We Know About Manchester Suicide Bomber Salman Abedi," *Telegraph* (UK), May 26, 2017.

25 **"The July [2005 London] bombers":** Crook, "Britain, Its Muslims, and the War on Terror."

26 **As of 2015, more British Muslims:** Mary Anne Weaver, "Her Majesty's Jihadists," *New York Times*, April 14, 2015.

26 **identification with Brussels:** Directorate-General for Communication, European Commission, "European Citizenship," *Standard Eurobarometer* 85 (Spring 2016), 18.

26 **"It is not for":** Matteo Salvini's Facebook page, trans. Matteo Godi, July 21, 2015, https://www.facebook.com/salviniofficial.

26 **The Irish, Italians:** David R. Roediger, *Working Toward Whiteness: How America's Immigrants Became White* (New York: Basic Books, 2005), 5–6, 16; James R. Barrett and David Roediger, "In-between Peoples: Race, Nationality, and the 'New Immigrant' Working Class," *Journal of American Ethnic History* 16, no. 3 (1997): 3–44; Michael O'Meara, "How the Irish Became White, Part 1," *Counter-Currents,* December 26, 2012, https://www.counter-currents.com/2012/12/how-the-irish-became-white-part-1.

26 **From the nation's:** Taken almost verbatim from Chua, *Day of Empire*, 248.

27 **waves of immigrants:** Kristofer Allerfeldt, *Beyond the Huddled Masses: American Immigration and the Treaty of Versailles* (London: I. B. Tauris & Co., 2006), 16–17, 21, 23; Roger Daniels and Otis L. Graham, *Debating American Immigration, 1882–Present* (Lanham, MD: Rowman & Littlefield Publishers, 2001), 12–18, 23–25, 27–28, 77, 129.

27 **Between 1820 and 1914:** Taken almost verbatim from Chua, *Day of Empire*, 248.

27   **between 1871 and 1911:** Taken almost verbatim from ibid., 251.

28   **children of U.S. citizens:** See Child Citizenship Act of 2000, 8 U.S. Code §§ 1431–33 (2012).

28   **one of only a very few:** Eyder Peralta, "3 Things You Should Know About Birthright Citizenship," NPR, August 18, 2015, http://www.npr.org/sec tions/thetwo-way/2015/08/18/432707866/3-things-you-should -know-about-birthright-citizenship.

28   **France . . . New Zealand:** Caroline Sawyer, "The Loss of Birthright Citizenship in New Zealand," *Victoria University of Wellington Law Review* 44 (2013): 653–74; Linda R. Monk, "Birth Rights: Citizenship and the Constitution" (National Constitution Center, January 2011), 9, https:// constitutioncenter.org/media/files/Monograph_BirthRights.pdf; see also Barbara Crossette, "Citizenship Is a Malleable Concept," *New York Times*, August 18, 1996.

28   **Ivy League universities:** Taken almost verbatim from Chua, *Day of Empire*, 257–58; see Geoffrey Kabaservice, *The Guardians: Kingman Brewster, His Circle, and the Rise of the Liberal Establishment* (New York: Henry Holt, 2004), 65–66, 156, 174, 259–67; Jerome Karabel, *The Chosen: The Hidden History of Admission and Exclusion at Harvard, Yale, and Princeton* (New York: Houghton Mifflin, 2005), 364–67, 379, 392; Dan A. Oren, *Joining the Club: A History of Jews and Yale* (New Haven, CT: Yale University Press, 1985), 183–84, 272–77.

29   **The 1965 Immigration and Nationality Act:** This paragraph is taken almost verbatim from Chua, *Day of Empire*, 258–59; see also Samuel P. Huntington, *Who Are We? The Challenges to America's National Identity* (New York: Simon & Schuster, 2004), 196, 223–25.

30   **increase in illegal entries:** Douglas S. Massey and Karen A. Pren, "Unintended Consequences of US Immigration Policy: Explaining the Post-1965 Surge from Latin America," *Population and Development Review* 38, no. 1 (2012): 1–5.

30   **In 1960 . . . In 2000:** Chua, *Day of Empire*, 259; Huntington, *Who Are We?*, 223–24.

30   **in the U.S. Congress:** "Faith on the Hill: The Religious Composition of the 114th Congress," Pew Research Center, January 5, 2015, http://www .pewforum.org/2015/01/05/faith-on-the-hill.

31   **46 percent of Americans:** "America's Changing Religious Landscape," Pew Research Center, May 12, 2015, http://www.pewforum.org/2015 /05/12/americas-changing-religious-landscape.

31   **20 percent of the class of 2017:** "2017 By the Numbers: Beliefs and Lifestyle," *Harvard Crimson*, http://features.thecrimson.com/2013/frosh-survey /lifestyle.html.

31   **appointment of Neil Gorsuch:** Daniel Burke, "What Is Neil Gorsuch's Religion? It's Complicated," CNN, March 22, 2017, http://www.cnn .com/2017/03/18/politics/neil-gorsuch-religion.

31 ***Billboard*'s top 10:** *Billboard*, "Artist 100," week of December 31, 2016, accessed January 5, 2017, http://www.billboard.com/charts/artist-100. (in order from 1 to 10: J. Cole, Pentatonix, The Weeknd, Bruno Mars, Drake, Ariana Grande, Twenty One Pilots, Taylor Swift, Shawn Mendes, and Rae Sremmurd).

32 **Adele instead of:** Maura Johnston, "Beyoncé's Grammy Snub Isn't Just an Oversight—It's a Real Problem," *Time,* February 13, 2017.

33 **"[Y]ou can go to live":** Ronald Reagan, "The Brotherhood of Man" speech in Fulton, MO, November 19, 1990, http://ec2-184-73-198-63 .compute-1.amazonaws.com/wgbh/americanexperience/features /primary-resources/reagan-brotherhood.

33 **only one among all the world's great powers:** Some super-groups arguably exist among the world's non-major powers. Canada, for example, is famous for its tolerance and multiculturalism. See Canadian Multiculturalism Act, R.S.C., 1985, c. 24 (4th Supp.). The question in Canada's case, especially in light of Quebec's distinctive French identity, is whether there exists a sufficiently strong, overarching national identity for Canada to qualify as a super-group. See, e.g., Nick Bryant, "Neverendum Referendum: Voting on Independence, Quebec-Style," BBC News, September 8, 2014.

34 **"[O]ne thing is clear":** Barack Obama, "Remarks by President Obama at High-Level Meeting on Libya," United Nations, New York, September 20, 2011, http://www.whitehouse.gov/the-press-office/2011/09/20 /remarks-president-obama-high-level-meeting-libya.

34 **140 different tribes:** Ramazan Erdağ, *Libya in the Arab Spring: From Revolution to Insecurity* (New York: Palgrave Macmillan, 2017), 26; Peter Apps, "Factbox: Libya's Tribal, Cultural Divisions," Reuters, August 25, 2011, http://www.reuters.com/article/us-libya-tribes-idUSTRE77O4 3R20110825.

34 **"The degree of tribal division":** Jeffrey Goldberg, "The Obama Doctrine," *Atlantic,* April 2016.

35 **"a failed state":** Richard Lardner, "The Top American General in Africa Says Libya Is a Failed State," *U.S. World & News Report,* March 8, 2016.

35 **"failing to plan":** "President Obama: Libya Aftermath 'Worst Mistake' of Presidency," BBC News, April 11, 2016.

Chapter Two: Vietnam

37 **"Vietnam is too close":** James S. Olson and Randy Roberts, *Where the Domino Fell: America and Vietnam, 1945–1990* (West Sussex, UK: Wiley-Blackwell, 2014), 3.

37 **"We will drive":** Nguyen Cao Ky, *How We Lost the Vietnam War* (New York: First Cooper Square Press, 2002), 22.

37 **"No war since the Civil War"**: Henry Kissinger, *Ending the Vietnam War: A History of America's Involvement in and Extrication from the Vietnam War* (New York: Simon and Schuster, 2003), 7.

37 **"We are humiliated"**: Louis B. Zimmer, *The Vietnam War Debate: Hans J. Morgenthau and the Attempt to Halt the Drift into Disaster* (Lanham, MD: Lexington Books, 2011), 2.

37 **"an utter, unmitigated"**: "Time to Wave the Flag, McGovern Urges Democrats," *Telegraph* (UK), January 26, 2004.

38 **"a piddling, piss-ant"**: Ronald Steel, "Blind Contrition" (review of *In Retrospect: The Tragedy and Lessons of Vietnam,* by Robert S. McNamara with Brian Van De Mark), *New Republic,* June 5, 1995, 35.

38 **"the best and the brightest"**: David Halberstam, *The Best and the Brightest* (New York: Random House, 1972).

38 **overlooked the potency:** See, e.g., William J. Duiker, *Ho Chi Minh* (New York: Hyperion, 2000), 123, 341–42, 570; Marilyn B. Young, *The Vietnam Wars, 1945–1990* (New York: HarperCollins, 1991), 23–24, 178–80; Fredrik Logevall, *Embers of War: The Fall of an Empire and the Making of America's Vietnam* (New York: Random House, 2012), epilogue; Thomas Friedman, "ISIS and Vietnam," *New York Times,* October 28, 2014.

38 **"to understand that"**: Friedman, "ISIS and Vietnam."

38 **red or blue group:** Yarrow Dunham, Andrew Scott Baron, and Susan Carey, "Consequences of 'Minimal' Group Affiliations in Children," *Child Development* 82, no. 3 (2011): 793–811.

39 **"pervasively distorted by mere membership"**: Ibid., 797–98, 807–8; see also Henri Tajfel et al., "Social Categorization and Intergroup Behaviour," *European Journal of Social Psychology* 1, no. 2 (1971): 149–77.

39 **"group identification is both innate"**: Adam Piore, "Why We're Patriotic," *Nautilus,* November 26, 2015, http://nautil.us/issue/30/identity/why-were-patriotic; João F. Guassi Moreira, Jay J. Van Bavel, and Eva H. Telzer, "The Neural Development of 'Us and Them,'" *Social, Cognitive, and Affective Neuroscience* 12, no. 2 (2017): 184–96.

39 **tended to "light up"**: Piore, "Why We're Patriotic"; Jay J. Van Bavel et al., "The Neural Substrates of In-Group Bias: A Functional Magnetic Resonance Imaging Investigation," *Psychological Science* 19, no. 11 (2008): 1131, 1137.

40 **"outgroup members" . . . negatively stereotype:** Gary G. Berntson and John T. Cacioppo, ed., *Handbook of Neuroscience for the Behavioral Sciences 2* (Hoboken, NJ: John Wiley & Sons, 2009), 977.

40 **activate our reward centers:** Piore, "Why We're Patriotic."

40 **Newborns shown images:** David J. Kelly et al., "Three-Month-Olds, but Not Newborns, Prefer Own-Race Faces," *Developmental Science* 8, no. 6 (2005): F31–36.

40 **"Caucasian babies prefer"**: Paul Bloom, *Just Babies: The Origins of Good and Evil* (London: The Bodley Head, 2013), 105.

40 **people of their own race:** Xiaojing Xu et al., "Do You Feel My Pain? Racial Group Membership Modulates Empathic Neural Responses," *Journal of Neuroscience* 29, no. 26 (2009): 8525–29; see Shihui Han, "Intergroup Relationship and Empathy for Others' Pain: A Social Neuroscience Approach," in *Neuroscience in Intercultural Contexts*, ed. Jason E. Warnick and Dan Landis (New York: Springer, 2015), 36–37.

41 **take "sadistic pleasure":** Piore, "Why We're Patriotic"; see Mina Cikara and Susan T. Fiske, "Bounded Empathy: Neural Responses to Outgroup Targets' (Mis)Fortunes," *Journal of Cognitive Neuroscience* 23, no. 12 (2011): 3791–3803.

41 **"as a form of":** Donald L. Horowitz, *Ethnic Groups in Conflict*, 2nd ed. (Berkeley: University of California Press, 2000), 57; see also Amy Chua, *World on Fire: How Exporting Free Market Democracy Breeds Ethnic Hatred and Global Instability* (New York: Anchor Books, 2004), 14–15.

41 **"The ethnic tie":** Horowitz, *Ethnic Groups in Conflict*, 60.

41 **Mixed together with:** Ibid., 63, 73; see Kanchan Chandra, "What Is Ethnic Identity and Does It Matter?," *Annual Review of Political Science* 9 (2006): 397–424; Michael Ignatieff, *Blood and Belonging: Journeys into the New Nationalism* (New York: Farrar, Straus & Giroux, 1995), 7.

42 **the Yellow Emperor:** Frank Dikkötter, "Culture, 'Race' and Nation: The Formation of National Identity in Twentieth Century China," *Journal of International Affairs* 49, no. 2 (1996): 596–97; James Leibold, "Competing Narratives of Racial Unity in Republican China: From the Yellow Emperor to Peking Man," *Modern China* 32, no. 2 (2006): 192.

42 **from the emperor Oduduwa:** Kanchan Chandra, ed., *Constructivist Theories of Ethnic Politics* (Oxford: Oxford University Press, 2012), 75.

42 **as "primordialists" believe:** See Francisco J. Gil-White, "Are Ethnic Groups Biological 'Species' to the Human Brain? Essentialism in Our Cognition of Some Social Categories," *Current Anthropology* 42, no. 4 (2001): 515–53; Francisco J. Gil-White, "How Thick Is Blood? The Plot Thickens . . . : If Ethnic Actors Are Primordialists, What Remains of the Circumstantialist/Primordialist Controversy?," *Ethnic and Racial Studies* 22, no. 5 (1999): 789–820; see generally Lawrence A. Hirschfeld, *Race in the Making: Cognition, Culture and the Child's Construction of Human Kinds* (Cambridge, MA: MIT Press, 1998); Eugeen Roosens, "The Primordial Nature of Origins in Migrant Ethnicity," in *The Anthropology of Ethnicity: Beyond "Ethnic Groups and Boundaries,"* ed. Hans Vermeulen and Cora Govers (Amsterdam: Het Spinhuis, 1994); Pierre L. van den Berghe, *The Ethnic Phenomenon* (New York: Elsevier, 1981).

42 **as "instrumentalists" believe:** See Chandra, *Constructivist Theories of Ethnic Politics*, 2–3; Fredrik Barth, ed., *Ethnic Groups and Boundaries: The Social Organization of Culture Difference* (Boston: Little, Brown and Company, 1969), 22–23, 28; Rogers Brubaker, *Ethnicity Without Groups* (Cambridge, MA: Harvard University Press, 2004), 43, 56; Michele Lamont, *The*

Dignity of Working Men: Morality and the Boundaries of Race, Class, and Immigration (Cambridge, MA: Harvard University Press, 2000), 241; Daniel Posner, *Institutions and Ethnic Politics in Africa* (New York: Cambridge University Press, 2005), 276.

42 **one group feels threatened:** See, e.g., Lauren M. McLaren, "Anti-Immigrant Prejudice in Europe: Contact, Threat Perception, and Preferences for the Exclusion of Migrants," *Social Forces* 81, no. 3 (2003): 909–36; Roger Brown et al., "Explaining Intergroup Differentiation in an Industrial Organization," *Journal of Occupational Psychology* 59, no. 4 (1986): 273–86.

42 **a form of "identity-by-blood":** Patrick Lloyd Hatcher, *The Suicide of an Elite: American Internationalists and Vietnam* (Stanford, CA: Stanford University Press, 1990), 124.

43 **a province of China:** Chua, *World on Fire*, 33; Christopher Goscha, *Vietnam: A New History* (New York: Basic Books, 2016), 16; Stanley Karnow, *Vietnam: A History* (New York: Viking Press, 1983), 99; Henry Kenny, *Shadow of the Dragon: Vietnam's Continuing Struggle with China and Its Implications for U.S. Foreign Policy* (Washington, DC: Brassey's, 2002), 23, 25.

43 **adopted much of Chinese culture:** See Kenny, *Shadow of the Dragon*, 45; Goscha, *Vietnam*, 19–21; Olson and Roberts, *Where the Domino Fell*, 3; Keith W. Taylor, *The Birth of Vietnam* (Berkeley: University of California Press, 1983), 73–83.

43 **refused to become Chinese:** Taylor, *The Birth of Vietnam*, 299.

43 **all the more "[i]ntensely ethnocentric":** Olson and Roberts, *Where the Domino Fell*, 3.

43 **preserved their own language:** Kenny, *Shadow of the Dragon*, 27–28; Taylor, *The Birth of Vietnam*, 298–300.

43 **independence from China in 938:** Taylor, *The Birth of Vietnam*, 269.

43 **remained under Chinese domination:** Kenny, *Shadow of the Dragon*, 31, 47.

43 **repelled over and over:** Ibid., 31, 47–48; see also Keith W. Taylor, "China and Vietnam: Looking for a New Version of an Old Relationship," in *The Vietnam War: Vietnamese and American Perspectives*, ed. Jayne S. Werner and Luu Doan Huynh (Armonk, NY: M. E. Sharpe, 1993), 271.

43 **Tales of Vietnamese bravery:** See Lan Cao, *Monkey Bridge* (New York: Penguin Books, 1997), 56–57; Taylor, *The Birth of Vietnam*, 90; see also Goscha, *Vietnam*, 21, 132, 231.

43 **twentieth-century construction:** Goscha, *Vietnam*, 130–33.

43 **"a new Vietnam":** Ibid., 132.

44 **the Trung sisters:** Taylor, *The Birth of Vietnam*, 38; see also Goscha, *Vietnam*, 21, 132, 231.

44 **"suffocating" . . . "Individual men":** Goscha, *Vietnam*, 132.

44 **the protracted fight:** Olson and Roberts, *Where the Domino Fell*, 3–4.

44 **"The struggle for the survival":** Tran Khanh, "Ethnic Chinese in Vietnam and Their Identity," in *Ethnic Chinese as Southeast Asians*, ed. Leo Suryadinata (Singapore: Institute of Southeast Asian Studies, 1997), 269.

44 **"a stalking horse":** Jeffery Record, *The Wrong War: Why We Lost in Vietnam* (Annapolis, MD: Naval Institute Press, 1998), 12.

44 **"Mr. McNamara," he recalls:** Transcript of *The Fog of War: Eleven Lessons from the Life of Robert S. McNamara*, directed by Errol Morris (Hollywood, CA: Sony Pictures Classics, 2003), http://www.errolmorris.com/film /fow_transcript.html.

45 **"puppet of China":** Robert P. Newman, *Owen Lattimore and the "Loss" of China* (Berkeley: University of California Press, 1992), 519.

45 **raised on tales:** Olson and Roberts, *Where the Domino Fell*, 5.

45 **Chinese prisons . . . leg irons:** Harrison E. Salisbury, introduction to *The Prison Diary of Ho Chi Minh*, by Ho Chi Minh, trans. Aileen Palmer (New York: Bantam Books, 1971), xiv; see also Mai Luan, Dac Xuan, and Tran Dan Tien, *Ho Chi Minh: From Childhood to President of Viet Nam* (Hansi, Vietnam: Gioi Publishers, 2005), 90.

45 **"soft-spoken" . . . Gandhi:** Neil L. Jamieson, *Understanding Vietnam* (Berkeley: University of California Press, 1995), 181; Duiker, *Ho Chi Minh*, 576.

45 **Ho barked: "You fools!":** There are many slightly different translations of Ho's statement. The one quoted is from Karnow, *Vietnam*, 153; see also Michael Maclear, *The Ten Thousand Day War: Vietnam, 1945–1975* (New York: St. Martin's Press, 1981), 17.

45 **wrote to President Truman . . . quoted the U.S. Declaration:** Duiker, *Ho Chi Minh*, 342, 357; Salisbury, introduction to *The Prison Diary of Ho Chi Minh*, x.

45 **An OSS report:** Maclear, *The Ten Thousand Day War*, 15.

46 **"To many Americans":** Nguyen, *How We Lost the Vietnam War*, 11.

46 **the term "market-dominant minority":** Chua, *World on Fire*, 6.

47 **Examples include ethnic Chinese:** Ibid.

47 **Parsis and Gujaratis:** Parsis: Zubin C. Shroff and Marcia C. Castro, "The Potential Impact of Intermarriage on the Population Decline of the Parsis of Mumbai, India," *Demographic Research* 25 (2011): 549; see also Jesse S. Palsetia, *The Parsis of India: Preservation of Identity in Bombay City* (Leiden, The Netherlands: Brill, 2001), xii; T. M. Luhrmann, *The Good Parsi: The Fate of a Colonial Elite in a Post-Colonial Society* (Cambridge, MA: Harvard University Press, 1996); "Not Fade Away: India's Vanishing Parsis," *Economist*, September 1, 2012. Gujaratis: Suketu Mehta, *Maximum City: Bombay Lost and Found* (New York: Knopf, 2004), 19; Dipankar Gupta, *Justice Before Reconciliation: Negotiating a "New Normal" in Post-Riot Mumbai and Ahmedabad* (London: Routledge, 2011), 169.

47 **very different reasons:** Chua, *World on Fire*, 63–65, 95, 99.

47 **as much as 70 percent:** Ibid., 43; see Leo Suryadinata, "Indonesian Politics Toward the Chinese Minority Under the New Order," *Asian Survey* 16 (1976): 770; "A Taxing Dilemma," *Asiaweek*, October 20, 1993, 57, 58 (reporting that, according to the Sakura Bank-Nomura Research Institute, in

1991 Indonesian Chinese comprised 3.5 percent of the population but commanded a 73 percent share of the country's listed equity); see also Linda Y. C. Lim and L. A. Peter Gosling, "Strengths and Weaknesses of Minority Status for Southeast Asian Chinese at a Time of Economic Growth and Liberalization," in *Essential Outsiders: Chinese and Jews in the Modern Transformation of Southeast Asia and Central Europe*, ed. Daniel Chirot and Anthony Reid (Seattle: University of Washington Press, 1997), 312 n. 2 (offering similar estimates).

47 For most of Bolivia's: Chua, *World on Fire*, 49–55.

47–48 In the Philippines, the 2 percent: The government of the Philippines does not provide information on ethnicity. The Taiwan government's Overseas Community Affairs Council estimates that there were 1,459,083 Chinese Filipinos in 2010, representing about 1.55 percent of the country's population. See Qiaoweihui Tongjishi (The Statistics Office of Overseas Community Affairs Council), *Feilübin 2010 nian Huaren Renkou Tongji Tuigu (A Statistical Estimate of the 2010 Population of Ethnic Chinese in the Philippines)*, Zhonghuaminguo Qiaowu Weiyuanhui (Overseas Community Affairs Council, Republic of China [Taiwan]), November 7, 2011, http://www.ocac.gov.tw/OCAC/File/Attach/245/File_241.pdf; see also Carmen N. Pedrosa, "Contribution of Chinese-Filipinos to the Country," *Philippine Star*, May 23, 2015 ("Today, there are 1.5 million Filipinos of pure Chinese ancestry or just over 1% of the total population").

48 controls the country's: Chua, *World on Fire*, 36–37.

48 according to *Forbes*: "Philippines' 50 Richest in 2015," *Forbes*; Doris Dumlao-Abadilla, "PH's 50 Richest Families Based on 2015 Forbes Ranking," *Philippine Daily Inquirer*, August 27, 2015, http://business.inquirer.net/197986/phs-50-richest-families-based-on-2015-forbes-ranking.

48 When a developing country: Chua, *World on Fire*, 124–25.

48 The Chinese in Vietnam: Ibid., 33–34; Frank H. Golay et al., *Underdevelopment and Economic Nationalism in Southeast Asia* (Ithaca, NY: Cornell University Press, 1969), 395; Tran Khanh, *The Ethnic Chinese and Economic Development in Vietnam* (Singapore: Institute of Southeast Asian Studies, 1993), 41–42; Pao-min Chang, *Beijing, Hanoi, and the Overseas Chinese* (Berkeley: Institute of East Asian Studies, 1982), 4, 16.

48 Cholon, Saigon's sister city: Justin Corfield, *Historical Dictionary of Ho Chi Minh City* (New York: Anthem Press, 2014), 60–62.

48 an estimated ten thousand: K. W. Taylor, *A History of the Vietnamese* (Cambridge: Cambridge University Press, 2013), 374.

48 burned and looted: George Dutton, *The Tây Sơn Uprising: Society and Rebellion in Eighteenth-Century Vietnam* (Chiang Mai, Thailand: Silkworm Books, 2008), 202–3.

48 "men, women, and children": Taylor, *A History of the Vietnamese*, 374.

48 "killed and their corpses": Dutton, *The Tây Sơn Uprising*, 203.

49 **When the French:** Goscha, *Vietnam*, 78.

49 **"vast economic power" . . . "a state within a state":** Chang, *Beijing, Hanoi, and the Overseas Chinese*, 4, 8.

49 **the "Petrol King":** Ungar, "Struggle Over the Chinese Community in Vietnam," 606.

49 **Vietnamese elite filled:** Olson and Roberts, *Where the Domino Fell*, 48; see also Goscha, *Vietnam*, 345–46.

49 **"stranglehold" on Vietnam's:** Alexander Woodside, "Nationalism and Poverty in the Breakdown of Sino-Vietnamese Relations," *Pacific Affairs* 52 (1979): 405; see also Olson and Roberts, *Where the Domino Fell*, 47.

49 **only a tiny percentage:** Olson and Roberts, *Where the Domino Fell*, 47.

49 **staggering 80 percent:** Woodside, "Nationalism and Poverty," 405; see also Steven J. Hood, *Dragons Entangled: Indochina and the China-Vietnam War* (Armonk, NY: M. E. Sharpe, 1992), 149; Li Tana, "In Search of the History of the Chinese in South Vietnam, 1945–75," in *The Chinese/Vietnamese Diaspora: Revisiting the Boat People*, ed. Yuk Wah Chan (Oxon, UK: Routledge, 2011), 58.

49 **The Hoa also dominated:** Chua, *World on Fire*, 33–34; Golay et al., *Underdevelopment and Economic Nationalism in Southeast Asia*, 395–96; Khanh, *The Ethnic Chinese and Economic Development in Vietnam*, 41, 47, 57. The Hoa produced much of the laundry powder, salad oil, candy bars, soft drinks, and cigarettes, not just for Vietnam but for all of Southeast Asia. Woodside, "Nationalism and Poverty," 393.

49 **they owned more than:** Khanh, *Ethnic Chinese and Economic Development in Vietnam*, 59.

49 **controlled 90 percent:** Chua, *World on Fire*, 33.

50 **in wealthy enclaves:** Philip Taylor, "Minorities at Large," in *Minorities at Large: New Approaches to Minority Ethnicity in Vietnam*, ed. Philip Taylor (Singapore: Institute of Southeast Asian Studies, 2011), 23.

50 **schools and temples:** Chang, *Beijing, Hanoi, and the Overseas Chinese*, 8, 16; Hood, *Dragons Entangled*, 137–38.

50 **typically marrying only:** King C. Chen, *China's War with Vietnam, 1979: Issues, Decisions, and Implications* (Stanford, CA: Hoover Institution Press, 1987), 51.

50 **"ethnic and cultural exclusivism":** Martin Stuart-Fox, *A Short History of China and Southeast Asia: Tribute, Trade, and Influence* (Crows Nest, Australia: Allen & Unwin, 2003), 131.

50 **seen as exploiting:** Taylor, "Minorities at Large," 23; Taylor, *The Birth of Vietnam*, 52; Hood, *Dragons Entangled*, 140.

50 **were impoverished peasants:** Joe Allen, *Vietnam: The (Last) War the U.S. Lost* (Chicago: Haymarket Books, 2008), 7; Golay et al., *Underdevelopment and Economic Nationalism in Southeast Asia*, 398.

50 **the Chinese minority stayed "apolitical":** Taylor, "Minorities at Large," 23.

50   **defeated the French:** Maclear, *The Ten Thousand Day War*, 45; Duiker, *Ho Chi Minh*, 462.

50   **Vietnam was divided:** Goscha, *Vietnam*, 279; Maclear, *The Ten Thousand Day War*, 49; Duiker, *Ho Chi Minh*, 458–60.

50   **The Geneva Accords . . . some 800,000:** Goscha, *Vietnam*, 280; Duiker, *Ho Chi Minh*, 465; Maclear, *The Ten Thousand Day War*, 51.

51   **"Frenchified" Vietnamese elite:** Record, *The Wrong War*, 136; see also Goscha, *Vietnam*, 349, 356.

51   **about 1 million out of 1.2 million:** Chang, *Beijing, Hanoi, and the Overseas Chinese*, 9.

51   **unified Vietnamese tribe:** Hatcher, *The Suicide of an Elite*, 125–26.

51   **"We have the same":** Walker Connor, "Beyond Reason: The Nature of the Ethnonational Bond," in *New Tribalisms: The Resurgence of Race and Ethnicity*, ed. Michael W. Hughey (New York: New York University Press, 1998), 47.

51   **In 1959, Ho:** Allen, *Vietnam*, 28.

51   **In 1965, we began:** Maclear, *The Ten Thousand Day War*, 128–29.

51   **We fought . . . more troops:** Record, *The Wrong War*, 141–42.

51   **chiefly benefiting—the Chinese:** Woodside, "Nationalism and Poverty," 404–5.

51   **also wealthy Vietnamese:** Khanh, *Ethnic Chinese and Economic Development in Vietnam*, 80.

51   **"the ethnic Chinese controlled":** Tana, "In Search of the History," 53.

51   **"the capitalist heart":** Ibid.

52   **more than $100 billion:** Ibid., 56.

52   **best position to deliver:** Khanh, *Ethnic Chinese and Economic Development in Vietnam*, 41–73, 80.

52   **"handled more than 60 per cent":** Ibid., 58.

52   **Many Chinese made:** Ibid.; Tana, "In Search of the History," 57.

52   **84 percent were:** Khanh, *Ethnic Chinese and Economic Development in Vietnam*, 58.

52   **"[g]old watches" . . . venereal disease:** Maclear, *The Ten Thousand Day War*, 144; see also Hood, *Dragons Entangled*, 141.

52   **owned twenty-eight of:** Khanh, *Ethnic Chinese and Economic Development in Vietnam*, 61.

52   **cultivated and bribed:** Ibid., 80; Nguyen, *How We Lost the Vietnam War*, 101–2.

52   **"[T]he slime of corruption":** Nguyen, *How We Lost the Vietnam War*, 104.

52   **created a rice shortage:** Ibid., 102.

53   **Being police chief:** Ibid., 106; William S. Turley, *The Second Indochina War: A Short Political and Military History, 1954–1975* (Boulder, CO: Westview Press, 1986), 167.

53   **more than one hundred thousand:** Nguyen, *How We Lost the Vietnam War*, 106.

53 **the U.S.-backed regime:** Maclear, *The Ten Thousand Day War*, 148.

53 **"Dinks and Gooks":** Nguyen, *How We Lost the Vietnam War*, 138.

53 **"We didn't even":** Jinim Park, *Narratives of the Vietnam War by Korean and American Writers* (New York: Peter Lang Publishing, 2007), 30.

53 **more than 2 million:** Olson and Roberts, *Where the Domino Fell*, 146.

53 **indiscriminate bombing, napalm:** Goscha, *Vietnam*, 326–28; Olson and Roberts, *Where the Domino Fell*, 160–61; Record, *The Wrong War*, 86.

54 **U.S. "friendly fire":** Olson and Roberts, *Where the Domino Fell*, 146.

54 **in a puppet state:** Maclear, *The Ten Thousand Day War*, 148; see also Record, *The Wrong War*, 125–26, 139.

54 **soldiers wore trinkets:** Olson and Roberts, *Where the Domino Fell*, 2.

54 **"[u]nfortunately our military":** Record, *The Wrong War*, 139 (quoting Henry Kissinger).

54 **"The South Vietnamese":** Ibid., 135 (quoting Guenter Lewy).

54 **lost their sons . . . to the other side:** Ibid., 86, 134–35, 138; Olson and Roberts, *Where the Domino Fell*, 63.

55 **The last U.S. troops:** Allen, *Vietnam*, 200–1.

55 **code name "X1":** Khanh, *The Ethnic Chinese and Economic Development in Vietnam*, 81; Ramses Amer, "The Boat People Crisis of 1978–79 and the Hong Kong Experience Examined Through the Ethnic Chinese Dimension," in Chan, *The Chinese/Vietnamese Diaspora*, 41.

55 **250 wealthy Chinese:** Khanh, *Ethnic Chinese and Economic Development in Vietnam*, 81–82.

55 **newspapers . . . hospitals . . . 70 percent:** Ibid., 81.

55 **estimated $2 billion:** Goscha, *Vietnam*, 379.

55 **relations between China and Vietnam:** Chang, *Beijing, Hanoi, and the Overseas Chinese*, 21, 23–25.

55 **"the campaign against":** Ibid., 25.

55 **In the south:** Ibid.

56 **fishermen, foresters, craftsmen:** Ramses Amer, "Vietnam's Policies and the Ethnic Chinese Since 1975," *Sojourn: Journal of Social Issues in Southeast Asia* 11, no. 1 (1996): 85.

56 **"purifying the border areas":** Chang, *Beijing, Hanoi, and the Overseas Chinese*, 24.

56 **began under "X2":** Amer, "Vietnam's Policies and the Ethnic Chinese Since 1975," 80; Chang, *Beijing, Hanoi, and the Overseas Chinese*, 27.

56 **fifty thousand Chinese businesses:** Chang, *Beijing, Hanoi, and the Overseas Chinese*, 27; Goscha, *Vietnam*, 379.

56 **"full of corpses":** Chang, *Beijing, Hanoi, and the Overseas Chinese*, 28.

56 **Similar raids took place:** Ibid., 27.

56 **Chinese were purged:** Amer, "Vietnam's Policies and the Ethnic Chinese Since 1975," 86.

56 thousands of Chinese: Chua, *World on Fire*, 34; see also Amer, "Vietnam's Policies and the Ethnic Chinese Since 1975," 83–85.

56 "My uncle was arrested": Goscha, *Vietnam*, 380.

56 "Hanoi is blaming": James N. Wallace, "A Ray of Hope," *U.S. News & World Report*, August 6, 1979, 50; see also Henry Kamm, "Vietnam Describes Economic Setbacks," *New York Times*, November 19, 1980, A9.

57 "China's allegations have now": Chang, *Beijing, Hanoi, and the Overseas Chinese*, 34.

57 By late 1978: Young, *The Vietnam Wars, 1945–1990*, 306; Amer, "Vietnam's Policies and the Ethnic Chinese Since 1975," 80, 83.

57 "Vietnamese boat people": Yuk Wah Chan, "Revisiting the Vietnamese Refugee Era," in Chan, *The Chinese/Vietnamese Diaspora*, 3.

57 most of those refugees: Ibid., 4.

57 three main waves: Ibid., 7–9.

57 70 percent of the refugees: Ibid., 7.

57 third wave . . . ethnic Vietnamese: Ibid., 3.

57 85 percent were Chinese: Chang, *Beijing, Hanoi, and the Overseas Chinese*, 35.

57 "intended to get rid": Ibid., 55–56.

57 at war with China: Maclear, *The Ten Thousand Day War*, 352; Chang, *Beijing, Hanoi, and the Overseas Chinese*, 53–56.

Chapter Three: Afghanistan

59 "In Afghanistan, you don't": Hermione Hoby, "Khaled Hosseini, 'If I Could Go Back Now, I'd Take the Kite Runner Apart,'" *Guardian*, June 1, 2013.

59 "May God keep you": There are many versions of this saying, which is sometimes attributed to Alexander the Great. See, e.g., "May God Keep You Away from Revenge of the Afghans," *London Post*, April 22, 2014 (remarks of Sir James Bevan KCMG, UK High Commissioner to India, to the Delhi Policy Group).

59 longest in our history: See Andrew J. Bacevich, "The Never-Ending War in Afghanistan," *New York Times*, March 13, 2017.

60 "a foreign policy disaster": Ann Jones, "America Lost in Afghanistan: Anatomy of a Foreign Policy Disaster," *Salon*, November 6, 2015, http://www.salon.com/2015/11/06/america_lost_in_afghanistan_partner.

60 a "never-ending war": Bacevich, "The Never-Ending War in Afghanistan."

60 "Fifteen years, thousands": Dana Rohrabacher, "How to Win in Afghanistan," *National Interest*, January 18, 2017.

60 Afghanistan's national anthem: Barnett R. Rubin, *Afghanistan from the Cold War Through the War on Terror* (Oxford: Oxford University Press, 2013), 161. The other ethnic groups recognized in the anthem are the Turkmen, Baluch, Pashai, Nuristani, Aymaq, Arab, Kyrgyz, Qizilbash, Gujar, and

Brahui. Ibid.; see also Anwar-ul-Haq Ahady, "The Decline of the Pashtuns in Afghanistan," *Asian Survey* 35, no. 7 (1995): 621.

60 **history of animosity:** Ahady, "The Decline of the Pashtuns in Afghanistan," 631–34.

60 **For more than two hundred:** Hassan Abbas, *The Taliban Revival: Violence and Extremism on the Pakistan-Afghanistan Border* (New Haven, CT: Yale University Press, 2014), 24.

60 **in 1992:** Seth G. Jones, *In the Graveyard of Empires: America's War in Afghanistan* (New York: W. W. Norton, 2009), 43–44; Ahady, "The Decline of the Pashtuns in Afghanistan," 623–24.

60 **The vast majority:** Abbas, *The Taliban Revival*, 5–7, 10; Jones, *In the Graveyard of Empires*, 59–60; Abubakar Siddique, *The Pashtun Question: The Unresolved Key to the Future of Pakistan and Afghanistan* (London: C. Hurst & Company, 2014), 56.

60 **It was founded:** Abbas, *The Taliban Revival*, 10, 62–63, 65; Steve Coll, *Ghost Wars: The Secret History of the CIA, Afghanistan, and bin Laden, from the Soviet Invasion to September 10, 2001* (New York: Penguin Press, 2004), 283–87; Siddique, *The Pashtun Question*, 198.

61 **as "Eastern Iranians":** Michael Barry, "Afghanistan," in *Princeton Encyclopedia of Islamic Political Thought*, ed. Gerhard Bowering et al. (Princeton, NJ: Princeton University Press, 2013), 20.

61 **a fifteen-hundred-mile-long border:** Jayshree Bajoria, "The Troubled Afghan-Pakistani Border," Council on Foreign Relations, March 20, 2009, http://www.cfr.org/pakistan/troubled-afghan-pakistani-border/p14905; see also Abbas, *The Taliban Revival*, 35.

61 **established in 1747:** Abbas, *The Taliban Revival*, 22; Peter Tomsen, *The Wars of Afghanistan: Messianic Terrorism, Tribal Conflicts, and the Failures of Great Powers* (New York: PublicAffairs, 2011), xxi.

61 **From 1747 to 1973:** Abbas, *The Taliban Revival*, 24.

61 **Europeans never conquered Afghanistan:** Tomsen, *The Wars of Afghanistan*, 29, 37–39.

61 **Pashto is the mother tongue:** Siddique, *The Pashtun Question*, 14.

61 **known as Pashtunwali:** Abbas, *The Taliban Revival*, 17–19; Siddique, *The Pashtun Question*, 14.

61 **often used interchangeably:** Siddique, *The Pashtun Question*, 11.

61 **"Pakistan" is an acronym:** See Choudhary Rahmat Ali, "Now or Never: Are We to Live or Perish Forever?" (1933), reprinted in *Pakistan Movement: Historic Documents*, ed. Gulam Allana (Karachi: Paradise Subscription Agency for the University of Karachi, 1967), 104; Willem van Schendel, *A History of Bangladesh* (Cambridge: Cambridge University Press, 2009), 89.

62 **Punjabis have politically:** Christophe Jaffrelot, *A History of Pakistan and Its Origins* (London: Anthem Press, 2002), 69; Theodore P. Wright Jr., "Center-Periphery Relations and Ethnic Conflict in Pakistan: Sindhis, Muhajirs, and Punjabis," *Comparative Politics* 23, no. 3 (1991): 299.

62 **somewhere around half:** See, e.g., CIA, "Pakistan," *The World Factbook*, https://www.cia.gov/library/publications/the-world-factbook/geos /pk.html (44.7%); Irm Haleem, "Ethnic and Sectarian Violence and the Propensity Towards Praetorianism in Pakistan," *Third World Quarterly* 24, no. 3 (2003): 467 (56%).

62 **Pakistan's famous military:** Alyssa Ayres, *Speaking Like a State: Language and Nationalism in Pakistan* (Cambridge: Cambridge University Press, 2009), 70; Wright, "Center-Periphery Relations and Ethnic Conflict in Pakistan," 299; Ayesha Shehzad, "The Issue of Ethnicity in Pakistan: Historical Background," *Pakistan Vision* 12, no. 2 (2011): 132; see also Jaffrelot, *A History of Pakistan and Its Origins*, 69, 315; Anatol Lieven, *Pakistan: A Hard Country* (New York: PublicAffairs, 2011), 179.

62 **most state institutions:** Ayres, *Speaking Like a State*, 65, 70–71; Farhan Hanif Siddiqi, *The Politics of Ethnicity in Pakistan: The Baloch, Sindhi and Mohajir Ethnic Movements* (London: Routledge, 2012), 43, 119; Wright, "Center-Periphery Relations and Ethnic Conflict in Pakistan," 301, 305.

62 **they are highly endogamous:** Hastings Donnan, "Mixed Marriage in Comparative Perspective: Gender and Power in Northern Ireland and Pakistan," *Journal of Comparative Family Studies* 21, no. 2 (1990): 208; Roomana Naz Bhutta et al., "Dynamics of Watta Satta Marriages in Rural Areas of Southern Punjab Pakistan," *Open Journal of Social Sciences* 3 (2015): 166; R. Hussain, "Community Perceptions of Reasons for Preference for Consanguineous Marriages in Pakistan," *Journal of Biosocial Science* 31 (1999): 449.

62 **leading to an "appalling":** Steven Swinford, "First Cousin Marriages in Pakistani Communities Leading to 'Appalling' Disabilities Among Children," *Telegraph* (UK), July 7, 2015.

62 **Ever since independence:** Siddique, *The Pashtun Question*, 38–39.

62 **only 15 percent:** CIA, "Pakistan," *The World Factbook*.

62 *more* **Pashtuns in Pakistan:** Abbas, *The Taliban Revival*, 14; see also Coll, *Ghost Wars*, 62; Siddique, *The Pashtun Question*, 12.

62 **most of Pakistan's Pashtuns:** Abbas, *The Taliban Revival*, 14, 34–35; Bajoria, "The Troubled Afghan-Pakistani Border."

62 **the Durand Line:** Abbas, *The Taliban Revival*, 27, 49–50; Siddique, *The Pashtun Question*, 35; American Institute of Afghanistan Studies, *The Durand Line: History, Consequences, and Future* (The Hollings Center, July 2007), 1–2.

62 **"[y]ou cannot separate":** Siddique, *The Pashtun Question*, 216.

62 **still identify themselves:** Ibid., 11.

63 **when Pakistan's Bengalis:** Ibid., 39.

63 **In 1978, Afghanistan's president:** Tomsen, *The Wars of Afghanistan*, 112–13.

63 **pro-Communist rebels led the coup:** Coll, *Ghost Wars*, 39; Tomsen, *The Wars of Afghanistan*, 119.

NOTES

63   **"even the KGB":** Vladislav M. Zubok, *A Failed Empire: The Soviet Union in the Cold War from Stalin to Gorbachev* (Chapel Hill: University of North Carolina Press, 2009), 259.

63   **accelerated the contradictions:** Rodric Braithwaite, *Afgantsy: The Russians in Afghanistan 1979–89* (Oxford: Oxford University Press, 2011), 43.

63   **no proletariat in Afghanistan:** Ibid., 38; see also Tomsen, *The Wars of Afghanistan*, 117.

63   **a festering feud:** Tomsen, *The Wars of Afghanistan*, 93, 106, 117, 119, 127, 131; Thomas J. Barfield, "Weapons of the Not So Weak in Afghanistan: Pashtun Agrarian Structure and Tribal Organization," in *Culture, Conflict, and Counterinsurgency*, ed. Thomas H. Johnson and Barry Scott Zellen (Stanford, CA: Stanford University Press, 2014), 115; see also Anthony Arnold, *Afghanistan's Two-Party Communism: Parcham and Khalq* (Stanford, CA: Hoover Press, 1983), 3–4.

64   **who "viewed 'Afghan'":** Tomsen, *The Wars of Afghanistan*, 131.

64   **hunting down rival:** Ibid., 133–34.

64   **"Afghan clients":** Jones, *In the Graveyard of Empires*, 143.

64   **Moscow feared that:** Ibid., 16–18.

64   **"It'll be over":** Ibid., 18; see also Tomsen, *The Wars of Afghanistan*, 142–43.

64   **Nine years later:** Jones, *In the Graveyard of Empires*, 36–40.

64   **Zbigniew Brzezinski, Carter's:** Coll, *Ghost Wars*, 50–51.

64   **still stinging from Vietnam:** Ibid., 59.

65   **"who got the most":** Ibid., 60.

65   **its geopolitical pawn:** Ibid.

65   **longstanding rivalries and conflicts:** See Tomsen, *The Wars of Afghanistan*, 30–31, 57; Barfield, "Weapons of the Not So Weak in Afghanistan," 96–97, 115; Michael Barry, *Kabul's Long Shadows: Historical Perspectives* (Princeton, NJ: Liechtenstein Institute on Self-Determination, 2011), 69–70.

65   **largest tribally organized:** Abbas, *The Taliban Revival*, 11; Siddique, *The Pashtun Question*, 13; see also Tomsen, *The Wars of Afghanistan*, 29–31.

65   **virtually all Pashtuns are Sunni Muslims:** Siddique, *The Pashtun Question*, 15.

65   **are more religious:** See, e.g., Abbas, *The Taliban Revival*, 14–15, 24; Siddique, *The Pashtun Question*, 13–14; Tomsen, *The Wars of Afghanistan*, 258; Thomas H. Johnson and M. Chris Mason, "Understanding the Taliban and Insurgency in Afghanistan," *Orbis: A Journal of World Affairs* 51, no. 1 (2007): 71, 74–75.

65   **Zia shrewdly favored:** Siddique, *The Pashtun Question*, 15, 39–40, 42–43; Tomsen, *The Wars of Afghanistan*, 9–10; see also Jones, *In the Graveyard of Empires*, 56 (the ISI deliberately favored the Ghilzai Pashtuns and marginalized the Durrani Pashtuns).

65   **He built madrassas:** Jones, *In the Graveyard of Empires*, 56.

65   **"Pakistan set out":** Ahmad Bilal Khalil, "Pakistan, Islamism, and the Fear of Afghan Nationalism," *Diplomat*, March 3, 2017, http://thediplomat

.com/2017/03/pakistan-islamism-and-the-fear-of-afghan-nationalism (quoting Hamid Karzai in a 2003 conversation with U.S. representative Dana Rohrabacher).

65   **the United States romanticized:** Coll, *Ghost Wars*, 91–92; Tomsen, *The Wars of Afghanistan*, 281–82.

65–66 **Congressman Charlie Wilson:** Tomsen, *The Wars of Afghanistan*, 281–82.

66   **Between 1980 and 1992:** Jones, *In the Graveyard of Empires*, 37.

66   **machine guns . . . Stinger missiles:** Coll, *Ghost Wars*, 337, 340; Jones, *In the Graveyard of Empires*, 38.

66   **Mullah Mohammed Omar:** Coll, *Ghost Wars*, 292–94, 312, 328; Jones, *In the Graveyard of Empires*, 52–54.

66   **brutal civil war:** Abbas, *The Taliban Revival*, 58; Jones, *In the Graveyard of Empires*, 46–49.

66   **U.S. government lost interest:** Abbas, *The Taliban Revival*, 59; Jones, *In the Graveyard of Empires*, 44–45, 48–50.

66   **caught completely off guard:** Abbas, *The Taliban Revival*, 61; Ahmed Rashid, "The Rise of Bin Laden," *New York Review of Books*, May 27, 2004 (reviewing Coll, *Ghost Wars*, and citing former CIA officials).

66   **two thirds of Afghanistan:** Coll, *Ghost Wars*, 335.

67   **Warlords ruled practically:** Abbas, *The Taliban Revival*, 61.

67   **Racketeers . . . and rape:** Coll, *Ghost Wars*, 282.

67   **it provided security:** Ibid., 335; Abbas, *The Taliban Revival*, 62–63; Jones, *In the Graveyard of Empires*, 60, 67; Barnett R. Rubin, "The Political Economy of War and Peace in Afghanistan," *World Development* 28, no. 10 (2000): 1789, 1793–95.

67   **dress code and bans:** Jones, *In the Graveyard of Empires*, 61.

67   **For hundreds of years:** Abbas, *The Taliban Revival*, 22–23; Ahady, "The Decline of the Pashtuns in Afghanistan," 621–22.

67   **After the fall:** Ali Reza Sarwar, "Ashraf Ghani and the Pashtun Dilemma," *Diplomat*, January 18, 2015, http://thediplomat.com/2015/01/ashraf-ghani-and-the-pashtun-dilemma; Ahady, "The Decline of the Pashtuns in Afghanistan," 622–24.

67   **the Tajik minority:** Jones, *In the Graveyard of Empires*, 44–45, 59; Tomsen, *The Wars of Afghanistan*, xxvi–xxvii, 486–87, 541–42.

67   **where Burhanuddin Rabbani:** Tomsen, *The Wars of Afghanistan*, xxvii, 526–27, 539.

67   **They had lost . . . Afghan military:** Ahady, "The Decline of the Pashtuns in Afghanistan," 621–24, 626.

68   **leadership . . . rank and file:** Abbas, *The Taliban Revival*, 10, 65; Siddique, *The Pashtun Question*, 176, 198.

68   **"lowest socio-economic rung":** Abbas, *The Taliban Revival*, 65.

68   **"[t]heir Pashtun identity:** Siddique, *The Pashtun Question*, 198.

68   **"The Taliban's strategy":** Jones, *In the Graveyard of Empires*, 59.

68–69 **"[T]he Taliban's Pashtun identity":** Abbas, *The Taliban Revival*, 65.

69   **primarily in non-Pashtun areas:** Ibid., 65.

69   **"more significant than":** Ahady, "The Decline of the Pashtuns in Afghanistan," 621, 623–24.

69   **"was an unlikely heir":** Coll, *Ghost Wars*, 287–88.

69   **spring of 1996:** Ibid., 328.

69   **Ahmad Shah Durrani:** Ibid., 280–82.

69   **"Cloak of the Holy Prophet":** Ibid., 328.

69   **never succeeded in unifying:** Siddique, *The Pashtun Question*, 198; Tomsen, *The Wars of Afghanistan*, 546–47; Sarwar, "Ashraf Ghani and the Pashtun Dilemma."

69–70 **More moderate, pro-Western:** Siddique, *The Pashtun Question*, 184; Tomsen, *The Wars of Afghanistan*, 546, 564–65.

70   **feared the "Pakistanization":** Tomsen, *The Wars of Afghanistan*, 546; see also Siddique, *The Pashtun Question*, 198.

70   **exploit Pashtun ethnonationalism:** Siddique, *The Pashtun Question*, 199; Sarwar, "Ashraf Ghani and the Pashtun Dilemma."

70   **Taliban massacred 2,000:** "Massacres of Hazaras in Afghanistan," Human Rights Watch, 2001, https://www.hrw.org/reports/2001/afghanistan/afghan101-02.htm; see also Sven Gunnar Simonsen, "Ethnicising Afghanistan?: Inclusion and Exclusion in Post-Bonn Institution Building," *Third World Quarterly* 25, no. 4 (2004): 711.

70   **tried to starve:** "U.N. Says Taliban Starving Hungry People for Military Agenda," Associated Press, January 7, 1998.

70   **persecuted and killed Tajiks:** Graeme Swincer, "Tajiks and Their Security in Afghanistan," Blue Mountains Refugee Support Group, September 2014, 1.

70   **weren't allowing girls . . . Buddha statues:** Abbas, *The Taliban Revival*, 69, 71; Coll, *Ghost Wars*, 362–63.

70   **it was the duty:** Abbas, *The Taliban Revival*, 73.

70   **refused to turn over:** Ibid., 74.

71   **toppled the Taliban:** Ibid., 76; Tomsen, *The Wars of Afghanistan*, 588.

71   **joined forces with the Northern Alliance:** Coll, *Ghost Wars*, xvi, 467–69, 494; Siddique, *The Pashtun Question*, 199.

71   **led by Tajik and Uzbek:** Coll, *Ghost Wars*, xvi; Siddique, *The Pashtun Question*, 199; Ahady, "The Decline of the Pashtuns in Afghanistan," 626.

71   **"was known for such tendencies":** Abbas, *The Taliban Revival*, 77.

71   **Although Dostum later insisted:** Luke Harding, "Afghan Massacre Haunts Pentagon," *Guardian*, September 13, 2002.

71   **"hundreds suffocated in":** Abbas, *The Taliban Revival*, 77.

72   **anti-Pashtun mass killer:** Sune Engel Rasmussen, "Afghanistan's Warlord Vice-President Spoiling for a Fight with the Taliban," *Guardian*, August 4, 2015.

72   **one of "America's warlords":** Abbas, *The Taliban Revival*, 85–86.

72 **alienating Pashtuns all over:** Ibid., 82–83, 116; Siddique, *The Pashtun Question*, 199, 206.

72 **conference convened in Bonn:** Abbas, *The Taliban Revival*, 82–83; "Filling the Vacuum: The Bonn Conference," *Frontline*, http://www.pbs.org/wgbh/pages/frontline/shows/campaign/withus/cbonn.html.

72 **"remotely associated with the Taliban":** Siddique, *The Pashtun Question*, 206.

72 **more moderate Pashtuns:** Abbas, *The Taliban Revival*, 77; Sarwar, "Ashraf Ghani and the Pashtun Dilemma."

72 **key positions of power:** Abbas, *The Taliban Revival*, 83; Siddique, *The Pashtun Question*, 206; Selig S. Harrison, "Afghanistan's Tyranny of the Minority," *New York Times*, August 16, 2009.

72 **top ministry positions:** Abbas, *The Taliban Revival*, 83, 116; Harrison, "Afghanistan's Tyranny of the Minority."

72 **Afghan National Army:** Harrison, "Afghanistan's Tyranny of the Minority"; see also Abbas, *The Taliban Revival*, 190–91.

72 **"[t]hey get the dollars":** Harrison, "Afghanistan's Tyranny of the Minority"; see also Siddique, *The Pashtun Question*, 206.

73 **grew increasingly alienated:** Siddique, *The Pashtun Question*, 16, 206.

73 **at the very bottom:** Ibid., 16.

73 **hiding in the mountains:** Abbas, *The Taliban Revival*, 77.

73 **turned our back:** Ibid., 86–88; Siddique, *The Pashtun Question*, 206.

73 **failed to implement:** Abbas, *The Taliban Revival*, 86–88; Siddique, *The Pashtun Question*, 206.

73 **extortions, rapes, gang robberies:** Coll, *Ghost Wars*, 282–83.

73 **corruption and lawlessness:** Abbas, *The Taliban Revival*, 86–88; Siddique, *The Pashtun Question*, 206.

73 **"The Taliban is out":** Tomsen, *The Wars of Afghanistan*, 588.

73 **By 2010, the Taliban:** Abbas, *The Taliban Revival*, 186.

73 **$650 billion on the war:** Siddique, *The Pashtun Question*, 205.

73 **43 percent:** Special Inspector General for Afghanistan Reconstruction, Quarterly Report to the United States Congress, January 30, 2017, 89–90.

73 **"the Taliban have":** Euan McKirdy and Ehsan Popalzai, "Afghan Troops Withdraw from Key Area in Fight with Taliban," CNN, March 24, 2017.

74 **the Pakistani Taliban:** Abbas, *The Taliban Revival*, 151; "Pakistan Taliban: Peshawar School Attack Leaves 141 Dead," BBC News, December 16, 2014.

74 **"not sufficiently studied":** Abbas, *The Taliban Revival*, 168–69.

74 **"The Pashtun Dilemma":** See, e.g., Siddique, *The Pashtun Question*; Sarwar, "Ashraf Ghani and the Pashtun Dilemma"; Tim Willasey-Wilsey, "The Return of the Pashtun Problem and NATO Withdrawal from Afghanistan in 2014," Gateway House, Indian Council on Global

Relations, June 18, 2012, http://www.gatewayhouse.in/return-pashtun
-problem-and-nato-withdrawal-afghanistan-2014.

Chapter Four: Iraq

75 **"A group of imams"**: Emma Sky, *The Unraveling: High Hopes and Missed Opportunities in Iraq* (New York: PublicAffairs, 2015), 35.

75 **"You don't kill"**: Sam Bailey, "Interview: General David Petraeus," *Frontline*, June 14, 2011, http://www.pbs.org/wgbh/frontline/article/interview-general-david-petraeu.

75 **Germany and Japan:** See President George W. Bush, speech to American Enterprise Institute, Washington, DC, February 26, 2003, https://georgewbush-whitehouse.archives.gov/news/releases/2003/02/20030226-11.html; Peter R. Mansoor, *Surge: My Journey with General David Petraeus and the Remaking of the Iraq War* (New Haven, CT: Yale University Press, 2013), 6; Sky, *The Unraveling*, 56.

75 **"There was a time"**: Bush, speech to American Enterprise Institute.

76 **"We will help"**: President George W. Bush, remarks at Whitehall Palace, London, November 19, 2003, http://www.presidency.ucsb.edu/ws/?pid=812.

76 **"The rise of freedom"**: President George W. Bush, speech at Fort Bragg, North Carolina, June 28, 2005, https://www.theguardian.com/world/2005/jun/29/iraq.usa.

76 **"the streets in Basra"**: "Eyes on Iraq; In Cheney's Words: The Administration Case for Removing Saddam Hussein," *New York Times*, August 27, 2002 (excerpts from Vice President Richard Cheney's speech at the Veterans of Foreign Wars National Convention, Nashville, TN, August 26, 2002) (quoting Fouad Ajami).

76 **"the freedom-loving peoples"**: Ibid.

76 **"sneaking hundreds of"**: Michael R. Gordon and General Bernard E. Trainor, *Cobra II: The Inside Story of the Invasion and Occupation of Iraq* (New York: Pantheon Books, 2006), 137.

76 **The problem was:** Amy Chua, *World on Fire: How Exporting Free Market Democracy Breeds Ethnic Hatred and Global Instability* (New York: Anchor Books, 2004), Afterword to the Anchor edition, 90.

77 **Like Iraq, Yugoslavia:** See ibid., 170–72; Tim Judah, *The Serbs: History, Myth and the Destruction of Yugoslavia* (New Haven, CT: Yale University Press, 1997), chapters 8 and 9; Stephen Engelberg, "Carving Out a Greater Serbia," *New York Times*, September 1, 1991; Tom Hundley, "Bosnia's Mixed Marriages Bear Special Burden," *Chicago Tribune*, September 8, 1996.

77 **But when democratization:** Chua, *World on Fire*, 172–74; Judah, *The Serbs*, 165, 180–81, 192, 225–41; Barbara Crosette, "U.N. Details Its Failure to Stop '95 Bosnia Massacre," *New York Times*, November 16, 1999.

77 **"We will kill Croats"**: Johanna McGeary, "Face to Face with Evil," *Time*, May 13, 1996, 46.

78 **In 2003, Iraq too:** Chua, *World on Fire*, 290; George Packer, "The Lesson of Tal Afar," *New Yorker*, April 10, 2006.

78 **roughly 15 percent:** John Hartley, "Post Election Iraq: A Case for Declining Optimism," in *Beyond the Iraq War: The Promises, Pitfalls and Perils of External Interventionism*, ed. Michael Heazle and Iyanatul Islam (Cheltenham, UK: Edward Elgar Publishing, 2006), 95; Peter Mansfield, *A History of the Middle East*, 4th ed. rev. by Nicolas Pelham (New York: Penguin Books, 2013), 441; Vali Nasr, *The Shia Revival: How Conflicts within Islam Will Shape the Future* (New York: W. W. Norton, 2006), 90–93; Yaroslav Trofimov, "After Minority Rule, Iraq's Sunnis Refuse Minority Role," *Wall Street Journal*, April 9, 2015.

78 **Shias comprised . . . slums:** Marion Farouk-Sluglett and Peter Sluglett, *Iraq Since 1958: From Revolution to Dictatorship* (London: KPI, 1987), 190–91; see also Jon Lee Anderson, "Out on the Street," *New Yorker*, November 15, 2004.

78 **Sunnis had dominated:** R. Stephen Humphreys, *Between Memory and Desire: The Middle East in a Troubled Age* (Berkeley: University of California Press, 1999), 78, 120; Bernard Lewis, *The Middle East: A Brief History of the Last 2,000 Years* (New York: Scribner, 1995), 114; Nasr, *The Shia Revival*, 90; Farouk-Sluglett and Sluglett, *Iraq Since 1958*, 192; William R. Polk, *Understanding Iraq: The Whole Sweep of Iraqi History, from Genghis Khan's Mongols to the Ottoman Turks to the British Mandate to the American Occupation* (London: I. B. Tauris, 2005), 121; Sky, *The Unraveling*, 38.

78 **the Baath Party:** Nasr, *The Shia Revival*, 186–87; see also John Keegan, *The Iraq War* (New York: Alfred A. Knopf, 2004), 43; Farouk-Sluglett and Sluglett, *Iraq Since 1958*, 197–98, 205–6.

78 **almost cultlike leader:** Farouk-Sluglett and Sluglett, *Iraq Since 1958*, 184, 229.

79 **filled the ranks:** Ibid., 206–7, 229; Sky, *The Unraveling*, 39.

79 **own hometown and clan:** Farouk-Sluglett and Sluglett, *Iraq Since 1958*, 206–7, 229; Sky, *The Unraveling*, 39.

79 **nationalized oil company:** Farouk-Sluglett and Sluglett, *Iraq Since 1958*, 229–30.

79 **rising influence of Shia:** See Saïd K. Aburish, *Saddam Hussein: The Politics of Revenge* (New York: Bloomsbury, 2000), 70–71, 122–23, 183–84; Farouk-Sluglett and Sluglett, *Iraq Since 1958*, 195–200.

79 **large Shia population:** Aburish, *Saddam Hussein*, 122; Alex Edwards, *"Dual Containment" Policy in the Persian Gulf: The USA, Iran, and Iraq, 1991–2000* (New York: Palgrave Macmillan, 2014), 45.

79 **banned Shia . . . executed:** Nasr, *The Shia Revival*, 186–87; Farouk-Sluglett and Sluglett, *Iraq Since 1958*, 197–200.

79 **Entire Shia villages:** Chris Hedges, "In a Remote Southern Marsh, Iraq Is Strangling the Shiites," *New York Times*, November 16, 1993.

79   **hundreds of thousands:** Mansfield, *A History of the Middle East*, 387; Polk, *Understanding Iraq*, 121–22.

79   **Saddam retaliated mercilessly:** John Kifner, "After the War; Iraqi Refugees Tell U.S. Soldiers of Brutal Repression of Rebellion," *New York Times*, March 28, 1991; Aburish, *Saddam Hussein*, 311–12.

79   **long-oppressed 60 percent:** Chua, *World on Fire*, 290.

79   **"There is not a history":** Paul Waldman, "On Iraq, Let's Ignore Those Who Got It All Wrong," *Washington Post*, June 13, 2014.

80   **"Most Arab countries":** David Corn, "Kristol Clear at Time," *Nation*, January 2, 2007.

80   **"[t]here has been":** Statement of Paul Wolfowitz, deputy secretary of defense, *Department of Defense Budget Priorities for Fiscal Year 2004: Hearing Before the House Committee on the Budget*, 108th Cong., February 27, 2003, 9, 39.

80   **"[O]ne can predict":** Noah Feldman, *What We Owe Iraq: War and the Ethics of Nation Building* (Princeton, NJ: Princeton University Press, 2004), 49.

80   **Sunni insurgents began:** See Thabit A. I. Abdullah, *A Short History of Iraq*, 2nd ed. (Harlow, UK: Longman, 2011), 165; Special Inspector General for Iraq Reconstruction, *Hard Lessons: The Iraq Reconstruction Experience* (Washington, DC: U.S. Government Printing Office, 2009), 59–60; Sky, *The Unraveling*, xi; see also John Diamond, "Prewar Intelligence Predicted Iraqi Insurgency," *USA Today*, October 24, 2004.

80–81 **Only one . . . "if they supported":** Abdullah, *A Short History of Iraq*, 162–63.

81   **"in the top four ranks":** Sky, *The Unraveling*, 56.

81   **de-Baathification "reinforced Sunnis' fears":** General Stanley McChrystal, *My Share of the Task: A Memoir* (New York: Penguin, 2014), 112.

81   **stripped the country . . . Hospitals found themselves:** Special Inspector General for Iraq Reconstruction, *Hard Lessons*, 74; Anderson, "Out on the Street."

81   **disbanding the entire:** Abdullah, *A Short History of Iraq*, 163; Miranda Sissons and Abdulrazzaq Al-Saiedi, "A Bitter Legacy: Lessons of De-Baathification in Iraq," International Center for Transitional Justice, March 2013, 21; Anderson, "Out on the Street"; see also Thomas E. Ricks, *Fiasco: The American Military Adventure in Iraq* (New York: Penguin Press, 2006), 78–79; Dexter Filkins, "Did George W. Bush Create ISIS?," *New Yorker*, May 15, 2015.

81   **some 250,000 to 350,000:** Filkins, "Did George W. Bush Create ISIS?" (250,000); Abdullah, *A Short History of Iraq*, 163 (350,000).

81   **Many of these men:** Anderson, "Out on the Street"; Filkins, "Did George W. Bush Create ISIS?"

81   **one expert estimated:** Davide Mastracci, "How the 'Catastrophic' American Decision to Disband Saddam's Military Helped Fuel the Rise of ISIL," *National Post*, May 23, 2015, http://news.nationalpost.com/news

/world/how-the-catastrophic-american-decision-to-disband-saddams
-military-helped-fuel-the-rise-of-isil.

81   **the U.S. solution:** Chua, *World on Fire*, 291; Mansoor, *Surge*, 25; George
     Packer, *The Assassins' Gate: America in Iraq* (New York: Farrar, Straus &
     Giroux, 2005), 358.

82   **With practically no:** Special Inspector General for Iraq Reconstruction,
     Hard Lessons, 116.

82   **"[t]he most organized":** David Rohde, "After the War: Occupation;
     Iraqis Were Set to Vote, but U.S. Wielded a Veto," *New York Times,* June
     19, 2003; see also Special Inspector General for Iraq Reconstruction,
     Hard Lessons, 116.

82   **"remarkable transformation" . . . "hundreds of parties":** President
     George W. Bush, speech to World Affairs Council, Philadelphia, Penn-
     sylvania, December 12, 2005, http://www.cnn.com/2005/POLITICS
     /12/12/bush.transcript.philly.speech.

82   **the political parties:** Abdullah, *A Short History of Iraq,* 168–70.

82   **Shias voted for Shias:** See ibid., 169–70. Iraq's Sunnis mostly boycotted
     the January 2005 elections; they voted in the December 2005 elections—
     but overwhelmingly for Sunnis. Ibid., 169; see also Packer, *The Assassins'
     Gate,* 438–39; Peter Beaumont, Rory McCarthy, and Paul Harris, "End of
     Iraq's Nightmare . . . or the Start," *Guardian,* January 22, 2005.

82   **"The elections hardened":** Thomas E. Ricks, "Petraeus Cites Errors in
     Iraq," *Washington Post,* January 23, 2007.

82   **roaming Shia death squads:** See "Iraq's Death Squads," *Washington Post,*
     December 4, 2005; Erwin Decker, "Iraq Woes: Death Squads Terrorize
     Baghdad," *Spiegel,* March 16, 2006, http://www.spiegel.de/international
     /spiegel/iraq-woes-death-squads-terrorize-baghdad-a-406342.html.

83   **declared "all-out war":** "Al-Zarqawi Declares War on Iraqi Shia," Al
     Jazeera, September 14, 2005, http://www.aljazeera.com/archive/2005
     /09/200849143727698709.html; Jackie Spinner and Bassam Sebti,
     "Militant Declares War on Iraqi Vote," *Washington Post,* January 24, 2005.

83   **twenty Sunni mosques:** Ellen Knickmeyer and K. I. Ibrahim, "Bombing
     Shatters Mosque in Iraq," *Washington Post,* February 23, 2006; Mansoor,
     Surge, 28.

83   **More than a thousand:** Ellen Knickmeyer, "Blood on Our Hands,"
     Foreign Policy, October 25, 2010.

83   **Sunni-Shia civil war:** Michael Crowley, "How the Fate of One Holy Site
     Could Plunge Iraq Back into Civil War," *Time,* June 26, 2014, http://time
     .com/2920692/iraq-isis-samarra-al-askari-mosque.

83   **in "exit-strategy" mode:** Packer, "The Lesson of Tal Afar"; Thomas E.
     Ricks, *The Gamble: General David Petraeus and the American Military Adventure
     in Iraq, 2006–2008* (New York: Penguin Press, 2009), 12–13.

83   **FOBs:** Packer, "The Lesson of Tal Afar"; Ricks, *The Gamble,* 12–13.

83   **"We're here to guard":** Packer, "The Lesson of Tal Afar."

84 **success . . . twenty thousand additional:** Mansoor, *Surge,* 55, 277–82; Sky, *The Unraveling,* 177, 212, 225; see also Michael E. O'Hanlon, *The Future of Land Warfare* (Washington, DC: Brookings Institution Press, 2015), 142.

84 **spin and finger-pointing:** See, e.g., Jeffrey M. Jones, "Iraq War Attitudes Politically Polarized," Gallup, April 8, 2008, http://www.gallup.com /poll/106309/iraq-war-attitudes-politically-polarized.aspx; "Democrats, Republicans, and Political Fault Lines on Iraq," Council on Foreign Relations, May 18, 2007, https://www.cfr.org/backgrounder/democrats -republicans-and-political-fault-lines-iraq; Peter Beinart, "The Surge Fallacy," *Atlantic,* September 2015; Alex Kingsbury, "Why the 2007 Surge in Iraq Actually Failed," *Boston Globe,* November 17, 2014.

84 **sent primarily to Baghdad:** Mansoor, *Surge,* 68, 278–79.

84 **a 180-degree shift:** Ricks, *The Gamble,* 27, 29–30.

84 **ethnically conscious policies:** Mansoor, *Surge,* xii, 126–27, 130–31, 269; Sky, *The Unraveling,* 177–92.

84 **city of Tal Afar:** Packer, "The Lesson of Tal Afar"; see also Ricks, *The Gamble,* 50–51.

84–85 **"When we came":** Packer, "The Lesson of Tal Afar."

85 **one that tried to understand:** Mansoor, *Surge,* 24–25; Packer, "The Lesson of Tal Afar."

85 **McMaster required his troops:** Packer, "The Lesson of Tal Afar."

85 **"[T]he regiment bought":** Ibid.

85 **"hajjis," for Arabs:** Ibid.

85 **"Every time you":** Ricks, *The Gamble,* 60.

85 **Arabic language classes:** Packer, "The Lesson of Tal Afar."

85 **McMaster sent his troops:** Ricks, *The Gamble,* 61; Packer, "The Lesson of Tal Afar."

86 **spent forty to fifty . . . "first the Shiite":** Packer, "The Lesson of Tal Afar."

86 **McMaster began building alliances:** Ibid.; see also Mansoor, *Surge,* 24–25.

86 **first successful . . . lonely bright spot:** Ricks, *The Gamble,* 50–51, 59–60; Mansoor, *Surge,* 24.

86 **Drawing on McMaster's:** Mansoor, *Surge,* 127–28.

87 **"[A]nyone who was caught" . . . "The corpses":** Ibid., 124.

87 **al-Qaeda's senior leaders . . . executed:** Ibid., 124, 130, 132.

87 **"Sunni Awakening" . . . seized this opening:** Ibid., 126, 129–30; Sky, *The Unraveling,* 183–84.

87 **working closely with Sunni tribal sheikhs:** Mansoor, *Surge,* 129–33.

87 **"[o]ver countless cups" . . . roadside bomb:** Ibid., 129, 133.

87 **new local police:** Ibid., 129–30.

87 **"cultural savvy and local":** Ibid., 130.

88 **as anachronisms, as the CPA initially did:** Ibid., 11.

88 **dismissing their importance:** See Ricks, *The Gamble*, 219.

88 **"[t]ribal society makes up":** Ibid.

88 **then "gated" them:** Mansoor, *Surge*, 135.

88 **By November 2006:** Ibid., 132, 136.

88 **became blueprints for:** Ibid., xiii, 127–28, 133.

88 **Shia al-Askari mosque:** Ibid., ix.

88 **four hundred thousand Iraqis:** Anthony H. Cordesman with assistance from Emma R. Davies, *Iraq's Insurgency and the Road to Civil Conflict* (Westport, CT: Praeger Security International, 2008), 656.

88 **"well over fifty":** Mansoor, *Surge*, ix.

88 **using overwhelming force:** Ricks, *The Gamble*, 26.

89 **"An operation that kills":** Ibid., 29; see Mansoor, *Surge*, x, xii.

89 **the "big idea":** Mansoor, *Surge,* 136.

89 **"key to victory":** Frederick W. Kagan, *Choosing Victory: A Plan for Success in Iraq, Phase I Report*, Iraq Planning Group, American Enterprise Institute, 2007, 14.

89 **a color-coded map:** Ibid., 16, fig. 2.

89 **so-called "brain trust":** Mansoor, *Surge*, 202; see also Ricks, *The Gamble*, 18–19, 24–26; Packer, "The Lesson of Tal Afar."

89 **"cultural ineptitude" . . . "[I]f I could sum":** Packer, "The Lesson of Tal Afar."

89 **remarkable Emma Sky:** Alissa J. Rubin, "In Iraq, a Blunt Civilian Is a Fixture by the General's Side," *New York Times,* November 20, 2009.

90 **had "encyclopedic knowledge":** Sky, *The Unraveling*, 177.

90 **"rather than raiding":** Ricks, *The Gamble,* 28 (quoting from an essay on counterinsurgency strategy by Australian army Lt. Colonel David Kilcullen, which the U.S. military under Petraeus later largely followed); see also Sky, *The Unraveling,* 161–62, 209.

90 **"By living among":** Mansoor, *Surge*, 269.

90 **"the groups just shy":** McChrystal, *My Share of the Task*, 244.

90 **Experts today agree:** Mansoor, *Surge*, 267–68; see also Peter D. Feaver, "The Right to Be Right: Civil-Military Relations and the Iraq Surge Decision," *International Security* 35, no. 4 (2011): 92, n. 10; Stephen Biddle, Jeffrey A. Friedman, and Jacob N. Shapiro, "Testing the Surge: Why Did Violence Decline in Iraq in 2007?," *International Security* 37, no. 1 (2012): 1–34.

91 **"stopped fighting Iraq's":** Ricks, *The Gamble*, 219.

91 **civilian deaths fell:** Mansoor, *Surge*, 280.

91 **a tipping point occurred:** Ibid., 210.

91 **"in the past 8 months":** Ibid., 281.

91 **Undoing the effects:** Ibid., 166, 177.

92 **2005 national elections:** Dexter Filkins, "What We Left Behind," *New Yorker,* April 28, 2014.

92 **ultimately threw its weight:** Ibid.; Ali Khedery, "Why We Stuck with Maliki—and Lost Iraq," *Washington Post,* July 3, 2014.

92   **a devout Shia who had spent:** Steven R. Hurst, "Analysis: Iraq PM's Silence Telling," *Washington Post,* January 12, 2007; Filkins, "What We Left Behind."

92   **Maliki's grandfather was:** Filkins, "What We Left Behind."

92   **sentenced to death:** Linda Robinson, *Tell Me How This Ends: General David Petraeus and the Search for a Way Out of Iraq* (New York: PublicAffairs, 2008), 147.

92   **"arrested everyone who":** Filkins, "What We Left Behind."

93   **excluding, detaining, persecuting:** Abigail Hauslohner, "In Baghdad, Middle-Class Sunnis Say They Prefer Militants to Maliki," *Washington Post,* July 12, 2014; Priyanka Boghani, "In Their Own Words: Sunnis on Their Treatment in Maliki's Iraq," *Frontline,* October 28, 2014, http://www.pbs.org/wgbh/pages/frontline/iraq-war-on-terror/rise-of-isis/in-their-own-words-sunnis-on-their-treatment-in-malikis-iraq.

93   **He forced Sunnis:** Sky, *The Unraveling,* 360; Boghani, "In Their Own Words."

93   **"ensuring a strong":** Sky, *The Unraveling,* 360.

93   **were terrorizing Sunnis:** Mohamad Bazzi, "How Saddam Hussein's Execution Contributed to the Rise of Sectarianism in the Middle East," *Nation,* January 15, 2016.

93   **Maliki was a puppet:** Steven R. Hurst, "Iraqi Sunni Claims 'Genocide Campaign,'" *Washington Post,* August 13, 2007. According to Kenneth M. Pollack, "It cannot be said often enough that Maliki himself is NOT an Iranian puppet. He dislikes and distrusts the Iranians, and sees himself as a nationalist who would like to free Iraq from Iran's clutches." Kenneth M. Pollack, "Iraqi Elections, Iranian Interests," *Markaz,* Brookings Institution, April 4, 2014, https://www.brookings.edu/blog/markaz/2014/04/04/iraqi-elections-iranian-interests.

93   **A fantasy caliphate:** Robyn Creswell and Bernard Haykel, "Why Jihadists Write Poetry," *New Yorker,* June 8, 2015.

93   **An al-Qaeda offshoot:** Tim Lister, "How ISIS Is Overshadowing al Qaeda," CNN, June 30, 2014, http://www.cnn.com/2014/06/30/world/meast/isis-overshadows-al-qaeda/index.html.

93   **Sunnis who feel shut out:** William McCants, *The ISIS Apocalypse: The History, Strategy, and Doomsday Vision of the Islamic State* (New York: St. Martin's Press, 2015), 10, 157; Jessica Stern and J. M. Berger, *ISIS: The State of Terror* (New York: HarperCollins, 2015), 20, 29–31, 44–45; Michael Weiss and Hassan Hassan, *ISIS: Inside the Army of Terror* (New York: Regan Arts, 2015), xvi, 164.

94   **killing Shia "apostates":** Graeme Wood, "What ISIS Really Wants," *Atlantic,* March 2015; see also Stern and Berger, *ISIS,* 16.

94   **"Shiites should be executed." Bin Laden's mother:** Mary Anne Weaver, "The Short, Violent Life of Abu Musab al-Zarqawi," *Atlantic,* June 8, 2006; Weiss and Hassan, *ISIS,* 11–12; Stern and Berger, *ISIS,* 16.

94   **they often fear and hate:** See, e.g., Tim Arango, "Iraqis Who Fled Mosul Say They Prefer Militants to Government," *New York Times,* June 12, 2014;

Nour Malas and Ghassan Adnan, "Sunni Tribes in Iraq Divided Over Battle Against Islamic State," *Wall Street Journal,* May 22, 2015.

94 **Even affluent, well-educated:** Hauslohner, "In Baghdad, Middle-Class Sunnis Say They Prefer Militants to Maliki."

94 **forced out in 2014:** Martin Chulov, Luke Harding, and Dan Roberts, "Nouri al-Maliki Forced from Post as Iraq's Political Turmoil Deepens," *Guardian,* August 12, 2014.

94 **"Mr. Maliki is not to blame":** Stern and Berger, *ISIS,* 30–31 (quoting Patrick Cockburn).

94 **"remain[ed] supportive of":** Renad Mansour, "The Sunni Predicament in Iraq" (Washington, DC: Carnegie Middle East Center, March 3, 2016), http://carnegie-mec.org/2016/03/03/sunni-predicament-in-iraq-pub -62924 (internal citations omitted).

95 **$1 trillion ... 4,500 American lives ... Iran's power:** Tim Arango, "Iran Dominates in Iraq After U.S. 'Handed the Country Over,'" *New York Times,* July 15, 2017.

95 **Market capitalism ... Democracy:** Taken almost verbatim from Chua, *World on Fire,* 8–9.

96 **"The spread of free markets'":** Thomas L. Friedman, *The Lexus and the Olive Tree* (New York: Anchor Books, 2000), xvi.

96 **"tends to turn":** Ibid., 12.

96 **Instead of global peace:** See generally Chua, *World on Fire.*

97 **As America celebrated:** Taken almost verbatim from ibid., 10.

97 **The point is not:** Taken almost verbatim from ibid., 293–94.

Chapter Five: Terror Tribes

99 **Most serial murderers:** U.S. Department of Justice, Federal Bureau of Investigation, *Serial Killers: Multi-Disciplinary Perspectives for Investigators,* July 2008, 14.

99 **psychologists studying terrorism:** John Horgan, *The Psychology of Terrorism,* 2nd ed. (London and New York: Routledge, 2014), 51–60.

99 **terrorists are "narcissistic":** Ibid., 53, 56–57.

99 **"driven by depression":** Ibid., 32 (inner quotes omitted) (quoting Adam Lankford, *The Myth of Martyrdom: What Really Drives Suicide Bombers, Rampage Shooters, and Other Self-Destructive Killers* [New York: Palgrave Macmillan, 2013]).

99 **from low self-esteem:** Ibid., 53.

99 **had abusive childhoods:** Ibid., 54 (citing Nehemia Friedland, "Becoming a Terrorist: Social and Individual Antecedents," in *Terrorism: Roots, Impacts, Responses,* ed. Lawrence Howard [New York: Praeger, 1992], 82).

99 **"[t]he terrorist group":** Ibid., 52 (quoting Martha Crenshaw, "The Psychology of Political Terrorism," in *Political Psychology: Contemporary Problems and Issues,* ed. Margaret G. Hermann [San Francisco: Jossey-Bass, 1986], 387).

99 **"vitamin deficiencies" . . . "faulty ear":** Ibid., 54 (citing Walter Reich, "Understanding Terrorist Behavior: The Limits and Opportunities of Psychological Inquiry," in *Origins of Terrorism: Psychologies, Ideologies, Theologies, States of Mind,* ed. Walter Reich [New York: Cambridge University Press, 1990], 261–79).

100 **"societies where fantasies":** Ibid., 54.

100 **now been rejected:** Ibid., 51–60; Marc Sageman, *Leaderless Jihad: Terror Networks in the Twenty-First Century* (Philadelphia: University of Pennsylvania Press, 2008), 16–18.

100 **simply no reliable evidence:** Horgan, *The Psychology of Terrorism,* 59–61.

100 **as "lovely," "friendly":** Sam Greenhill and Keith Gladdis, "'He Was Friendly and Polite': Hairdresser Ex-Girlfriend of Terror Suspect Says Adebolajo Was a 'Normal, Regular Boy,'" *Daily Mail,* May 23, 2013.

100 **"very personable":** Sageman, *Leaderless Jihad,* 4.

100 **"a nice guy":** Emily Bazelon, "There's a Strong Consensus That He Was Pretty Normal," *Slate,* April 19, 2013, http://www.slate.com/articles/news_and_politics/crime/2013/04/dzhokhar_tsarnaev_seemed_like_a_nice_kid_two_high_school_classmates_remember.html.

100 **"terrorists are essentially":** Horgan, *The Psychology of Terrorism,* 59 (quoting Andrew Silke, "Cheshire-Cat Logic: The Recurring Theme of Terrorist Abnormality in Psychological Research," *Psychology, Crime & Law* 4 [1998]: 53).

100 **a *group* phenomenon:** Scott Atran, *Talking to the Enemy: Faith, Brotherhood, and the (Un)making of Terrorists* (New York: HarperCollins, 2010), 33, 179–81; Horgan, *The Psychology of Terrorism,* 105.

100 **Robbers Cave experiment:** Muzafer Sherif et al., *The Robbers Cave Experiment: Intergroup Conflict and Cooperation* (Middletown, CT: Wesleyan University Press, 1988), 14–48.

101–2 **Dan Kahan . . . those with stronger numeracy:** Dan Kahan et al., "Motivated Numeracy and Enlightened Self-Government," *Behavioural Public Policy* 1, no. 1 (2017): 54–86.

102 **climate change—and extended:** See Dan Kahan et al., "The Polarizing Impact of Science Literacy and Numeracy on Perceived Climate Change Risks," *Nature Climate Change* 2 (2012): 732–35; Lawrence C. Hamilton, Matthew J. Cutler, and Andrew Schaefer, "Public Knowledge and Concern About Polar-Region Warming," *Polar Geography* 35, no. 2 (2012): 155–68.

102 **The better informed . . . better educated:** See Kahan et al., "The Polarizing Impact of Science Literacy and Numeracy on Perceived Climate Change Risks," 732–35; Lawrence C. Hamilton, "Education, Politics and Opinions About Climate Change Evidence for Interaction Effects," *Climatic Change* 104, no. 2 (2011): 231–42; Brian Resnick, "7 Psychological Concepts That Explain the Trump Era of Politics," *Vox,* March 20, 2017,

http://www.vox.com/science-and-health/2017/3/20/14915076/7
-psychological-concepts-explain-trump-politics.

102　**In Solomon Asch's:** Solomon E. Asch, "Effects of Group Pressure upon the Modification and Distortion of Judgments," in *Groups, Leadership, and Men,* ed. Harold Guetzkow (New York: Russell & Russell Inc., 1963), 177–90.

103–4　**Robb Willer . . . "breaking the spell":** Robb Willer et al., "The False Enforcement of Unpopular Norms," *American Journal of Sociology* 115, no. 2 (2009): 451, 454, 462–69.

104　**experiments similar to Asch's:** See, e.g., Jolanda Jetten, Tom Postmes, and Brendan J. McAuliffe, "'We're *All* Individuals': Group Norms of Individualism and Collectivism, Levels of Identification and Identity Threat," *European Journal of Social Psychology* 32, no. 2 (2002): 189.

104　**"descends several rungs" . . . "a sentiment of invincible power":** Gustave Le Bon, *The Crowd: A Study of the Popular Mind,* 2nd ed. (Dunwoody, GA: Norman S. Berg, 1968), 9, 12–13.

104　**a physiological basis:** See, e.g., Ian Robertson, "The Science Behind ISIL's Savagery," *Telegraph* (UK), November 17, 2014; Mina Cikara and Susan T. Fiske, "Bounded Empathy: Neural Responses to Outgroup Targets' (Mis)Fortunes," *Journal of Cognitive Neuroscience* 23, no. 12 (2011): 3791–3803.

104–5　**"black flags" . . . "It is groups":** Robertson, "The Science Behind ISIL's Savagery."

105　**out-group homogeneity effect:** George Quattrone et al., "The Perception of Variability Within In-groups and Out-groups: Implications for the Law of Small Numbers," *Journal of Personality and Social Psychology* 38, no. 1 (1980): 141–52.

105　**with negative traits:** Yona Teichman, "The Development of Israeli Children's Images of Jews and Arabs and Their Expression in Human Figure Drawings," *Developmental Psychology* 37, no. 6 (2001): 749–61.

105　**less than human:** Ruth Gaunt, Jacques-Philippe Leyens, and Denis Sindic, "Motivated Reasoning and the Attribution of Emotions to Ingroup and Outgroup," *Revue Internationale de Psychologie Sociale* 17, no. 1 (2004): 5–20; Ruth Gaunt, Jacques-Philippe Leyens, and Stéphanie Demoulin, "Intergroup Relations and the Attribution of Emotions: Control Over Memory for Secondary Emotions Associated with the Ingroup and Outgroup," *Journal of Experimental Social Psychology* 38, no. 5 (2002): 508–14; Jacques-Philippe Leyens et al., "The Emotional Side of Prejudice: The Attribution of Secondary Emotions to Ingroups and Outgroups," *Personality and Social Psychology Review* 4, no. 2 (2000): 186–97.

105　**These effects have:** Gaunt, Leyens, and Demoulin, "Intergroup Relations and the Attribution of Emotions," 509 (Belgians and Arabs); Amy J. C. Cuddy, Mindi S. Rock, and Michael I. Norton, "Aid in the Aftermath of Hurricane Katrina: Inferences of Secondary Emotions and Intergroup

Helping," *Group Processes & Intergroup Relations* 10, no. 1 (2007): 107–18 (whites and blacks in New Orleans); Michael J. Wohl, Matthew J. Hornsey, and Shannon H. Bennett, "Why Group Apologies Succeed and Fail: Intergroup Forgiveness and the Role of Primary and Secondary Emotions," *Journal of Personality and Social Psychology* 102, no. 2 (2012): 306 (Canadians and Afghans).

106 **"significantly more aggressive":** Teichman, "The Development of Israeli Children's Images of Jews and Arabs and Their Expression in Human Figure Drawings," 756.

106 **Roughly 64 percent . . . "very happy":** Hujierat Mussa, "Attitudes Gaps to Jewish Out-Group and Arab In-Group as an Expression of the Self-Identity of the Arab Minority in Israel," *Journal of Social and Development Sciences* 1, no. 5 (2011): 173–82.

106 **"funny but respectful":** Ted Thornhill, "The Curly-Haired, Bearded Hipster from a Wealthy Family Who Has Become a Sword-Wielding ISIS Poster Boy," *Daily Mail* (UK), August 7, 2014.

106 **"hot girlfriend" . . . "Every guy dreams":** Mona El-Naggar, "From a Private School in Cairo to ISIS Killing Fields in Syria," *New York Times,* February 18, 2015.

106–7 **In 2012 . . . "poster boy":** Ibid.; Thornhill, "The Curly-Haired, Bearded Hipster."

107 **a gradual process:** Horgan, *The Psychology of Terrorism,* 99–100, 120–24, 132.

107 **"fell down in a black hole":** Ben Taub, "Journey to Jihad," *New Yorker,* June 1, 2015.

107 **Enter Sharia4Belgium:** Ibid.

108 **"selfless heroes" . . . "You sit for months":** Ibid.

108 **called "the palace":** Ibid.

108 **"He is the youngest emir":** Ibid.

109 **Hundreds of Western women:** Katrin Bennhold, "Jihad and Girl Power: How ISIS Lured 3 London Girls," *New York Times,* August 17, 2015.

109 **wives stood guard:** William McCants, *The ISIS Apocalypse* (New York: St. Martin's Press, 2015), 114.

109 **"In this world":** Bennhold, "Jihad and Girl Power."

109 **"world's richest terrorist group" . . . millions of dollars a day:** Amanda Macias and Jeremy Bender, "Here's How the World's Richest Terrorist Group Makes Millions Every Day," *Business Insider,* August 27, 2014, http://www.businessinsider.com/isis-worlds-richest-terrorist-group -2014-8; Sarah Almukhtar, "ISIS Finances Are Strong," *New York Times,* May 19, 2015.

109 **"We have here mujahideen":** McCants, *The ISIS Apocalypse,* 101.

109 **"court poets" . . . "jihadi power couple":** Robyn Creswell and Bernard Haykel, "Battle Lines," *New Yorker,* June 8, 2015.

110 ***Their bullets shattered:*** Ibid.

110 ***Ask Mosul, city of Islam:*** Ibid.

110–11 she wrote a thirty-page essay: Ibid.

111 "the root cause": David Sterman, "Don't Dismiss Poverty's Role in Terrorism Yet," *Time,* February 4, 2015.

111 inherited $25 million: Rohan Gunaratna, *Inside Al-Qaeda: Global Network of Terror* (New York: Columbia University Press, 2002), 19.

111 has a Ph.D.: William McCants, "The Believer," Brookings, September 1, 2015, http://www.brookings.edu/content/research/essays/2015/the believer.

112 low per capita national income: Alberto Abadie, "Poverty, Political Freedom, and the Roots of Terrorism," *American Economic Review* 96, no. 2 (2006): 50–56.

112 individual poverty does not predict: Christopher Shea, "Another Blow to the Poverty-Causes-Terrorism Thesis," *Wall Street Journal,* August 9, 2012; Graeme Blair et al., "Poverty and Support for Militant Politics: Evidence from Pakistan," *American Journal of Political Science* 57, no. 1 (2013): 30–48.

112 Tamil Tigers of Sri Lanka: See Shri D. R. Kaarthikeyan, "Root Causes of Terrorism?: A Case Study of the Tamil Insurgency and the LTTE," in *Root Causes of Terrorism: Myths, Reality and Ways Forward,* ed. Tore Bjørgo (London: Routledge, 2005), 132 (noting that Tamil terrorism was "[b]orn out of discrimination, bred under oppression and strengthened through orchestrated state violence" against Sri Lanka's Tamil minority); see generally Gamini Samaranayake, "Political Terrorism of the Liberation Tigers of Tamil Eelam (LTTE) in Sri Lanka," *South Asia: Journal of South Asian Studies* 30, no. 1 (2007): 172 ("The causes which have contributed to the political terrorism of the LTTE need to be viewed in the context of the ongoing ethnic conflict between the Sinhalese, who comprise 74.5 percent of the population, and the Sri Lankan or indigenous Tamils who comprise 12.5 percent"); Robert A. Pape, *Dying to Win: The Strategic Logic of Suicide Terrorism* (New York: Random House, 2005), 31, 139–47.

112 Chechen separatists in Russia: See James Hughes, *Chechnya: From Nationalism to Jihad* (Philadelphia: University of Pennsylvania Press, 2007), 10 (describing the "colonial enmity in the Russian-Chechen relationship" and Stalin's "genocidal deportation" of the entire Chechen population to Central Asia in 1944 as "a defining event" for Chechens); Mariya Yevsyukova, "The Conflict Between Russia and Chechnya" (working paper no. 95-5[1], Conflict Research Consortium, Department of Sociology, University of Colorado, Boulder, 1995), http://www.colorado.edu/conflict /full_text_search/AllCRCDocs/95-5.htm ("The notion of humiliation and respect played a significant role [in the Chechen conflict] . . . [The Chechens] have fought for their independence for centuries").

112 Nigeria's Boko Haram: See Daniel Egiegba Agbiboa, "Why Boko Haram Exists: The Relative Deprivation Perspective," *African Conflict and Peacebuilding Review* 3, no. 1 (2013): 144, 151 (noting that Boko Haram has been fueled by the fact that "the wealthy elite throughout the country tend to be Christian, while the most impoverished communities in the country" are found among primarily Muslim ethnic groups); Seth G. Jones et al., *Rolling Back the Islamic State* (Santa Monica, CA: RAND Corporation, 2017), 126, https://www.rand.org/pubs/research_reports /RR1912.html (To aid with recruitment, "Boko Haram . . . play[s] on Kanuri perceptions that they are disadvantaged relative to other Nigerians, including southern Christians and Hausa- and Fulani-speaking Muslims"); see also Mike Smith, *Boko Haram: Inside Nigeria's Unholy War* (New York: I. B. Tauris, 2015), 62; Adaobi Tricia Nwaubani, "The Karma of Boko Haram," *New York Times,* February 22, 2015.

112 **militant Islamic movements:** See, e.g., Fawaz A. Gerges, *Journey of the Jihadist: Inside Muslim Militancy* (New York: Harcourt, 2006), 11, 32, 40, 43, 49; Pape, *Dying to Win*, 31, 117–19, 129–33.

112 **But when stark inequalities:** See Martha Crenshaw, "The Causes of Terrorism," *Comparative Politics* 13, no. 4 (1981): 383 ("The first condition that can be considered a direct cause of terrorism is the existence of concrete grievances among an identifiable subgroup of a larger population, such as an ethnic minority discriminated against by the majority"); see also Ted Robert Gurr, "Why Men Rebel Redux: How Valid Are Its Arguments Forty Years On?," E-International Relations, November 17, 2011, http://www.e-ir.info/2011/11/17/why-men-rebel-redux-how-valid-are-its-arguments-40-years-on ("It is not enough to point to big economic and social structures as the 'explanation.' . . . it is not sufficient, maybe not even important, to analyze the abstract content of ideologies. . . . Group identity is more important: What are people's clan, ethnic, religious, and political identities? With what people do they feel kindred, what networks of social interaction and communication connect them? The politics of identity are central to understanding people's reference group, their sense of collective injustice, and their susceptibility to appeals for political action").

112 **will often be led by the better situated:** See, e.g., Laurence R. Iannaccone and Eli Berman, "Religious Extremism: The Good, the Bad, and the Deadly," *Public Choice* 128 (2006): 109–29; Shelley A. Kirkpatrick and Edwin A. Locke, "Leadership: Do Traits Matter?," *Executive* 5, no. 2 (1991): 48, 49–50, 55; J. Michael Crant and Thomas S. Bateman, "Charismatic Leadership Viewed from Above: The Impact of Proactive Personality," *Journal of Organizational Behavior* 21, no. 1 (2000): 63, 66, 69, 72; Jessie Bernard, "Political Leadership Among North American Indians," *American Journal of Sociology* 34, no. 2 (1928): 296, 301–313; Ted Robert Gurr, *Why Men Rebel* (Princeton, NJ: Princeton University Press, 2011), 336–37.

113 **Inspired by Sayyid Qutb:** Gerges, *Journey of the Jihadist*, 35–37, 202–3; Paul Berman, "The Philosopher of Islamic Terror," *New York Times,* March 22, 2003.

NOTES

113 **"the head of the snake"... "Great Satan":** Gerges, *Journey of the Jihadist*, 22.

113 **"[T]he United States":** "Jihad Against Jews and Crusaders," February 23, 1998, https://fas.org/irp/world/para/docs/980223-fatwa.htm.

114 **"simpletons who have deluded":** McCants, *The ISIS Apocalypse*, 128.

114 **calling for all Shias:** Graeme Wood, "What ISIS Really Wants," *Atlantic*, March 2015.

114 **"[T]he time has come":** Karl Vick, "ISIS Militants Declare Islamist 'Caliphate,'" *Time*, June 29, 2014.

114 **"gather around your khalifah":** "This Is the Promise of Allah" (ISIS propaganda document), http://ia902505.us.archive.org/28/items/poa_25984/EN.pdf.

115 **They offer their members:** George Packer, "Why ISIS Murdered Kenji Goto," *New Yorker*, February 3, 2015; David D. Kirkpatrick, "New Freedoms in Tunisia Drive Support for ISIS," *New York Times*, October 21, 2014; Yaroslav Trofimov, "Islamic State's Scariest Success: Attracting Western Newcomers," *Wall Street Journal*, February 26, 2015.

115 **"what inspires ... is not":** Scott Atran, "Mindless Terrorists? The Truth about ISIS is Much Worse," *Guardian*, November 15, 2015.

115 **"almost never kill":** Atran, *Talking to the Enemy*, 33.

115 **"The Spanish authorities":** Ibid., 52–53.

Chapter Six: Venezuela

117 **"[A] trumpet tootles":** Rachel Nolan, "The Realest Reality Show in the World," *New York Times Magazine*, May 4, 2012.

117 **largest proven oil reserves:** CIA, "Country Comparison: Crude Oil—Proved Reserves," *The World Factbook*, accessed May 11, 2017, https://www.cia.gov/library/publications/the-world-factbook/rankorder/2244rank.html.

117 **funded his opposition:** Mark Weisbrot, "U.S. Support for Regime Change in Venezuela Is a Mistake," *Guardian*, February 18, 2014; Mark Eric Williams, "The New Balancing Act: International Relations Theory and Venezuela's Foreign Policy," in *The Revolution in Venezuela: Social and Political Change Under Chávez*, ed. Thomas Ponniah and Jonathan Eastwood (Cambridge, MA: Harvard University Press, 2011), 257.

117 **turned to Russia and China:** Editorial Board, "Latin America's 'Pink Tide' Is Fading Fast," *Chicago Tribune*, May 10, 2016.

117 **called President George W. Bush the "devil":** Ibid.

118 **Venezuela was not foremost:** Williams, "The New Balancing Act," 272.

118 **more international beauty queens:** Matt Roper, "Butt Implants Aged 12," *Daily Mail* (UK), December 12, 2014; Kate Briquelet, "Inside the Beauty Pageant Mills of Venezuela," *New York Post*, January 25, 2015; see also Marcia Ochoa, *Queen for a Day: Transformistas, Beauty Queens, and the Performance of Femininity in Venezuela* (Durham, NC: Duke University Press, 2014), 7 ("Venezuela has produced eleven title winners in the Miss

253

Universe and Miss World beauty pageants alone and winning entrants in a score of other international beauty pageants.").

118 **two thirds . . . intestines:** Roper, "Butt Implants Aged 12."

118 **Irene Sáez, a Miss Venezuela:** Elizabeth Gackstetter Nichols, *Beauty, Virtue, Power, and Success in Venezuela, 1850–2015* (Lanham, MD: Lexington Books, 2016), 141–45; Kathy Kiely, "A Beauty Queen Who Would Be Prez," *New York Daily News*, October 13, 1997.

119 **Sáez was a six-foot-one-inch:** Bart Jones, "Miss Universe–Turned–Politician Wows Voters," Associated Press, February 11, 1996; Nichols, *Beauty, Virtue, Power, and Success in Venezuela, 1850–2015*, 141.

119 **"big mouth" . . . "because it's African":** Cecily Hilleary, "Are Race and Class at the Root of Venezuela's Political Crisis?," *Voice of America News*, April 6, 2014.

119 **After sweeping to power:** Amy Chua, *World on Fire: How Exporting Free Market Democracy Breeds Ethnic Hatred and Global Instability* (New York: Anchor Books, 2003), 142–45; "Hugo Chávez Ramps Up Nationalisation Drive in Venezuela," *Telegraph* (UK), October 11, 2010; Simon Romero, "Chávez Seizes Assets of Oil Contractors," *New York Times*, May 8, 2009. See generally David Smilde and Daniel Hellinger, ed., *Venezuela's Bolivarian Democracy* (Durham, NC: Duke University Press, 2011).

119 **political instability . . . led to billions:** See Mark Weisbrot, "Venezuela in the Chávez Years: Its Economy and Influence on the Region," in Ponniah and Eastwood, *The Revolution in Venezuela*, 195; "Consolidating Power in Venezuela," *New York Times*, August 2, 2000.

119 **some spectacular successes:** "How Did Venezuela Change Under Hugo Chávez?," *Guardian*, October 4, 2012.

119 **in 2005, with the cooperation:** David Sharp, "Venezuela's Troubles Put U.S. Heating Oil Charity in Limbo," Associated Press, March 21, 2017.

119 **Today, however, Venezuela:** William Finnegan, "Venezuela, a Failing State," *New Yorker*, November 14, 2016; Nicholas Casey, "No Food, No Medicine, No Respite," *New York Times*, December 25, 2016.

120 **with criminal elements:** Moisés Naím, "Nicolas Maduro Doesn't Really Control Venezuela," *Atlantic*, May 25, 2017.

120 **Grief-stricken parents are:** Peter Walker, "We're Living in the End of Times," *Independent* (UK), December 16, 2016.

120 **highest murder rates:** Ioan Grillo and Jorge Benezra, "Venezuela's Murder Epidemic Rages on Amid State of Emergency," *Time*, May 20, 2016; Jim Wyss and Joey Flechas, "Beauty Queen Murder Shines Light on Venezuelan Violence," *Miami Herald*, January 7, 2014.

120 **life on Mars:** Erik Hayden, "Chávez: Capitalism Killed Life on Mars," *Atlantic*, March 22, 2011.

120 **thug-buffoon . . . threatening to spread:** See Franklin Foer, "The Talented Mr. Chávez," *Atlantic*, May 2006.

121 **"there is no racism" . . . "everyone is a *mestizo*":** Hilleary, "Are Race and Class at the Root of Venezuela's Political Crisis?"; George Ciccariello-Maher, *We Created Chávez: A People's History of the Venezuelan Revolution* (Durham, NC: Duke University Press, 2013), 153; Chua, *World on Fire*, 49–50, 142–44.

121 **Latin American society is:** This section on pigmentocracy in Latin America is taken almost verbatim from Chua, *World on Fire*, 57–59.

121 **"beautiful, and not":** Magnus Mörner, *Race Mixture in the History of Latin America* (Boston: Little, Brown and Company, 1967), 24.

121 **"[v]ery handsome and":** Ibid., 22.

121 **"the Spanish Conquest":** Ibid., 22–23.

122 **Intermarriage, concubinage, and polygamy:** Ibid., 25–26.

122 **Spaniard and Indian:** This list was compiled by Magnus Mörner in ibid., 58–59. My discussion of pigmentocracy and the Society of Castes draws heavily on Mörner, especially ibid., 1–2, 21–27, 53–68.

123 **That the Spaniards:** Ibid., 13.

123 **"pure white" . . . "impure, atavistically":** Ibid., 41–43, 60, 99, 140–41; Magnus Mörner, *The Andean Past* (New York: Columbia University Press, 1985), 181; David Bushnell and Neill Macaulay, *The Emergence of Latin America in the Nineteenth Century* (New York: Oxford University Press, 1988), 5.

123 **one hundred thousand:** Jesús María Herrera Salas, "Ethnicity and Revolution: The Political Economy of Racism in Venezuela," *Latin American Perspectives* 32, no. 2 (2005): 74.

123 **more than half:** Richard Gott, "Latin America as a White Settler Society," *Bulletin of Latin American Research* 26, no. 2 (2007): 278–79.

124 **"the constant" . . . to "whiten" Venezuela:** Salas, "Ethnicity and Revolution," 75, 78; Hilleary, "Are Race and Class at the Root of Venezuela's Political Crisis?"; see also Gott, "Latin America as a White Settler Society," 269, 284.

124 **After World War II:** Hilleary, "Are Race and Class at the Root of Venezuela's Political Crisis?"; Gott, "Latin America as a White Settler Society," 287.

124 **"slowed the longstanding":** Clarence J. Munford, *Race and Reparations: A Black Perspective for the 21st Century* (Trenton, NJ: Africa World Press, Inc.), 181.

124 **"[I]n Venezuela we complain":** Salas, "Ethnicity and Revolution," 72 (quoting Hans Neumann).

124 **hid the fact:** Ibid., 78, 86.

124 **80 percent:** Reynaldo Trombetta, "In Venezuela 82% of People Live in Poverty—Where Are Our Friends Now?," *Guardian*, April 5, 2017.

125 **"the most perfect":** Nichols, *Beauty, Virtue, Power, and Success in Venezuela, 1850–2015*, 141.

125 ***pelo malo* (bad hair):** Jasmine Garsd, "'Pelo Malo' Is a Rare Look into

Latin American Race Relations," NPR, December 10, 2014, http://www
.npr.org/2014/12/10/369645207/pelo-malo-is-a-rare-look-into-latin
-american-race-relations; see Ochoa, *Queen for a Day*, 34–37.

125 **Many black, indigenous:** Ochoa, *Queen for a Day*, 34, 37.

125 **they controlled not only:** Chua, *World on Fire*, 142; Nikolas Kozloff,
Hugo Chávez: Oil, Politics, and the Challenge to the United States (New York:
Palgrave Macmillan, 2006), 8, 11, 20, 27–29 (oil); Fernando Coronil,
"State Reflections: The 2002 Coup Against Hugo Chavez," in Ponniah
and Eastwood, *The Revolution in Venezuela*, 42, 45 (media); Gregory Wilpert, "Venezuela's Experiment in Participatory Democracy," in Ponniah
and Eastwood, *The Revolution in Venezuela*, 100 (politics); see also David
Theo Goldberg, *The Threat of Race: Reflections on Racial Neoliberalism* (Malden, MA: Blackwell, 2009), 226; Barry Cannon, "Class/Race Polarisa-
tion in Venezuela and the Electoral Success of Hugo Chávez: A Break
with the Past or the Song Remains the Same?," *Third World Quarterly* 29,
no. 4 (2008): 736–37.

126 **"In Venezuela there are":** Verbatim from Chua, *World on Fire*, 142.

126 **elected Hugo Chávez:** See Miguel Tinker Salas, *Venezuela: What Everyone
Needs to Know* (New York: Oxford University Press, 2015), 135.

126 **"the Indian from Barinas":** Larry Rohter, "Chávez Shaping Country to
His Vision," *New York Times,* July 28, 2000.

126 **"Hate against me":** Hilleary, "Are Race and Class at the Root of Venezuela's Political Crisis?"

126 **with "thick mouths" . . . "He is one":** Taken almost verbatim from Chua,
World on Fire, 142.

126 **called Chávez "El Negro":** Hilleary, "Are Race and Class at the Root of
Venezuela's Political Crisis?"; Ciccariello-Maher, *We Created Chávez*,
159–60.

126 **"Death to the Monkey":** Salas, "Ethnicity and Revolution," 84.

126–7 **new constitution . . . Law Against Racial Discrimination:** "Tackling Racism in Venezuela to Build a Society of Equals," *Telesur*, March 20, 2015,
http://www.telesurtv.net/english/analysis/Tackling-Racism-In-Venezuela
-to-Build-a-Society-of-Equals—20150319-0032.html; Dan Kovalik, "The
Venezuelan Revolution & the Indigenous Struggle," *Huffington Post*, October 15, 2014, http://www.huffingtonpost.com/dan-kovalik/the-venezue
lan-revolution_b_5989882.html.

127 **"[t]he rich people":** Hilleary, "Are Race and Class at the Root of Venezuela's Political Crisis?"

127 **"movement demanding that":** Ibid.; see also Ciccariello-Maher, *We Created Chávez*, 155–57.

127 **"his enthusiastic willingness":** Moisés Naím, "The Venezuelan Story:
Revisiting the Conventional Wisdom," *Vcrisis*, April 2001, http://www
.vcri sis.com/?content=analysis/moises1001); see also Chua, *World on
Fire*, 142.

127   **Like all demagogues:** Taken almost verbatim from Chua, *World on Fire*, 143.

127   **"catere[ed] to" . . . "inchoate but":** Naím, "The Venezuelan Story."

127   **the first president:** Ochoa, *Queen for a Day*, 43.

128   **two oil tankers:** Ibid., 53–55.

128   **first nonwhite Miss Venezuela:** Ibid., 35.

128   **more than $8 billion:** Chua, *World on Fire*, 144; "Consolidating Power in Venezuela."

128   **about 95 percent:** OPEC, "Venezuela Facts and Figures," http://www.opec.org/opec_web/en/about_us/171.htm; see also Kozloff, *Hugo Chávez*, 7, 18.

128   **Although technically state owned:** Taken almost verbatim from Chua, *World on Fire*, 144.

128   **left-wing academic:** Coronil, "State Reflections," 43; Christina Hoag, "Venezuela Faces Protest at Petroleum Company," *Houston Chronicle*, March 1, 2002, http://www.chron.com/business/energy/article/Venezuela-faces-protest-at-petroleum-company-2067379.php.

128   **"a victory for democracy":** Juan Forero, "Uprising in Venezuela," *New York Times*, April 13, 2002; Chua, *World on Fire*, 144–45.

128–29 **as is rumored:** See Kozloff, *Hugo Chávez*, 27; Williams, "The New Balancing Act," 257; "U.S. Papers Hail Venezuelan Coup as Pro-Democracy Move," *Fairness and Accuracy in Reporting*, April 18, 2002, http://fair.org/take-action/media-advisories/u-s-papers-hail-venezuelan-coup-as-pro-democracy-move-2.

129   **The coup was:** Taken almost verbatim from Chua, *World on Fire*, 144–45; see also Ciccariello-Maher, *We Created Chávez*, 170; Kozloff, *Hugo Chávez*, 28–29.

129   **major U.S. newspapers:** "U.S. Papers Hail Venezuelan Coup as Pro-Democracy Move."

129   **returned Chávez to power:** Ciccariello-Maher, *We Created Chávez*, 169–71; Coronil, "State Reflections," 51–53.

129–30 **Except for the United States . . . "rather stupid":** Paul Krugman, "Losing Latin America," *New York Times*, April 16, 2002; see also Julian Borger and Alex Bellos, "US 'Gave the Nod' to Venezuelan Coup," *Guardian*, April 17, 2002.

130   **our influence in the region:** Williams, "The New Balancing Act," 267.

130   **In December 2002:** Amy Chua, "Power to the Privileged," *New York Times*, January 7, 2003; Weisbrot, "U.S. Support for Regime Change in Venezuela is a Mistake."

130   **spearheaded by the country's wealthy:** Chua, "Power to the Privileged"; Coronil, "State Reflections," 42–46; Kozloff, *Hugo Chávez*, 28–30.

130   **January 2003 op-ed:** Chua, "Power to the Privileged."

131   **"As a Venezuelan":** Antonio Guzmán-Blanco, e-mail message to author, January 8, 2003.

131 **"Race has never":** Rafael Echeverria G., e-mail message to author, January 8, 2003.

132 **"Having grown up":** Francisco Alzuru, e-mail message to author, January 8, 2003.

132 **The e-mail campaign:** The anti-Chávez opposition controlled major media outlets. See Ciccariello-Maher, *We Created Chávez,* 173–74.

132 **now widely acknowledged:** See, e.g., Ochoa, *Queen for a Day,* 32–37; Hilleary, "Are Race and Class at the Root of Venezuela's Political Crisis?"; Salas, "Ethnicity and Revolution."

132 **Similarly ethnically tinged:** Chua, *World on Fire,* 72–74; Jonathan Watts, "Evo Morales Celebrates 10 Years as Bolivia's 'Indigenous Socialist' President," *Guardian,* January 22, 2016.

133 **"by half" ... "A victory":** Mark Weisbrot, "Why Chávez Was Reelected," *New York Times,* October 9, 2012; see generally Ciccariello-Maher, *We Created Chávez.*

133 **more democratic under:** See, e.g., Weisbrot, "Why Chávez Was Reelected"; Wilpert, "Venezuela's Experiment in Participatory Democracy," 99–100, 122–23, 125; Daniel Hellinger, "Defying the Iron Law of Oligarchy I: How Does 'El Pueblo' Conceive Democracy?," in Smilde and Hellinger, *Venezuela's Bolivarian Democracy,* 28–30, 56–57.

133 **with autocratic leanings:** Wilpert, "Venezuela's Experiment in Participatory Democracy," 120–21, 124–25; Naím, "Nicolas Maduro Doesn't Really Control Venezuela," *Atlantic,* May 25, 2017.

133 **By 2006, government:** Justin Fox, "How Hugo Chávez Trashed Latin America's Richest Economy," Bloomberg, August 27, 2015.

133 **more than $55 billion:** Marianna Parraga and Brian Ellsworth, "Venezuela Falls Behind on Oil-for-Loans Deals with China, Russia," Reuters, February 9, 2017, http://www.reuters.com/article/us-venezuela-oil-insight-idUSKBN15O2BC.

133 **Chávez imposed price controls:** William Neuman, "With Venezuelan Food Shortages, Some Blame Price Controls," *New York Times,* April 20, 2012.

133 **Oil production, drained:** Mark Shenk, "Venezuela Oil No Easy Fix After Brain Drain, Asset Seizures," Bloomberg, April 10, 2017, https://www.bloomberg.com/news/articles/2017-04-10/venezuela-oil-no-easy-fix-after-brain-drain-asset-seizures; Finnegan, "Venezuela, a Failing State"; Parraga and Ellsworth, "Venezuela Falls Behind."

133 **massive grief among:** Emilia Diaz and Juan Forero, "Poor Masses Mourn Chávez's Death as Venezuela Braces for Who Comes Next," *Washington Post,* March 5, 2013.

134 ***"Exprópiese!"* (Expropriate it!):** Nolan, "The Realest Reality Show in the World."

134 **Chávez joined Twitter:** Samuel Burke, "Hugo Chávez Was First Tweeter-

NOTES

in-Chief," CNN, January 26, 2017, http://money.cnn.com/2017/01/26
/technology/hugo-chavez-first-twitter-president-venezuela-trump; Associated Press, "Hugo Chávez Rewards Three-Millionth Twitter Follower
with New Home," *Guardian,* June 1, 2012.

134 **everything from trips:** Rory Carroll, "Hugo Chávez's Twitter Habit
Proves a Popular Success," *Guardian,* August 10, 2010.

134 **might be secretly infecting:** Tom Phillips, "Hugo Chávez Hints at U.S.
Cancer Plot," *Guardian,* December 29, 2011.

135 **global oil prices:** Fox, "How Hugo Chávez Trashed Latin America's
Richest Economy;" E.L., "Why the Oil Price Is Falling," *Economist,* December 8, 2014.

135 **plunging Venezuela into:** Finnegan, "Venezuela, a Failing State"; Casey,
"No Food, No Medicine, No Respite"; Grillo and Benezra, "Venezuela's
Murder Epidemic Rages on Amid State of Emergency."

135 **In 2016, inflation:** Carina Pons, "Venezuela 2016 Inflation Hits 800
Percent," Reuters, January 20, 2017, http://www.reuters.com/article
/us-venezuela-economy-idUSKBN154244.

135 **it does not appear:** Oliver Stuenkel, "Why Venezuela's Nicolás Maduro
Doesn't Look Quite Finished Yet," *Americas Quarterly,* April 10, 2017,
http://www.americasquarterly.org/content/why-venezuelas-nicolas
-maduro-doesnt-look-finished-quite-yet.

135 **"destroy[ing] Chávez's good name":** Kenneth Rapoza, "In Venezuela,
'Chavista' Says Maduro Must Go," *Forbes,* June 30, 2016.

135 **"constituent assembly" . . . widely viewed:** Nicholas Casey and Ana
Vanessa Herrero, "Venezuela's New Assembly Members Share a Goal:
Stifle Dissent," *New York Times,* August 3, 2017; Associated Press, "The
Latest: Regional Top Diplomats Reject Venezuela Assembly," *Richmond
Times-Dispatch,* August 8, 2017.

135 **"puppet" for Cuba:** Naím, "Nicolas Maduro Doesn't Really Control
Venezuela."

Chapter Seven: Inequality and the Tribal Chasm in America

138–39 **"shifted sharply to Donald Trump":** David Leonhardt, "How Democrats Can Get Their Mojo Back," *New York Times,* May 16, 2017.

139 **A City University of New York:** Ruth Milkman et al., *Changing the Subject:
A Bottom-Up Account of Occupy Wall Street in New York City* (New York: The
Murphy Institute, CUNY, 2013), 9, 47, appendix C.

139 **"Our research shows":** Douglas Schoen, "Polling the Occupy Wall
Street Crowd," *Wall Street Journal,* October 18, 2011; see also Matthias
Schwartz, "Pre-Occupied," *New Yorker,* November 28, 2011.

139 **Yet another poll:** Sean Captain, "Infographic: Who Is Occupy Wall
Street?," *Fast Company,* November 2, 2011, http://www.fastcompany.com
/1792056/infographic-who-occupy-wall-street.

140 **more racial and ethnic:** Milkman et al., *Changing the Subject*, 10, fig. 1; Ruth Milkman, "Revolt of the College-Educated Millennials," *Contexts* 11, no. 2 (2012): 13.

140 **there is consensus:** Milkman et al., *Changing the Subject*, 10, fig. 1; Milkman, "Revolt of the College-Educated Millennials," 13.

140 **"had previously participated in":** Milkman et al., *Changing the Subject*, 15.

140 **"[Occupy Wall Street] was not":** Ibid., 2.

140 **The Other 98%:** "Join the Other 98%," *Other 98%*, accessed January 10, 2016, https://other98.com/mission/join (screenshot on file with author).

140 **The team of six:** "The Team," *Other 98%*, accessed July 11, 2015, http://other98.com/about-us/the-team (screenshot on file with author).

141 **Micah White, a "failure":** "Protest is Broken," Interview with Micah White by *Folha de São Paulo*, May 26, 2015, accessed August 13, 2017, https://www.micahmwhite.com/protest-is-broken.

141 **many attribute to Occupy:** Michael Levitin, "The Triumph of Occupy Wall Street," *Atlantic*, June 10, 2015.

141 **"more a meme than a movement":** George Packer, "'By the People' and 'Wages of Rebellion,'" *New York Times*, June 29, 2015, Sunday Book Review.

141 **The most common:** See, e.g., Andy Ostroy, "The Failure of Occupy Wall Street," *Huffington Post*, July 31, 2012, http://www.huffingtonpost.com/andy-ostroy/the-failure-of-occupy-wal_b_1558787.html.

141 **authentic and potent:** Bernd Simon and Bert Klandermans, "Politicized Collective Identity: A Social Psychological Analysis," *American Psychologist* 56 (2001): 320, 324–25; Martijn Van Zomeren et al., "Toward an Integrative Social Identity Model of Collective Action: A Quantitative Research Synthesis of Three Socio-Psychological Perspectives," *Psychological Bulletin* 134 (2008): 524, 526.

142 **"Social media has":** "Protest is Broken."

142 **"You have generations":** Milkman et al., *Changing the Subject*, 13.

142 **"We kick the ass":** Robert Hughes, *Walker Finds a Way: Running Into the Adult World with Autism* (London: Jessica Kingsley Publishers, 2016), 79.

142 **But Occupy gave this sense of belonging:** See Michael Kazin, "The End of Outrage?," *Slate*, February 17, 2015, http://www.slate.com/articles/news_and_politics/politics/2015/02/inequality_and_american_protest_history_why_are_no_movements_rising_up_against.html; Alex Evans, "What Can G7's Dwindling Anti-Poverty Protesters Learn from Climate Activists?," *Guardian*, June 6, 2015; cf. Chidi Anselm Odinkalu, "Why More Africans Don't Use Human Rights Language," Carnegie Council on Ethics and International Affairs, 1999 (noting that the human rights world "appears almost by design to exclude the participation of the people whose welfare it purports to advance").

142 **"Many lower class":** Essay by Joe Chatham, 2016 (on file with author).

143 **"The White Savior":** Teju Cole, "The White-Savior Industrial Complex," *Atlantic*, March 21, 2012.

143 **America's poor are:** See David Callahan and J. Mijin Cha, "Stacked Deck: How the Dominance of Politics by the Affluent & Business Undermines Economic Mobility in America," Demos, 2013, http://www.demos.org/sites/default/files/publications/Demos-Stacked-Deck.pdf; K. L. Schlozman et al., "Civic Participation and the Equality Problem," in *Civic Engagement in American Democracy*, ed. Theda Skocpol and Morris P. Fiorina (Washington, DC: Brookings Institute Press, 1999), 431, 433–34.

143 **less likely to work on political:** Schlozman et al., "Civic Participation and the Equality Problem," 433–34.

143 **contact elected officials:** "The Politics of Financial Insecurity," Pew Research Center, January 8, 2015, http://www.people-press.org/2015/01/08/the-politics-of-financial-insecurity-a-democratic-tilt-undercut-by-low-participation.

143 **or vote. In part:** Callahan and Cha, "Stacked Deck," 11.

143 **less likely to join:** Robert D. Putnam, *Our Kids: The American Dream in Crisis* (New York: Simon & Schuster, 2015): 207–10, 225.

143 **church attendance among:** Ibid., 225; Charles Murray, *Coming Apart: The State of White America, 1960–2010* (New York: Crown, 2012), 200–208; see also J. D. Vance, *Hillbilly Elegy: A Memoir of a Family and Culture in Crisis* (New York: HarperCollins, 2016), 93.

143 **"we have witnessed":** Putnam, *Our Kids*, 206.

144 **The ranks of America's police:** Harlan Hahn, "A Profile of Urban Police," *Law & Contemporary Problems* 36 (1971): 449; Jerry R. Sparger and David J. Giacopassi, "Police Resentment of the Upper Class," *Criminal Justice Review* 11 (1986): 25.

144 **armed forces:** Amy Lutz, "Who Joins the Military?: A Look at Race, Class, and Immigration Status," *Journal of Political and Military Sociology* 36, no. 2 (2008): 167–88.

144 **famous for group loyalty:** William K. Muir Jr., *Police: Streetcorner Politicians* (Chicago: University of Chicago Press, 1977), 29–31; Stephen M. Passamaneck, *Police Ethics and the Jewish Tradition* (Springfield, IL: Charles C. Thomas Publisher, 2003), 20–21; John Mueller, *The Remnants of War* (Ithaca, NY: Cornell University Press, 2004), 12; Johan M. G. Van der Dennen, "Combat Motivation," *Journal of Social Justice* 17 (2005): 81–82.

144 **single greatest threat:** Maxwell Barna, "Move Over Jihadists—Sovereign Citizens Seen as America's Top Terrorist Threat," *Vice*, August 15, 2014, https://news.vice.com/article/move-over-jihadists-sovereign-citizens-seen-as-americas-top-terrorist-threat. Many thanks to Spencer Todd for

bringing sovereign citizens to my attention and for his contributions to this section.

144 **bizarre antigovernment group:** Anti-Defamation League, *The Lawless Ones: The Resurgence of the Sovereign Citizen Movement* (ADL Special Report, 2012), http://www.adl.org/assets/pdf/combating-hate/Lawless-Ones-2012-Edition-WEB-final.pdf; Southern Poverty Law Center, "Sovereign Citizens Movement," http://www.splcenter.org/fighting-hate/extremist-files/ideology/sovereign-citizens-movement.

144 **economic dislocation:** Southern Poverty Law Center, "Sovereign Citizens Movement"; Mark Potok, "The 'Patriot' Movement Explodes," *Intelligence Report*, no. 145 (Southern Poverty Law Center, Spring 2012).

144 **Gavin Long, who shot:** Ryan Lenz, "Gunman Who Killed Three Police Officers in Baton Rouge Member of Black Antigovernment 'Sovereign Citizen' Group," Southern Poverty Law Center, July 18, 2016, https://www.splcenter.org/hatewatch/2016/07/18/gunman-who-killed-three-police-officers-baton-rouge-member-black-antigovernment-sovereign.

144 **central beliefs include:** Southern Poverty Law Center, "Sovereign Citizens Movement"; Anti-Defamation League, *The Lawless Ones*; Leslie R. Masterson, "'Sovereign Citizens': Fringe in the Courtroom," *American Bankruptcy Institute Journal* 30 (2011): 66; J. J. MacNab, "Context Matters: The Cliven Bundy Standoff—Part 3," *Forbes*, May 6, 2014, http://www.forbes.com/sites/jjmacnab/2014/05/06/context-matters-the-cliven-bundy-standoff-part-3.

146 **"paper terrorism" . . . "the nonsensical":** Southern Poverty Law Center, "Sovereign Citizens Movement."

146–7 **Richard Posner . . . "but had no governmental authority":** Joe Patrice, "Judge Posner Lights into Pro Se 'Sovereign Citizen,'" Above the Law, February 23, 2015, http://abovethelaw.com/2015/02/judge-posner-lights-into-pro-se-sovereign-citizen.

148 **Like America's Founding Fathers:** Southern Poverty Law Center, "Sovereign Citizens Movement."

148 **The Washitaw Nation:** Lenz, "Gunman Who Killed Three Police Officers."

148 **"sovereigns believe that":** Southern Poverty Law Center, "Sovereign Citizens Movement."

149 **twenty-seven thousand street gangs:** Arlen Egley and Christina E. O'Donnell, *Highlights of the 2007 National Youth Gang Survey* (Office of Juvenile Justice and Delinquency Preventions, U.S. Department of Justice, Washington, DC, April 2007); see also Irving A. Spergel, *The Youth Gang Problem: A Community Approach* (New York: Oxford University Press, 1995), 9–16, 26–33; James Diego Vigil, Steve C. Yun, and Jesse Cheng, "A Shortcut to the American Dream? Vietnamese Youth Gangs in Little Saigon," in *Asian American Youth: Culture, Identity and Ethnicity*, ed. Jennifer Lee and Min Zhou (New York: Routledge, 2004), 207, 211, 215–17.

149 **have a racial or ethnic:** Dana Peterson, Inger-Lise Lien, and Frank van Gemert, "Concluding Remarks: The Roles of Migration and Ethnicity in Street Gang Formation, Involvement and Response," in *Street Gangs, Migration and Ethnicity,* ed. Frank van Gemert, Dana Peterson, and Inger-Lise Lien (Portland, OR: Willan Publishing, 2008), 262.

149 **famously violent Mara Salvatrucha:** Matthew DeLuca, "Central American Gang MS-13 Cuts Swath of Murder and Mayhem Across Long Island," *Daily Beast,* June 3, 2012, http://www.thedailybeast.com/articles /2012/06/03/central-american-gang-ms-13-cuts-swath-of-murder-and -mayhem-across-long-island.html.

149 **All About Cash, Cash Ave:** Federal Bureau of Investigation, National Gang Intelligence Center, *National Gang Threat Assessment: Emerging Trends* (2011), 58, 64, 65, http://www.fbi.gov/stats-services/publications/2011 -national-gang-threat-assessment; see also Claudia Durst Johnson, *Youth Gangs in Literature* (Westport, CT: Greenwood Press, 2004), 5.

149 **Most active gang members:** See John Johnson, "The Violence: Fear Stalks the Hallways as Shootings Touch Lives," *Los Angeles Times,* September 19, 1993; Mary M. Jensen, *Introduction to Emotional and Behavioral Disorders* (Upper Saddle River, NJ: Pearson/Merrill Prentice Hall, 2004), 134; Cecilia M. Harper, "How Do I Divorce My Gang?: Modifying the Defense of Withdrawal for a Gang-Related Conspiracy," *Valparaiso University Law Review* 50, no. 3 (2016): 774; Tom Branson, "Gang Members on Path of 'Assumed Destiny'—Dying by Age 20," *Northwest Indiana Times,* February 5, 2014, http://www.nwitimes.com/news/gang-members-on-path-of -assumeddestiny-dying-by-age/article_a9110339-5381-56dc-af4c -8d1224a162a9.html.

149 **"with few skills":** Orlando Patterson, "The Real Problem with America's Inner Cities," *New York Times,* May 9, 2015.

149 **status, a strong tribe:** Andrew J. Diamond, *Mean Streets: Chicago Youths and the Everyday Struggle for Empowerment in the Multiracial City, 1908–1969* (Berkeley: University of California Press, 2009), 33, 198; Patterson, "The Real Problem with America's Inner Cities"; see also João H. Costa Vargas, *Catching Hell in the City of Angels: Life and Meanings of Blackness in South Central Los Angeles* (Minneapolis: University of Minnesota Press, 2006), 181–82; Curtis W. Branch, ed., *Adolescent Gangs: Old Issues, New Approaches* (Philadelphia: Brunner/Mazel, 1999), 10, 178; Eric C. Schneider, *Vampires, Dragons, and Egyptian Kings: Youth Gangs in Postwar New York* (Princeton, NJ: Princeton University Press, 1999), 98, 179.

150 **San Francisco's Mission District:** "Santa Muerte in the Mission San Fco California," http://www.santamuerte.org/santuarios/usa/3036-santa -muerte-in-the-mission-san-fco-california.html. For a fascinating, in-depth study of Santa Muerte and her devotees, see R. Andrew Chesnut, *Devoted to Death: Santa Muerte, the Skeleton Saint,* 2nd ed. (New York: Oxford University Press, 2018).

150 **Melrose Avenue in:** "Templo Santa Muerte Los Angeles, CA," http://
www.santamuerte.org/santuarios/usa/3034-templo-santa-muerte-los
-angeles-ca.html.

150 **New Orleans . . . black, white, or red robes:** Henrick Caroliszyn,
"Santa Muerte in New Orleans," http://www.bestofneworleans.com
/gambit/santa-muerte-in-new-orleans/Content?oid=2690150.

150 **started in Mexico:** R. Andrew Chesnut, "Saint Without Borders: Santa
Muerte Goes Global," June 5, 2014, http://skeletonsaint.com/2014/06
/05/saint-without-borders-santa-muerte-goes-global.

150 **"the fastest growing":** Carmen Sesin, "Growing Devotion to Santa
Muerte in U.S. and Abroad," NBC News, December 29, 2014, http://
www.nbcnews.com/news/latino/growing-devotion-santa-muerte-u-s
-abroad-n275856; Rick Paulas, "Our Lady of the Holy Death Is the
World's Fastest Growing Religious Movement," *Vice*, November 13, 2014,
https://www.vice.com/read/our-lady-of-the-holy-death-is-the-worlds
-fastest-growing-religious-movement-456.

150 **"Mexico's saint of delinquents":** Erin Lee, "La Santa Muerte: Mexico's
Saint of Delinquents and Outcasts," *Vice*, November 1, 2014, http://www
.vice.com/read/la-santa-muerte-is-a-saint-for-mexicos-delinquents
-and-outcasts.

150 **LGBT . . . transgender sex workers:** Lois Ann Lorentzen et al., ed., *Religion at the Corner of Bliss and Nirvana: Politics, Identity, and Faith in New Migrant Communities* (Durham, NC: Duke University Press, 2009), 30–31.

150 **"She's the saint":** Caroliszyn, "Santa Muerte in New Orleans."

150–51 **"[Y]ou can ask" . . . Heisenberg:** Jake Flanagin, "The Rise of the
Narco-Saints: A New Religious Trend in Mexico," *Atlantic*, September
2014; see Paulas, "Our Lady of the Holy Death Is the World's Fastest
Growing Religious Movement."

151 **has been "meteoric" . . . Bony Lady:** Chesnut, "Saint Without Borders:
Santa Muerte Goes Global."

151 **10 to 12 million devotees:** Caroliszyn, "Santa Muerte in New Orleans."

151 **cigars, shots of rum:** "Templo Santa Muerte Los Angeles, CA."

151 **presence in Miami:** Sesin, "Growing Devotion to Santa Muerte in U.S.
and Abroad."

151 **movement works to raise:** John Nova Lomax, "Santa Muerte: Patron
Saint of the Drug War," *Houston Press*, September 12, 2012, http://www
.houstonpress.com/news/santa-muerte-patron-saint-of-the-drug-war
-6595544.

151 **legendary bandit Jesús Malverde:** Morgan Smith, "La Santa Muerte and
Jesús Malverde: Narco Saints?," *New Mexico Mercury*, November 7, 2013;
Sam Quinones, "Jesus Malverde," *Frontline*, http://www.pbs.org/wgbh
/pages/frontline/shows/drugs/business/malverde.html; Sam Quinones,
True Tales from Another Mexico (Albuquerque: University of New Mexico
Press, 2001), 225–32.

151   **Sinaloa drug cartel ... "El Chapo":** Monte Reel, "Underworld: How the Sinaloa Drug Cartel Digs Its Tunnels," *New Yorker*, August 3, 2015.

151   **"Thank you Malverde":** Quinones, "Jesus Malverde."

152   **"Most Mexican-Americans today":** Essay by Nicolas Molina, February 3, 2015 (on file with author).

153   **with more than 10,000:** Hartford Institute for Religious Research, "Database of Megachurches in the U.S.," http://hirr.hartsem.edu/cgi-bin/mega/db.pl?db=default&uid=default&view_records=1&ID=*&sb=3&so=descend.

153   **almost half ... 8,500 members:** Kate Bowler, *Blessed: A History of the American Prosperity Gospel* (Oxford: Oxford University Press, 2013), 181–82.

153   **7 million viewers weekly:** Cathleen Falsani, "The Prosperity Gospel," *Washington Post*, December 20, 2009.

153   **Creflo Dollar preaches:** Abby Ohlheiser, "Pastor Creflo Dollar Might Get His $65 Million Private Jet After All," *Washington Post*, June 3, 2015.

153   **televangelist Mark Burns:** Rob Barnett, "Easley Pastor to Address Republican National Convention," *Florida Today*, July 14, 2015.

153   **"There is no":** Elizabeth Dias, "Donald Trump's Prosperity Preachers," *Time*, April 14, 2016, http://time.com/donald-trump-prosperity-preachers.

153   **"As soon as Jesus":** Bowler, *Blessed*, 96.

153   **who owns two Rolls-Royces:** Olivia Nuzzi, "Jesus Wants Me to Have This Jet," *Daily Beast*, March 14, 2015, http://www.thedailybeast.com/jesus-wants-me-to-have-this-jet.

154   **"anointing to prosper":** Bowler, *Blessed*, 96 (italics added).

154   **wore designer clothes:** Ibid., 96; John Avanzini, "Believers Voice of Victory," Trinity Broadcasting Network, January 20, 1991.

154   **"[A]ccording to Deuteronomy":** Bowler, *Blessed*, 96.

154   **"surrounded Adam and Eve":** Ibid., 97.

154   **"He took your place":** Ibid., 95.

155   **"Faith requires action":** Ibid., 127–28.

155   **has many detractors:** Falsani, "The Prosperity Gospel"; Pastor Rick Henderson, "The False Promise of the Prosperity Gospel: Why I Called Out Joel Osteen and Joyce Meyer," *Huffington Post*, August 21, 2013; Hanna Rosin, "Did Christianity Cause the Crash?," *Atlantic*, December 2009.

155   **enormous appeal for have-nots:** Bowler, *Blessed*, 233–34; Rosin, "Did Christianity Cause the Crash?"

155   **popular with disadvantaged minorities:** Bowler, *Blessed*, 6, 111–13, 119, 161; Milmon F. Harrison, *Righteous Riches: The Word of Faith Movement in Contemporary African American Religion* (New York: Oxford University Press, 2005), 148–52; Emily Raboteau, "My Search for Creflo Dollar," *Salon*, January 6, 2013, http://www.salon.com/2013/01/06/my_search_for_creflo_dollar ("most of them poor and working-class blacks"); Rosin, "Did Christianity Cause the Crash?"

155   **"lift believers' chins":** Bowler, *Blessed*, 232.

155 **not "victims" but "victors":** Rosin, "Did Christianity Cause the Crash?"

155 **even the poor control:** Raboteau, "My Search for Creflo Dollar."

156 **75 million fans:** Lawrence W. Hugenberg and Barbara S. Hugenberg, "If It Ain't Rubbin', It Ain't Racin': NASCAR, American Values, and Fandom," *Journal of Popular Culture* 41, no. 4 (2008): 635.

156 **white, working-class . . . moonshiners:** Larry J. Griffin and Peggy G. Hargis, ed., *The New Encyclopedia of Southern Culture, Social Class* 20 (Chapel Hill: University of North Carolina Press, 2012), 265, 410.

156 **40 percent of NASCAR fans:** Hugenberg and Hugenberg, "If It Ain't Rubbin', It Ain't Racin'," 637.

156 **remains overwhelmingly Republican:** Joshua I. Newman, "A Detour Through 'Nascar Nation,'" *International Review for the Sociology of Sport* 42, no. 3 (2007): 298–99.

156 **racing-speak is filled:** Rebecca R. Scott, "Environmental Affects: NASCAR, Place and White American Cultural Citizenship," *Social Identities for the Study of Race, Nation and Culture* 19 (2013): 13–14.

156 **NASCAR is all about:** Hugenberg and Hugenberg, "If It Ain't Rubbin', It Ain't Racin'," 640; Steve Odland, "NASCAR's Back!," *Forbes*, February 27, 2012; Lynsay Clutter, "Nascar Fans Are Brand Loyal," WTHR, http://www.wthr.com/story/3689698/nascar-fans-are-brand-loyal.

156 **NASCAR fans are more:** Clutter, "Nascar Fans Are Brand Loyal."

157 **"I have an Interstate battery":** Ibid.

157 **three times more likely:** Ibid.

157 **"I have a Nextel phone":** Ibid.

157 **the "NASCAR congregation":** Newman, "A Detour Through 'Nascar Nation,'" 299, 300.

157 **"pilgrimages" that fans:** Hugenberg and Hugenberg, "If It Ain't Rubbin', It Ain't Racin'," 643.

157 **"that of *belonging*":** Newman, "A Detour Through 'Nascar Nation,'" 300.

157 **quarter of a million . . . "pure joy":** "NASCAR Power Real, 'Til It's Over," *Florida Times-Union*, February 17, 2002; see also Hugenberg and Hugenberg, "If It Ain't Rubbin', It Ain't Racin'," 636.

157 **owner and CEO, Brian France:** Griffin and Hargis, *The New Encyclopedia of Southern Culture*, 265–66; Shubhankar Chhokra, "NASCAR Asks Fans Not to Display Confederate Flag, NASCAR Fans Rebel," *National Review*, July 7, 2015.

158 **"Spotting a Confederate flag":** Ibid.

158 **Brian France endorsed him:** Jeff Gluck, "NASCAR CEO, Some Drivers Endorse Trump for President," *USA Today*, February 29, 2016.

159 **"world of wrestling":** Roland Barthes, *Mythologies*, trans. Annette Lavers (New York: Hill and Wang, 2001), 15. This section on WWE draws heavily on the work of Alex Wang.

159 **working-class Americans:** Wrestling fans tend to be lower or middle class. See R. J. Smith, "Among the Mooks," *New York Times Magazine,* August 6, 2000, 40–41; Frank B. Ashley, John Dollar, and Brian Wigley, "Professional Wrestling Fans: Your Next-Door Neighbors?," *Sports Marketing Quarterly* 9, no. 3 (2000): 143.

159 **real and fictive:** Sharon Mazer, *Professional Wrestling: Sport and Spectacle* (Jackson: University Press of Mississippi, 1998), 167.

159 **narratives about modern romance:** Betty Jo Barrett and Dana S. Levin, "What's Love Got to Do with It? A Qualitative Grounded Theory Content Analysis of Romance Narratives in the PG Era of World Wrestling Entertainment (WWE) Programming," *Sexuality and Culture* (2014): 564.

159 **form of melodrama:** Henry Jenkins III, "'Never Trust a Snake': WWF Wrestling as Masculine Melodrama," in *Steel Chair to the Head: The Pleasure and Pain of Professional Wrestling,* ed. Nicholas Sammond (Durham, NC: Duke University Press, 2005), 36.

159 **drama of good versus evil:** Mazer, *Professional Wrestling,* 2, 3.

159 **He once entered the ring:** Vann R. Newkirk II, "Donald Trump, Wrestling Heel," *Atlantic,* March 15, 2016.

159 **"both mesmerizing and gross":** Christina Wilkle, "That Time Donald Trump Clotheslined Vince McMahon on 'Wrestlemania,'" *Huffington Post,* February 23, 2016.

159 **a "WWE Superstar":** "Donald Trump," WWE, accessed January 9, 2017, http://www.wwe.com/superstars/donald-trump; "Donald Trump Enters the Hall: 2013 WWE Hall of Fame Induction Ceremony," WWE, accessed January 9, 2017, http://www.wwe.com/videos/donald -trump-enters-the-hall-2013-wwe-hall-of-fame-induction-ceremony.

159 **Linda McMahon, whom he chose:** See Kate Vinton, "Meet Linda McMahon, Wife of WWE Billionaire and Trump's Pick for Small Business Administrator," *Forbes,* December 7, 2016.

160 **in July 2017 Trump proudly:** Michael M. Grynbaum, "Trump Tweets a Video of Him Wrestling 'CNN' to the Ground," *New York Times,* July 2, 2017.

160 **black and Latino working class following:** Chris Harrington, "WWE Viewer Demographics," Indeed Wrestling, July 29, 2014, http:// indeedwrestling.blogspot.com/2014/07/wwe-viewer-demographics .html.

160 **the prototypical:** Claire Shaeperkoetter, Jordan Bass, and Kyle S. Bunds, "Wrestling to Understand Fan Motivations: Examining the MSSC Within the WWE," *Journal of Entertainment and Media Studies* 2, no. 1 (2016): 123; Ashley, Dollar, and Wigley, "Professional Wrestling Fans," 143.

160 **some experts, disaffected:** Douglas Battema and Philip Sewell, "Trading in Masculinity: Muscles, Money, and Market Discourse in the WWF," in Sammond, *Steel Chair to the Head,* 282; Michael Atkinson, "Fifty Million

Viewers Can't Be Wrong: Professional Wrestling, Sports-Entertainment, and Mimesis," *Sociology of Sport Journal* 19 (2002): 62; Vaughn May, "Cultural Politics and Professional Wrestling," *Popular Culture Association in the South* 21, no. 3 (1999): 81; Smith, "Among the Mooks," 40–41.

160 **former industrial heartland and the South:** Google search data from 2004 to 2016 shows that most searches for "WWE" come from users in the Rust Belt, Midwest, and South. The WWE is most often searched in West Virginia, followed by Rust Belt cities in upstate New York (Utica and Buffalo in particular). Of the top ten states in which users search "WWE," five are in the South (Louisiana, South Carolina, Texas, Mississippi, arguably Virginia), two are in the Midwest (Kentucky, West Virginia), and three are on the East Coast (Pennsylvania, New Jersey, New York)—though searches in Pennsylvania and New York are noticeably clustered around fading industrial hubs. Despite its vast population, California is not listed in the top twenty-five state searches for the WWE. Independent analysis, Google Trends Search Data, 2004 to present, accessed January 10, 2017, https://www.google.com/trends/explore?date=all&geo=US&q=WWE.

160 **"[a] political novice":** Gail Collins, "Who Wants to Elect a Millionaire?," *New York Times*, May 26, 2010.

160 **"Linda has a":** Vinton, "Meet Linda McMahon, Wife of WWE Billionaire and Trump's Pick for Small Business Administrator."

161 **"don't take him literally":** Nolan D. McCaskill, "Trump Adviser: Don't Take Trump Literally, 'Take Him Symbolically,'" *Politico*, December 20, 2016, http://www.politico.com/story/2016/12/trump-symbolically-anthony-scaramucci-232848.

161 **"As this election fades":** Jenée Desmond-Harris, "Trump's Win Is a Reminder of the Incredible, Unbeatable Power of Racism," *Vox*, November 9, 2016.

162 **"[N]obody did this":** Kevin Williamson, "Chaos in the City, Chaos in the State: The White Working Class's Dysfunction," *National Review*, March 28, 2016.

163 **"who won't sacrifice" . . . "[N]o educated person":** Robert Donachie, "Tech Founder: Middle America Is Too 'Violent, Stupid, and Racist' for New Jobs," *Daily Caller*, January 8, 2017.

163 **"treason":** Ann Coulter, *Treason: Liberal Treachery from the Cold War to the War on Terrorism* (New York: Crown, 2003).

163 **"Liberals hate":** Ann Coulter, *Slander: Liberal Lies About the American Right* (New York: Crown, 2002), 7.

163 **so little interaction:** Joan C. Williams, *White Working Class: Overcoming Class Cluelessness in America* (Boston: Harvard Business Review Press, 2017), 2–4; Arlie Russell Hochschild, *Strangers in Their Own Land: Anger and Mourning on the American Right* (New York: The New Press, 2016), 5,

135–43; Charles Murray, *Coming Apart*, 69–94; Putnam, *Our Kids*, 39–41; Janie Boschma, "Why Obama Is Worried About 'Class Segregation,'" *Atlantic,* May 12, 2015.

163   **"I may be white":** Vance, *Hillbilly Elegy*, 3.

Chapter Eight: Democracy and Political Tribalism in America

165   **"There is nothing which I dread":** John Adams, letter to Jonathan Jackson, October 2, 1780, in *The Works of John Adams, Second President of the United States,* ed. Charles Francis Adams (Boston: Little, Brown and Company, 1854), 511.

165   **"America is woven":** Ralph Ellison, *Invisible Man* (New York: Vintage, 1980), 577.

166   **unlike the United Kingdom and the European Union:** Ian Bremmer, "These 5 Facts Explain Why Brexit Could Lead to a U.K. Breakup," *Time,* July 1, 2016; Tony Barber, "Europe Starts to Think the Unthinkable: Breaking Up," *Financial Times,* March 2, 2017.

166   **In 1965, whites:** "Modern Immigration Wave Brings 59 Million to U.S., Driving Population Growth and Change Through 2065," Pew Research Center: Hispanic Trends, September 28, 2015, 9, http://www.pewhispanic.org/2015/09/28/modern-immigration-wave-brings-59-million-to-u-s-driving-population-growth-and-change-through-2065.

166   **nearly 59 million:** Ibid., 8, 11, table 1; D'vera Cohn and Andrea Caumont, "10 Demographic Trends That Are Shaping the U.S. and the World," Pew Research Center, March 31, 2016, http://www.pewresearch.org/fact-tank/2016/03/31/10-demographic-trends-that-are-shaping-the-u-s-and-the-world.

166   **Unlike previous waves:** "Modern Immigration Wave Brings 59 Million to U.S.," 8.

166–67   **Between 1965 and 2015:** Ibid., 27.

167   **Already, non-Hispanic whites:** Drew Desilver, "Share of Counties Where Whites Are a Minority Has Doubled Since 1980," Pew Research Center, July 1, 2015, http://www.pewresearch.org/fact-tank/2015/07/01/share-of-counties-where-whites-are-a-minority-has-doubled-since-1980.

167   **By 2020, more than:** U.S. Census Bureau, "Projecting Majority-Minority: Non-Hispanic Whites May No Longer Comprise Over 50 Percent of the U.S. Population by 2044" (chart based on 2014 national projections), http://www.census.gov/content/dam/Census/newsroom/releases/2015/cb15-tps16_graphic.pdf.

167   **According to Pew Foundation:** "Modern Immigration Wave Brings 59 Million to U.S.," 10.

167   **The U.S. Census predicts:** Sandra L. Colby and Jennifer M. Ortman, *Projections of the Size and Composition of the U.S. Population: 2014 to 2060,* U.S. Census Bureau, March 2015, 9.

167 **the Census typically categorizes**: Richard Alba, "The Likely Persistence of a White Majority," *American Prospect,* January 11, 2016.

167 **might self-identify as white**: Hua Hsu, "The End of White America?," *Atlantic,* January/February 2009.

167 **largest group of new immigrants**: "The Rise of Asian Americans," Pew Research Center, April 4, 2013, http://www.pewsocialtrends.org/2012 /06/19/the-rise-of-asian-americans.

167 **"beiging" is more apt**: Hsu, "The End of White America?" (citing Michael Lind).

168 **"In a little more than fifty years"**: President William J. Clinton, Commencement Address at Portland State University, Oregon, June 13, 1998, http://www.presidency.ucsb.edu/ws/?pid=56140.

168 **"nothing positive about"**: Hsu, "The End of White America?" (quoting Noel Ignatiev).

168 **"the sickness of race"**: Ibid., (quoting William "Upski" Wimsatt's 1994 book *Bomb the Suburbs*).

168 **After the Civil War**: Taken almost verbatim from Amy Chua, *World on Fire: How Exporting Free Market Democracy Breeds Ethnic Hatred and Global Instability* (New York: Anchor Books, 2004), 199 (citing C. Vann Woodward, *The Strange Career of Jim Crow* [New York: Oxford University Press, 1966], 23, and James Oakes, *The Ruling Race: A History of American Slaveholders* [New York: W. W. Norton, 1998], 234).

168 **"we will have black"**: Oakes, *The Ruling Race,* 234 (quoting a Georgia commissioner speaking before the Virginia secession convention).

168 **Southern whites responded**: Taken almost verbatim from Chua, *World on Fire,* 199–200.

169 **Many believe that**: See, e.g., Carol Anderson, "Donald Trump Is the Result of White Rage, Not Economic Anxiety," *Time,* November 16, 2016; see also Charles Blow, "Trump: Making America White Again," *New York Times,* November 21, 2016.

169 **two thirds . . . "that discrimination"**: Robert P. Jones et al., *How Immigration and Concerns about Cultural Changes Are Shaping the 2016 Election,* PRRI/Brookings, June 23, 2016, https://www.prri.org/research/prri -brookings-poll-immigration-economy-trade-terrorism-presidential-race.

170 **"there is more racism"**: "Racism as a Zero-Sum Game," NPR, July 13, 2011 (interview by Michel Martin of Michael Norton and Tim Wise), http://www.npr.org/2011/07/13/137818177/racism-as-a-zero-sum-game.

170 **"by nearly any metric"**: Evan Osnos, "The Fearful and the Frustrated," *New Yorker,* August 31, 2015 (quoting Michael I. Norton and Samuel R. Sommers, "Whites See Racism as a Zero-Sum Game That They Are Now Losing," *Perspectives on Psychological Science* 6, no. 3 [2011]: 215–18).

170 **"decline of whiteness"**: Robb Willer et al., "Threats to Racial Status Promote Tea Party Support Among White Americans," Stanford Graduate School of Business, Working Paper No. 3422, May 4, 2016,

https://www.gsb.stanford.edu/faculty-research/working-papers/
threats-racial-status-promote-tea-party-support-among-white.

170 **"most unsettled"**: Janet Adamy and Paul Overberg, "Places Most Unsettled by Rapid Demographic Change Are Drawn to Donald Trump," *Wall
Street Journal,* November 1, 2016.

170 **"52 percent of"**: Claire Foran, "The Optimism and Anxiety of Trump Vot-
ers," *Atlantic,* January 20, 2017 (summarizing Robert P. Jones, Daniel Cox,
Betsy Cooper, and Rachel Lienesch, "Nearly One in Five Female Clinton
Voters Say Husband or Partner Didn't Vote," PRRI, December 1, 2016).

171 **discrimination against whites**: "Low Approval of Trump's Transition
but Outlook for his Presidency Improves," Pew Research Center, December 8, 2016, 27, http://www.people-press.org/2016/12/08/low-approval-of
-trumps-transition-but-outlook-for-his-presidency-improves.

171 **that "average Americans"**: Michael Tesler, "Trump Voters Think African Americans Are Much Less Deserving Than 'Average Americans,'"
Huffington Post, December 19, 2016.

171 **"perceptions that whites"**: Michael Tesler, "Views About Race Mattered More in Electing Trump Than in Electing Obama," *Washington
Post,* November 22, 2016.

171 **unemployment and addiction**: See Centers for Disease Control and Pre-
vention, "Today's Heroin Epidemic," last updated July 7, 2015, https://
www.cdc.gov/vitalsigns/heroin; Aria Bendix, "The Collapse of the White
Working Class," *Atlantic,* March 24, 2017; Victor Tan Chen, "All Hollowed
Out: The Lonely Poverty of America's White Working Class," *Atlantic,*
January 16, 2016; Rod Dreher, "Trump: Tribune of Poor White People,"
American Conservative, July 22, 2016 (interview with J. D. Vance); J. D. Vance,
"Why Race Relations Got Worse," *Atlantic,* August 29, 2016.

171 **Life expectancy is**: Monica Potts, "What's Killing Poor White Women,"
American Prospect, September 3, 2013 (citing S. Jay Olshanky et al., "Differences in Life Expectancy Due to Race and Educational Differences Are
Widening, and Many May Not Catch Up," *Health Affairs* 31, no. 8 [August
2012]); Betsy McKay, "Life Expectancy for White Americans Declines,"
Wall Street Journal, April 20, 2016; see also Jessica Boddy, "The Forces Driving Middle-Aged White People's 'Deaths of Despair,'" NPR, March 23,
2017, http://www.npr.org/sections/health-shots/2017/03/23/521083335
/the-forces-driving-middle-aged-white-peoples-deaths-of-despair.

171 **Educational prospects for**: See generally Joan C. Williams, *White Working Class: Overcoming Class Cluelessness in America* (Boston: Harvard Business
Review Press, 2017), 43–52; J. D. Vance, *Hillbilly Elegy: A Memoir of a Family
and Culture in Crisis* (New York: HarperCollins, 2016), 197–207.

171 **most elite colleges**: Jodi Wilgoren, "Elite Colleges Step Up Courting of
Minorities," *New York Times,* October 25, 1999.

171 **one poor white**: Informal survey at Yale Law School conducted by Blake
Neal, April 25, 2017 (on file with author).

NOTES

172　**America's elite universities:** Ross Douthat, "The Roots of White Anxiety," *New York Times,* July 18, 2010 (citing Thomas J. Espenshade and Alexandria Walton Radford, *No Longer Separate, Not Yet Equal: Race and Class in Elite College Admission and Campus Life* [Princeton, NJ: Princeton University Press, 2009]).

172　**White employees increasingly feel:** Arlie Russell Hochschild, *Strangers in Their Own Land: Anger and Mourning on the American Right* (New York: The New Press, 2016), 136–39.

172　**city of New Haven:** *Ricci v. DeStefano,* 557 U.S. 557, 563 (2009).

172　**While whites generally are:** Haeyoun Park, Josh Keller, and Josh Williams, "The Faces of American Power, Nearly as White as the Oscar Nominees," *New York Times,* February 24, 2016.

172　**Between 1999 and 2008:** Nicholas Carnes, *White-Collar Government: The Hidden Role of Class in Economic Policy Making* (Chicago: University of Chicago Press, 2013), 20.

172　**"Although women and racial":** Nicholas Carnes, "Does the Numerical Underrepresentation of the Working Class in Congress Matter?," *Legislative Studies Quarterly* 37, no. 1 (2012), 6.

172　**among the lowest upward mobility:** Amy Chua and Jed Rubenfeld, *The Triple Package: How Three Unlikely Traits Explain the Rise and Fall of Cultural Groups in America* (New York: Penguin, 2014), 174–80; see also Nancy Isenberg, *White Trash: The 400-Year Untold History of Class in America* (New York: Viking, 2016), 319–21.

173　**Just 24 percent:** Andrew Kohut, "What Will Become of America's Kids?," Pew Research Center, May 12, 2014, http://www.pewresearch.org/fact-tank/2014/05/12/what-will-become-of-americas-kids.

173　**"cop killer entertainment":** Carma Hassan, Gregory Krieg, and Melonyce McAfee, "Police Union Calls for Law Enforcement Labor to Boycott Beyonce's World Tour," CNN, February 20, 2016.

173　**"whitesplaining" jazz:** Emily Yahr, "Your Guide to the 'La La Land' Backlash," *Washington Post,* January 25, 2017.

173　**clueless white male:** Hsu, "The End of White America?"

173　**in part a "whitelash":** "'This Was a Whitelash': Van Jones' Take on the Election Results," CNN, November 9, 2016, http://www.cnn.com/2016/11/09/politics/van-jones-results-disappointment-cnntv.

174　**"choked to death":** Ta-Nehisi Coates, "Letter to My Son," *Atlantic,* July 4, 2015; see also Chris Hayes, *A Colony in a Nation* (New York: W. W. Norton, 2017), 37, 115–16.

174　**"imprisons a larger":** Michelle Alexander, *The New Jim Crow: Mass Incarceration in the Age of Color Blindness* rev. ed. (New York: The New Press, 2012), 6.

174　**"three out of four":** Alexander, *The New Jim Crow,* 6–7.

175　**"target African Americans with":** Jason Hanna, John Newsome, and Ariane de Vogue, "North Carolina Voter ID Law Overturned on Appeal,"

272

CNN, July 29, 2016, http://www.cnn.com/2016/07/29/politics/north
-carolina-voter-id.

175 **"so dirty" . . . followed around:** Beverly Daniel Tatum, Ph.D. *"Why Are
All the Black Kids Sitting Together in the Cafeteria?" And Other Conversations About
Race* (New York: Basic Books, 1997), 36, 96.

175 **Whites do not have to:** Ibid., 77–79, 85–86; Hayes, *A Colony in a Nation*,
37–38, 197–98.

175 **"They went to Taipei":** Angie Thomas, *The Hate U Give* (New York: Balzer + Bray, 2017), 77.

175 **"We felt in":** Omer Aziz, "What President Donald Trump Means for
Muslims," *New Republic*, November 10, 2016.

176 **Reports abound of:** See, e.g., Arelis R. Hernández, Wesley Lowery, and
Abigail Hauslohner, "Federal Immigration Raids Net Many Without
Criminal Records, Sowing Fear," *Washington Post*, February 16, 2016.

176 **Women in America:** See, e.g., Gillian Chadwick, "Predator in Chief:
President Trump and the Glorification of Sexual Violence," *Huffington
Post,* November 30, 2016.

176 **Gay and transgender:** Liam Stack, "Trump Victory Alarms Gay and
Transgender Groups," *New York Times,* November 10, 2016.

176 **"Citizens can be afraid" . . . "I saw a YouTube":** Colleen Culbertson,
"Elites, Identity Politics and Islamophobia: A Snapshot of Eastern Washington State," May 15, 2017 (on file with author).

177 **"I feel like":** Sabrina Tavernise, "Are Liberals Helping Trump?," *New
York Times,* February 18, 2017.

177 **the WASP elites:** Geoffrey Kabaservice, *The Guardians: Kingman Brewster,
His Circle, and the Rise of the Liberal Establishment* (New York: Henry Holt,
2004), 65, 174, 259–60, 264, 267, 271; Jerome Karabel, *The Chosen: The
Hidden History of Admission and Exclusion at Harvard, Yale, and Princeton* (New
York: Houghton Mifflin, 2005), 364–67, 379, 392; Dan A. Oren, *Joining
the Club: A History of Jews and Yale* (New Haven, CT: Yale University Press,
1985), 183–84, 272–77.

178 **"This is one country":** John F. Kennedy, radio and television report to
the American people on civil rights, June 11, 1963, https://www.jfkli
brary.org/Research/Research-Aids/JFK-Speeches/Civil-Rights-Radio
-and-Television-Report_19630611.aspx.

178 **"When the architects of our republic":** Martin Luther King Jr., "I have
a dream" speech, Washington, DC, August 28, 1963, http://www.ameri
canrhetoric.com/speeches/mlkihaveadream.htm (internal quotation marks
omitted).

179 **in an "original position" . . . "veil of ignorance":** John Rawls, *A Theory of
Justice* (rev. ed. Cambridge, MA: Belknap Press, 1999), 11.

179 **"race, gender, religious":** "Original Position," *Stanford Encyclopedia of
Philosophy* (first published February 27, 1996; last substantive revision September 9, 2014), https://plato.stanford.edu/entries/original-position.

179 **"Rather than protecting":** Will Kymlicka, *Multicultural Citizenship: A Liberal Theory of Minority Rights* (Oxford: Clarendon Press, 1995), 2–3.

179 **with many calling:** See, e.g., Martha C. Nussbaum, "Patriotism and Cosmopolitanism," *Boston Review*, October 1, 1994, http://bostonreview .net/martha-nussbaum-patriotism-and-cosmopolitanism.

179 **"city upon a hill" . . . free markets:** Ronald Reagan, "Farewell Address to American People," *New York Times,* January 12, 1989, http://www.nytimes .com/1989/01/12/news/transcript-of-reagan-s-farewell-address -to-american-people.html.

180 **"We are committed":** "Reagan Quotes King Speech in Opposing Minority Quotas," *New York Times,* January 19, 1986.

180 **"welfare queens" as a term:** Rachel Black and Aleta Sprague, "The 'Welfare Queen' is a Lie," *Atlantic,* September 28, 2016,

180 **"Race-Baiter in Chief":** Jillian Rayfield, "Fox News Host: Obama Is 'Race-Baiter in Chief,'" *Salon,* July 19, 2013, http://www.salon.com /2013/07/19/fox_news_host_obama_is_race_baiter_in_chief.

180 **called the speech "disgraceful":** Aliyah Shaid, "Conservatives Blast President Obama's Remarks on Trayvon Martin: He's Race Baiting!," *New York Daily News,* March 24, 2012.

181 **"politics of recognition":** See Nancy Fraser, "From Redistribution to Recognition? Dilemmas of Justice in a 'Post-Socialist' Age," *New Left Review* 1, no. 212 (July–August 1995): 68–93, https://newleftreview.org/I/212/nancy -fraser-from-redistribution-to-recognition-dilemmas-of-justice-in-a -post-socialist-age.

181 **"[W]hat makes identity":** Sonia Kruks, *Retrieving Experience: Subjectivity and Recognition in Feminist Politics* (Ithaca, NY: Cornell University Press, 2001), 85.

181 **"If black people":** Jamelle Bouie, "The Democratic Party's Racial Reckoning," *Slate,* October 2, 2016, http://www.slate.com/articles/news_and _politics/cover_story/2016/10/hillary_clinton_s_reverse_sister_soul jah_moment.html (quoting Sister Souljah).

181 **"There's not a":** Barack Obama, keynote address at the 2004 Democratic National Convention, Boston, July 27, 2004, transcript available at http:// www.washingtonpost.com/wp-dyn/articles/A19751-2004Jul27.html.

182 **"America has always":** Essay by Catherine Crooke, February 5, 2017 (on file with author).

182 **"confront rather than":** Ibid.

183 **"'Hey, I'm a Latina'":** Eliza Collins, "Sanders: Not Enough to Say, 'I'm a Woman, Vote for Me'," *USA Today,* November 21, 2016.

183 **"comments regarding identity":** Robby Soave, "White Identity Politics Gave Us Trump. But Did the Left Give Us White Identity Politics?," *Reason,* http://reason.com/blog/2016/11/29/white-identity-politics-gave -us-trump-bu, November 29, 2016; see also Quentin James, "The Left Has a White Supremacy Problem, Too," Medium, November 22, 2016,

https://medium.com/@quentinjames/the-left-has-a-white-supremacy
-problem-too-2071ebd1022.

183 **or "black experience":** Kimberlé Crenshaw, "Demarginalizing the Inter-
section of Race and Sex: A Black Feminist Critique of Antidiscrimination
Doctrine, Feminist Theory and Antiracist Politics," *University of Chicago Legal Forum* 140 (1989): 140; see also Laura Flanders, "No Single-Issue Politics,
Only Intersectionality: An Interview with Kimberlé Crenshaw," Truthout,
May 8, 2017, http://www.truth-out.org/opinion/item/40498-no-single
-issue-politics-only-intersectionality-an-interview-with-kimberle-crenshaw.

183 **"look at the ratio":** Farah Stockman, "Women's March on Washington
Opens Contentious Dialogues About Race," *New York Times,* January 9,
2017.

184 **"identity politics on steroids":** Flanders, "No Single-Issue Politics, Only
Intersectionality" (quoting Kimberlé Crenshaw). In a keynote speech at
the 2016 Women of the World Festival, Crenshaw said, "Some colleagues
in Germany undertook to count how many intersections there are. Last
count there were like seventeen or something. It was an attempt to map
them all. That's not my articulation of intersectionality. Intersectionality
is not primarily about identity, it's about how structures make certain
identities the consequence of and the vehicle for vulnerability." Kimberlé
Crenshaw, "On Intersectionality-Keynote-WOW 2016, at https://www
.youtube.com/watch?v=-DW4HLgYPlA.

184 **the acronym LGBTQ:** "Is it LGBT? GLBT? TBLG? LGBTQQ? Behind
the Acronym Controversy," *My Castro News,* April 8, 2014. Many thanks
to Aislinn Klos and Taonga Leslie for their insights on intersectionality
and identity politics.

184 **an "Oppression Olympics":** Shannon Ridgway, "Oppression Olympics:
The Games We Shouldn't Be Playing," Everyday Feminism, November 4,
2012, http://everydayfeminism.com/2012/11/oppression-olympics; see also
Michelle Goldberg, "Feminism's Toxic Twitter Wars," *Nation,* January 29,
2014, https://www.thenation.com/article/feminisms-toxic-twitter-wars.

184 **a staggering 4.2 million:** Sarah Frostenson, "The Women's Marches May
Have Been the Largest Demonstration in U.S. History," *Vox,* January 31,
2017, http://www.vox.com/2017/1/22/14350808/womens-marches
-largest-demonstration-us-history-map; Tim Wallace and Alicia Parlapi-
ano, "Crowd Scientists Say Women's March in Washington Had 3 Times as
Many People as Trump's Inauguration," *New York Times,* January 22, 2017.

184 **a stupendous success:** Emily Kalah Gade, "Why the Women's March
May Be the Start of a Serious Social Movement," *Washington Post,* January
30, 2017.

184 **"crowds on Saturday":** Jia Tolentino, "The Radical Possibility of the
Women's March," *New Yorker,* January 22, 2017.

184 **"Million Woman March":** Jia Tolentino, "The Somehow Controversial
Women's March on Washington," *New Yorker,* January 18, 2017.

185 **"I take issue":** Ashley Dejean, "'Million Women March' protest was appropriating black activism so organizers did this," *Splinter News*, November 12, 2016, http://splinternews.com/million-women-march-protest-was-appropriating-black-act-1793863713.

185 **"This is the perfect":** Brittany T. Oliver, "Why I do not support the Women's March on Washington," *Brittany T. Oliver* (blog), November 16, 2016, accessed August 17, 2017, http://www.brittanytoliver.com/blog/2016/11/16/why-i-do-not-support-the-one-million-women-march-on-washington.

185 **nonwhite activists as cochairs:** Tolentino, "The Somehow Controversial Women's March on Washington."

185 **But tensions continued:** Candice Huber, "The Problem with the Women's March on Washington and White Feminism," *Nerdy-But-Flirty* (blog), December 2, 2016, accessed August 17, 2017, https://nerdybutflirty.com/2016/12/02/the-problem-with-the-womens-march-on-washington-and-white-feminism.

185 **53 percent of:** Phoebe Lett, "White Women Voted Trump. Now What?," *New York Times*, November 10, 2016.

185 **"they didn't want to be":** ShiShi Rose, "After March, a Letter to White Women" (blog), January 23, 2017, accessed August 17, 2017, http://www.shishirose.com/blog.

185 **"I was born scared" ... "Now is the time":** Stockman, "Women's March on Washington Opens Contentious Dialogues About Race."

185 **"to feel not very welcome":** Ibid.

186 **"This is a women's march":** Ibid.

186 **"understand their privilege" ... "Fuck You":** Tolentino, "The Somehow Controversial Women's March on Washington."

186 **"this is a black and brown":** Todd Starnes, "Black DNC Protest Tells Crowd: 'White People to the Back,'" Fox News video, 1:28, July 27, 2016, http://www.foxnews.com/opinion/2016/07/27/black-dnc-protest-tells-crowd-white-people-to-back.html.

186 **Beyoncé was criticized:** Reneysh Vittal, "How I Fell In and Out of Love with Cultural Appropriation," *Vice*, November 2, 2016, http://www.vice.com/en_us/article/the-fine-line-between-celebrating-and-appropriating-foreign-culture.

186 **Amy Schumer, in turn:** Ibid.

186 **Students at Oberlin:** Conor Friedersdorf, "A Food Fight at Oberlin College," *Atlantic*, December 21, 2015.

187 **"a lot of ethnic women":** Quoted in Katherine Timpf, "Student Op-Ed: Some Eyebrows Are Cultural Appropriation," *National Review*, January 27, 2017.

187 **"If we allowed ourselves":** Giovanni Sanchez, "Crying Wolf: How Elite Liberal Outrage Is Undermining the Left's Goals," February 7, 2017 (on file with author).

187 **Samuel P. Huntington was:** See Samuel P. Huntington, *The Clash of Civilizations and the Remaking of World Order* (New York: Simon & Schuster, 1996), 209–18; Samuel P. Huntington, *Who Are We? The Challenges to America's National Identity* (New York: Simon & Schuster, 2004), 59, 316–24.

187 **"a total and complete shutdown":** Jenna Johnson, "Trump Calls for 'Total and Complete Shutdown of Muslims Entering the United States,'" *Washington Post,* December 7, 2015.

188 **"rapists" . . . "an inherent conflict":** Jia Tolentino, "Trump and the Truth: The 'Mexican' Judge," *New Yorker,* September 20, 2016.

188 **"is a vicious cancer":** Andrew Kaczynski, "Michael Flynn in August: Islamism a 'Vicious Cancer' in Body of All Muslims That 'Has to Be Excised,'" CNN, November 22, 2016, http://www.cnn.com/2016/11/22/politics/kfile-michael-flynn-august-speech/index.html.

188 **war with Islam:** Ishaan Tharoor, "U.S. Republicans See a Clash of Civilizations. French President Says No," *Washington Post,* November 16, 2015.

188 **Even moderate Republicans:** Steve Benen, "Jeb Bush Would Back Refugees Who 'Prove' They're Christian," MSNBC, November 18, 2015, http:// www.msnbc.com/rachel-maddow-show/jeb-bush-would-back-refugees-who-prove-theyre-christian.

188 **"Unite the Right":** "Unite the Right: David Duke and Mike Enoch Speak Out at the Rally at Charlottesville, Virginia," video, 6:20, August 14, 2017, https://www.youtube.com/watch?v=GDizQPZMEhI&feature=youtu.be&t=6m17s; see Emma Green, "Why the Charlottesville Marchers Were Obsessed with Jews," *Atlantic,* August 15, 2017.

188 **"[e]ngineering schools" . . . "can't get a job":** Philip Bump, "Steve Bannon Once Complained That 20 Percent of the Country Is Made Up of Immigrants. It Isn't," *Washington Post,* February 1, 2017.

188 **"[T]wo-thirds . . . civic society":** Willa Frej, "Steve Bannon Suggests There Are Too Many Asian CEOs in Silicon Valley," *Huffington Post,* November 23, 2016, http://www.huffingtonpost.com/entry/steve-bannon-disgusted-asian-ceos-silicon-valley_us_582c5d19e4b0e39c1fa71e48.

188 **a wild exaggeration:** Maya Kosoff, "Steve Bannon's Racist Comments About Silicon Valley Are Also Wildly Inaccurate," *Vanity Fair,* November 17, 2016; Buck Gee, Denise Peck, and Janet Wong, *Hidden in Plain Sight: Asian American Leaders in Silicon Valley* (The Ascend Foundation, 2015), 2–3, 8.

189 **"maybe I'm just":** Chris Bodenner, "If You Want Identity Politics, Identity Politics Is What You Get," *Atlantic,* November 11, 2016, http://www.theatlantic.com/notes/2016/11/if-you-want-identity-politics-identity-politics-is-what-you-will-get/507437.

189 **"The Democratic party":** Quoted in Ian Schwartz, "Maher: People Fed Up with 'Fake Outrage,' 'Politically Correct Bullshit' and Response to Islam from Democrats," *Real Clear Politics,* November 12, 2016, http://www.realclearpolitics.com/video/2016/11/12/maher_people_fed_up_with

_fake_outrage_politically_correct_bullshit_and_response_to_islam
_from_democrats.html.

189 **"I'm a white guy":** Rod Dreher, "Creating the White Tribe," *American Conservative,* January 25, 2017, http://www.theamericanconservative.com /dreher/creating-the-white-tribe (quoting "Reader Zapollo").

191 **"Most on the right":** Joe Chatham, "Group Identity on the Right," November 13, 2016 (on file with author).

191 **"I get it":** Hsu, "The End of White America?" (quoting Christian Lander).

192 **"result is a racial pride":** Ibid.

192 **"The GOP Is":** Max Boot, "The GOP Is America's Party of White Nationalism," *Foreign Policy,* March 14, 2017.

192 **an "ethno-nationalist president":** Jonathan S. Blake, "How Ethno-Nationalism Explains Trump's Early Presidency," *Vice,* February 27, 2017, http://www.vice.com/en_us/article/53qnxx/how-etho-nationalism -explains-trumps-early-presidency.

192 **"White Nationalism is":** Jamelle Bouie, "Government by White Nationalism Is Upon Us," *Slate,* February 6, 2017, http://www.slate.com/arti cles/news_and_politics/cover_story/2017/02/government_by_white _nationalism_is_upon_us.html.

192 **"fashy" . . . "ethno-state":** John Woodrow Cox, "'Let's Party Like It's 1933': Inside the Alt-Right World of Richard Spencer," *Washington Post,* November 22, 2016.

193 **"ethnic cleansing" . . . "peaceful":** Chris Graham, "Nazi Salutes and White Supremacism: Who Is Richard Spencer, the 'Racist Academic' Behind the 'Alt-Right' Movement?," *Telegraph* (UK), November 22, 2016.

193 **"Look, maybe it":** Cox, "'Let's Party Like It's 1933.'"

193 **Many hear echoes:** Josh Harkinson, "The Dark History of the White House Aides Who Crafted Trump's 'Muslim Ban,'" *Mother Jones,* January 30, 2017, http://www.motherjones.com/politics/2017/01/stephen-bannon -miller-trump-refugee-ban-islamophobia-white-nationalist; Chauncey De-Vega, "A White Nationalist Fantasy: Donald Trump's America Is Not 'Made for You and Me,'" *Salon,* February 12, 2017, http://www.salon .com/2017/02/12/a-white-nationalist-fantasy-donald-trumps-america -is-not-made-for-you-and-me.

193 **two Indian American engineers:** Mark Berman and Samantha Schmidt, "He Yelled 'Get Out of My Country,' Witnesses Say, and Then Shot 2 Men from India, Killing One," *Washington Post,* February 24, 2017.

193 **right outside his home:** "Indian-Origin Businessman Shot Dead in the US," *Times of India,* March 5, 2017, http://timesofindia.indiatimes.com /nri/us-canada-news/indian-origin-businessman-shot-dead-in-the-us /articleshow/57462656.cms.

193 **"Go back to your country, terrorist":** Cleve R. Wootson Jr., "'Go Back to Your Country, Terrorist': Man Accused of Attacking Restaurant Employee with a Pipe," *Washington Post,* March 12, 2017.

193　**In May 2017:** Matthew Haag and Jacey Fortin, "Two Killed in Portland While Trying to Stop Anti-Muslim Rant, Police Say," *New York Times,* May 27, 2017.

193　**"targets of threats, vandalism, or arson":** Doug Criss, "This Map Shows How Many Mosques Have Been Targeted Just This Year," CNN, March 20, 2017, http://www.cnn.com/2017/03/20/us/mosques-targeted -2017-trnd/index.html.

193　**August 2017 NPR/PBS Marist poll:** NPR/PBS News Hour/Marist Poll, August 14–15, 2017, http://maristpoll.marist.edu/wp-content/misc/us apolls/us170814_PBS/NPR_PBS%20NewsHour_Marist%20Poll _National%20Nature%20of%20the%20Sample%20and%20Tables _August%2017,%202017.pdf#page=3, 13.

193　**"neither good nor bad":** Bradley Jones and Jocelyn Kiley, "More 'Warmth' for Trump Among GOP Voters Concerned by Immigrants, Diversity," Pew Research Center, June 2, 2016, http://www.pewresearch .org/fact-tank/2016/06/02/more-warmth-for-trump-among-gop-voters -concerned-by-immigrants-diversity.

194　**"Colin, I support":** Video and as quoted in part at Jake Hancock, "Tomi Lahren Blitzes Kaepernick's Backfield," *The Blaze,* August 30, 2016, http://www.theblaze.com/stories/2016/08/30/tomi-lahren-blitzes-kaeper nicks-backfield.

195　**66 million people:** Mike Wendling, "Tomi Lahren: The Young Republican Who's Bigger Than Trump on Facebook," BBC News, November 30, 2016, http://www.bbc.com/news/world-us-canada-38021995.

195　**"Do you know":** Tomi Lahren, Facebook video, June 28, 2016, accessed May 26, 2017, https://www.facebook.com/TomiLahren/videos/101750 6241675896.

196　**of "majoritarian pigs":** Ta-Nehisi Coates, "Blue Lives Matter," *Atlantic,* December 22, 2014.

196　**"questioned whether Barack Obama":** Toni Morrison, "Making America White Again," *New Yorker,* November 21, 2016.

196　**"traditional to destroy":** Coates, "Letter to My Son."

Epilogue

197　**"human beings first":** Carolyn Bostick, "In Era of Division, Interfaith Coalition Promotes Unity," *Observer-Dispatch,* February 4, 2017, http:// www.uticaod.com/news/20170204/in-era-of-division-interfaith-coalition -promotes-unity.

197　**"Make America Relate":** "Make America Relate Again Northwestern NJ," January 28, 2017, https://www.meetup.com/Make-America-Relate -Again-Northwestern-NJ.

197　**Silicon Valley's Ro Khanna:** Nitasha Tiku, "Silicon Valley Rebrands Itself as Good for the Rest of America," *Wired,* May 15, 2017, https://www .wired.com/2017/05/silicon-valley-rebrands-good-rest-america.

198 **Van Jones ... "Help me understand":** "Van Jones Sits Down with Trump Supporters," CNN, December 6, 2016, http://www.cnn.com/videos/tv /2016/12/06/exp-van-jones-special-cnntv.cnn.

198 **comedian W. Kamau Bell:** Alex Cipolle, "Comedian W. Kamau Bell Reaches Across the Aisle," *Register-Guard*, May 19, 2017, http://register guard.com/rg/entertainment/35571393-67/comedian-w.-kamau-bell -reaches-across-the-aisle.csp.

198 **University of Minnesota . . . "the divisions":** "Call for Applications: Cross-Country Reporting Fellowship 'Crossing the Divide,'" April 25, 2017, https://cla.umn.edu/sjmc/news-events/news/call-applications-cross -country-reporting-fellowship-crossing-divide.

198 **"closed to compromise":** Charles M. Blow, "The Death of Compassion," *New York Times,* February 23, 2017.

198 **tremendous progress can be made:** See, e.g., Thomas F. Pettigrew and Linda R. Tropp, "A Meta-Analytic Test of Intergroup Contact Theory," *Journal of Personality and Social Psychology* 90, no. 5 (2006): 766.

199 *The Nature of Prejudice:* Gordon W. Allport, *The Nature of Prejudice* (Cambridge, MA: Addison-Wesley, 1954).

199 **face-to-face contact:** See Pettigrew and Tropp, "A Meta-Analytic Test of Intergroup Contact Theory," 751–83.

199 **England to Italy to Sri Lanka:** See Nico Schulenkorf, "Sport Events and Ethnic Reconciliation: Attempting to Create Social Change Between Sinhalese, Tamil and Muslim Sportspeople in War-Torn Sri Lanka," *International Review for the Sociology of Sport* 45, no. 3 (2010): 273; Dora Capozza, Gian Antonio Di Bernardo, and Rossella Falvo, "Intergroup Contact and Outgroup Humanization: Is the Causal Relationship Uni- or Bidirectional?," *PLOS One* 12, no. 1 (2017), 1–3; Katharina Schmid, Ananthi Al Ramiah, and Miles Hewstone, "Neighborhood Ethnic Diversity and Trust: The Role of Intergroup Contact and Perceived Threat," *Psychological Science* 25, no. 3 (2014): 665–74.

199 **all forms of group prejudice:** Pettigrew and Tropp, "A Meta-Analytic Test of Intergroup Contact Theory," 751–83.

199 **nearly two thirds:** Gregory M. Herek, "Lesbians and Gay Men in the U.S. Military: Historical Background," Sexual Orientation: Science, Education, and Policy, University of California, Davis, accessed August 7, 2017, http://psychology.ucdavis.edu/rainbow/html/military_history.html.

199 **Internal opposition was:** Jim Garamone, "Historian Charts Six Decades of Racial Integration in U.S. Military," American Forces Press Service, U.S. Department of Defense, July 23, 2008, http://archive.defense.gov /news/newsarticle.aspx?id=50560.

199 **"cooperation in integrated units":** Herek, "Lesbians and Gay Men in the U.S. Military."

199 **"When your life":** Garamone, "Historian Charts Six Decades of Racial Integration in U.S. Military."

199 **"an 18-year old Hispanic":** Karl Marlantes, "Vietnam: The War That Killed Trust," *New York Times,* January 7, 2017.

201 **opinions about same-sex marriage:** Todd Venook, "The Group Instinct and the Modern American Moment," March 3, 2017 (on file with author).

201 **just 11 percent:** Scott Clement, "Gay Marriage's Road to Popularity, in 5 Charts," *Washington Post,* April 28, 2015.

201 **today, 62 percent:** "Changing Attitudes on Gay Marriage," Pew Research Center, June 26, 2017, http://www.pewforum.org/fact-sheet /changing-attitudes-on-gay-marriage.

201 **"a friend, relative, or coworker":** Jeffrey M. Jones, "More Americans See Gay, Lesbian Orientation as Birth Factor," Gallup, May 16, 2013, http://www.gallup.com/poll/162569/americans-gay-lesbian-orientation -birth-factor.aspx.

201 **"Once [gay] people began":** Marcia Coyle, "Justice Ginsburg Laments 'Real Racial Problem' in U.S.; Discusses Major Rulings, Law Schools in Sweeping Q&A," *National Law Journal,* August 22, 2014.

201 **One study by Harvard professor:** Ryan D. Enos, "How the Demographic Shift Could Hurt Democrats, Too," *Washington Post,* March 8, 2013.

201 **negative interactions with people:** Stefania Paolini, Jake Harwood, and Mark Rubin, "Negative Intergroup Contact Makes Group Memberships Salient: Explaining Why Intergroup Conflict Endures," *Personality and Social Psychology Bulletin* 36, no. 12 (2010): 1723.

202 **"[H]umility is a mediator":** Humans of New York (May 18, 2015), http://www.humansofnewyork.com/post/119284859436/my-daughters -greatest-quality-is-her-humility.

203 **"THEY CAME TO":** See Giovanni Sanchez, "Crying Wolf: How Liberal Elite Outrage Is Undermining the Left's Goals" (February 7, 2017, on file with author) (quoting meme posted on Facebook).

203 **"'WHITE WORKING CLASS'":** Kirsten West Savali, "'White Working Class' Narrative Is Nothing but a Racist Dog Whistle," *The Root,* November 17, 2016, http://www.theroot.com/white-working-class-narrative-is -nothing-but-a-racist-1790857771.

203 **"America is neither":** "America: Land of the Oppressed, Home of the Cowards," *Opposingviews,* May 26, 2010, http://www.opposingviews .com/i/america-land-of-the-oppressed-home-of-the-cowards.

204 **"a nation founded on":** Tiffany Gabbay, "Michael Moore: U.S. Was 'Founded on Genocide and Built on the Backs of Slaves,'" *The Blaze,* January 20, 2012, http://www.theblaze.com/news/2012/01/20/michael -moore-u-s-was-founded-on-genocide-and-built-on-the-backs-of-slaves.

204 **"Unlike any nation":** Toni Morrison, "Making America White Again," *New Yorker,* November 21, 2016.

204 **The peril we face:** This insight and way of putting it is from Yasin Hegazy, "Achieving Our Country: James Baldwin's Prophetic Model of America's Post-Racial Identity" (draft of May 2017, on file with author).

205 **"Walter helped us"**: Sanchez, "Crying Wolf," 5.

205 **"a critical paradox"**: Ibid., 12.

206 **"the countless iterations"**: Ibid., 13.

207 **"collection of myths"**: James Baldwin, "The Fire Next Time," in *Collected Essays* (New York: Library of America, 1998), 294, 344, 347.

208 **"standing up for"**: Eric J. Sundquist, "King's Dream," *New York Times*, January 16, 2009.

208 **"[A]s much as"**: President Barack Obama, "Remarks at a Church Service Honoring Martin Luther King Jr.," Vermont Avenue Baptist Church, Washington, DC, January 17, 2010, http://www.presidency.ucsb.edu/ws/index.php?pid=87399.

209 **Failures are part and parcel:** Many thanks to Yena Lee for her insights and eloquent words.

209 ***"Let America be the dream"***: Langston Hughes, "Let America be America Again," in *The Collected Poems of Langston Hughes*, ed. Arnold Rampersad and David Roessel (New York: Vintage Books, 1995), 189–91.

Index

INDEX

Basra, Iraq, 76
Belgians/Belgium, 26, 105, 107–9
Believer's Voice of Victory, 154
Belkacem, Fouad, 107
Bell, W. Kamau, 198
Bennett, Brit, 9
Beyoncé, 32, 173, 186
Billboard, 31
bin Laden, Osama, 59, 66, 70, 94, 111,
    113–14
Black Lives Matter, 173–74, 186, 196, 202
blacks, 18, 171, 181, 191, 194–95, 206
    and American Dream, 138–39
    blame whites, 189
    discrimination against, 8–9, 17–18,
        170, 196
    disenfranchised, 168–69, 174–75
    radical movements of, 178
    and tribal instincts, 105
    and upward mobility, 173
    in Venezuela, 124–26, 128, 132
    and WWE, 160
    See also African Americans;
        slaves/slavery
Blessed (Bowler), 154–55
Bloom, Paul, 40
Blow, Charles, 198
Bolívar, Simón, 128
Bolivia, 47, 97, 123, 132
Bontinck, Jejoen, 107–8
Bosnians, 77, 197
Bowler, Kate, 154–55
Brazil, 27, 133
Breaking Bad, 151
Brezhnev, Leonid, 64
Brooks, Nycki, 90
Brown v. Board of Education, 28, 169
"browning" of America, 8, 166–69
    See also United States, "browning of"
Brussels, 26
Brzezinski, Zbigniew, 64
Burns, Mark, 153
Bush, George W.
    on freedom/democracy, 3, 7, 75–76,
        82, 128–29
    and Hugo Chávez, 117, 128–29
    and Iraq, 3, 75–76, 81–82, 84, 115
Bush, Jeb, 188
Byerley, Melinda, 163

California, 17, 150–51, 160, 167, 181
Cambodians, 18, 149
Cameron, David, 25
Canada/Canadians, 20, 27–28, 30, 105
Cao Ky, Nguyen, 46
capitalism, 2, 27, 50–52, 55–56, 63, 95,
    120, 138, 180–81
Caribbean, 47
Carmichael, Stokely, 178
Carmona, Pedro, 129
Carnes, Nick, 172
Carter, Jimmy, 64
castes/*castas*, 15, 122–23
Castro, Fidel, 120
Catholics, 31, 51, 77, 150
Charlottesville, Virginia, 188
Chávez, Hugo, 12–13, 117–20,
    125–35, 138
Chechnya, 108
Cheney, Dick, 73, 76
Chesnut, Andrew, 150–51
Chi Minh, Ho, 45–46, 50–51, 55
Chicago Tribune, 129
Chile, 123
China, 109, 117, 133
    dominates Vietnam, 42–57
    as ethnic nation, 11, 22, 42
    and Han Chinese, 22, 42
    See also Vietnam: Chinese in
Chinese Americans, 30. *See also* Asian
    Americans
Cholon, Vietnam, 48, 51–53, 56
Christians, 4, 9, 22–23, 78, 116, 127,
    153–54, 172–73, 188, 197, 203–4
CIA, 71, 76
Cikara, Mina, 40–41
citizenship, 11, 1726–28. *See also* sovereign
    citizens
City University of New York (CUNY)
    study, 139–40
Civil Rights Act of 1964, 27–28, 169, 178
civil rights movement, 12, 141, 208
Civil War, 12, 27–28, 37, 168, 195
Clash of Civilizations, The (Huntington), 187
class, 4–6, 126–27, 130–31, 142–44,
    148–49, 158, 190
Clinton, Bill, 7, 167–68, 176, 181
Clinton, Hillary, 132, 183
CNN, 73, 160, 198

Hawaii, 167
Hazaras, 60, 70, 72
Helmand Province, 73
Hillbilly Elegy (Vance), 163
Hispanic Americans, 4, 9, 150–52,
    166–67, 187–88, 191, 199–200
Hollywood, 8, 31–32
Horowitz, Donald, 41
"How Democrats Can Get Their Mojo
    Back" (Leonhardt), 138–39
Hsu, Hua, 192
Huffington Post, 6, 159, 171
Hughes, Langston, 209–10
human rights, 7, 18, 178–80, 202
Hungary/Hungarians, 11, 22, 26, 64
Huntington, Samuel P., 187
Hussein, Saddam, 3, 78–79, 81, 92, 95, 97

ICE, 176
identity politics, 9–11, 166, 177–92
    See also group identity; national
    identity; subgroups; super-groups
Ignatiev, Noel, 168
Illinois, 170, 176
immigrants
    Hispanic, 187–88, 192
    mass influx of, 26–30, 166–68,
        170, 207
    nation of, 19–20, 27–28, 197, 203,
        207–8
    opposition to, 10, 23, 27, 29, 32, 201
    and racial categories, 18, 26–27
    in United States, 32, 194, 205–6
Immigration and Nationality Act (1965),
    29–30
imperialism, 15–16, 196
India/Indians, 16, 30, 47, 69, 109,
    121, 193
Indiana, 170, 188
indigenous
    -blooded masses, 121, 123, 125, 126
    movements, 38, 132
individual rights, 7–8, 10, 95, 178–79
individualism, 10, 20–21, 143, 179,
    190–91
Indonesia, 47
inequality
    and democracy, 7–9, 120, 130
    and extremism, 112–16

high levels of, 9, 32
in United States, 19, 137–41, 148–49,
    155, 162, 164
in Venezuela, 120, 130, 132
See also racial: inequality
Internet, 114, 194
intersectionality, 183–86
Iowa, 28, 170
Iran/Iranians, 32, 61, 66, 93, 95
Iraq, 20, 34, 73
    democracy in, 79–83, 92–96
    ISIS in, 109–10, 115
    as multiethnic nation, 34, 76–78
    Sunni minority in, 78–80
    U.S. invasion of, 2–3, 16, 75–76,
        78–80, 95
    U.S. surge in (2007), 84–92
Ireland/Irish, 24, 26, 28, 163
ISIS, 74, 76, 81, 93–95, 97, 104–5, 107,
    109–11, 113–15
Islam, 65–70, 97, 108–9, 114, 163, 178,
    188. *See also* Afghanistan; al-Qaeda
    militants; ISIS; Taliban
Islamic
    culture, 187
    holy sites, 83, 88
    militant groups, 25–26, 60–61, 107–16
    Revolution, 66
    schools, 65
    State, 93–95, 107, 110, 114–15
Israel, 105–6, 113, 116, 202
Italy/Italians, 22, 26, 30, 33, 124, 199
Ivy League universities, 28–29, 177. *See
    also specific universities*

Jamaican Americans, 18, 32
James, Quentin, 183
Japan, 22, 75–78
Jeter, Derek, 32
Jews, 42, 123, 188, 191, 202
    and Arabs in Israel, 105–6
    discrimination against, 9, 17, 56
    at elite colleges, 29, 177
    in Europe, 23, 25
    immigrate to United States, 26, 32
    in Russia, 47, 97
    on U.S. Supreme Court, 31
jihadis, 25–26, 66, 72, 107–9, 115, 203
Jim Crow, 169, 174, 177

Welsh, 24
West Africa, 47
white Americans, 17, 181
    divisions among, 161–64
    dominance of, 29–31, 176–77, 180, 182,
        196, 203–4
    elected Trump, 5, 13, 138–39, 160–64
    ethnonationalism among, 192–93, 196
    feel discrimination, 8–10, 169–75,
        189–92, 195
    and identity politics, 10–11, 32, 177–78,
        189–92
    as minority, 31–32, 165–68
    and NASCAR, 156–58
    and political activism, 139–40
    supremacists, 6, 8, 144, 183, 185, 196,
        203–4
    See also elites: in United States;
        Protestants; WASPS
White, Micah, 141–42
Who Are We? (Huntington), 187
Willer, Robb, 103–4, 170
Wilson, Charlie, 65–66
Wilson, Woodrow, 17, 19
Wimsattcalls, William, 168
Winfrey, Oprah, 32
Wisconsin, 170
Wolfowitz, Paul, 80, 88
women, 178
    black, 183–86
    and equal rights, 140, 183, 186

    as NASCAR fans, 156–57
    and Spanish Conquest, 121–22
    support Trump, 185–86, 194
    terrorists, 108–11
    in United States, 29, 172, 176, 180–81
    in Venezuela, 118–20, 125, 128, 131
    white, 183–87
Women's March, 184–86
working class, 6
    and American Dream, 138–39, 203
    discrimination against, 169–74, 189
    dislike protests, 4–5, 142–43
    in Europe, 26
    and NASCAR, 156–58
    poor prospects for, 171–73
    and prosperity gospel, 4–5
    in United States, 130, 143–44, 163, 206
    and WWE, 158–61
World War II, 45, 75, 77, 124
World Wrestling Entertainment (WWE),
    158–61

Yaken, Islam, 106–8
Yale Law School, 101, 132, 171–72
Yale University, 29, 40, 202
Yoruba, 18, 42
YouTube, 106, 176
Yugoslavia, 47, 77–79, 96–97

Zia-ul-Haq, Muhammad, 65
Zito, Salena, 161